The Marx Reader

The Marx Reader

Edited by

Christopher Pierson

Polity Press

First published in 1997 by Polity Press
in association with Blackwell Publishers Ltd.

Reprinted 2005

Polity Press
65 Bridge Street
Cambridge CB2 1UR, UK

Polity Press
350 Main Street
Maldon, MA 02148, USA

ISBN 0-7456-1727-1
ISBN 0-7456-1728-X(pbk)

A CIP catalogue record for this book is available from the British Library.

Typeset in 10 on 12 Times
by Ace Filmsetting Ltd, Frome,

This book is printed on acid-free

For further information on Polity, v

Contents

Acknowledgements

Most of the selections in this reader are drawn from the edition of the *Complete Works of Marx and Engels* published by Lawrence and Wishart. Other readings are taken from *The German Ideology (Part One)*, *Capital: Volumes One and Three*, Marx and Engels' *Selected Work in Two Volumes: Volume Two* and *Selected Correspondence* (all published by Lawrence and Wishart). David McLellan's 1971 translation (published by Macmillan) was the source for material from *Grundrisse*. Several of the works included here are jointly attributed to Marx and his lifelong collaborator Friedrich Engels. The actual authorship of key passages has been the source of some scholarly dispute. Here it will suffice to say that most of the material in this reader was solely authored by Marx.

Special thanks are due to Anthony Giddens, Julia Harsant and all the staff at Polity who eased the preparation of this volume.

The editor and publishers wish to thank the following for permission to reproduce material in this book: Lawrence and Wishart for Karl Marx and Friedrich Engels, *Collected Works*; Karl Marx (ed. C. J. Arthur), *The German Ideology*; Karl Marx, *Capital*; Karl Marx and Friedrich Engels, *Selected Works in Two Volumes*; Karl Marx and Friedrich Engels, *Selected Correspondence*; Macmillan for Karl Marx (translated and edited by D. McLellan), *Grundrisse*.

Every effort has been made to trace all copyright holders, but if any has been inadvertently overlooked, the publishers will be pleased to make the necessary arrangement at the first opportunity.

Editor's Note

An ellipsis has been used whenever material from the original has been omitted. Where more than a paragraph has been excluded, a line space appears above and below [. . .].

1

Introduction

A spectre is haunting Europe – the spectre of Communism
Karl Marx, The Communist Manifesto

Communism is Dead
Francis Fukuyama, The End of History

1989 was the year of Velvet Revolutions in Eastern Europe. In 1990, the 'leading role' of the Communist Party was expunged from the Soviet Constitution. In 1991, the Communist Party of the Soviet Union was disbanded and the Soviet Union dissolved. Thus perished that distinctive brand of Soviet communism which had been created in the aftermath of the Russian Revolution of 1917 and exported into the satellite states of Eastern Europe in the wake of the Second World War. The New Socialist Age which the Bolshevik Revolution had promised to usher in had lasted less than a lifetime. Since Marxism had been the 'guiding thread' of the revolutionary process and the legitimating ideology of the postrevolutionary society, it seemed to many observers that the demise of Soviet communism and the death of Marxism were one and the same thing. With the collapse of the Soviet Empire, why should anyone, except the historian of now obsolete ideas, still read Marx?

Marxisms *after* Marx

This argument is just a little too neat to be true. First, the relationship between Marx's own work and (the diverse forms of) Marxism that arose from it is far from straightforward. Marxism is largely a product of the period *after* Marx's death (in 1883). Although there were some anticipations of a Marxist 'system' in Marx's own lifetime, the first 'orthodox' Marxism consisted in the codification, under the defining authority of Marx's long-standing collaborator Friedrich Engels, of certain key ideas mostly drawn from the economic texts of Marx's maturity. It was an interpretation of Marx that received its clearest expression in the founding Erfurt Programme of the German Social Democratic Party (SPD), written by Karl Kautsky and published in 1891. Yet within a decade, this 'orthodox' reading of Marx was under sustained challenge. The 'true' nature of Marxism and, with it, the question of what Marx *really* meant have been vigorously contested ever since.

This diversity extends to Marxist understandings of the Soviet Union. The earliest critique of Lenin's practice from a Marxist perspective actually *predates* the Bolshevik seizure of power in 1917 and criticism of Soviet Marxism by Marxists persisted throughout the 1930s and into the postwar period. The history of this dissent is complex. Some followed Karl Kautsky, in arguing that Lenin's political practice was at odds with Marx's teaching. Others held that Lenin, the great practitioner of revolution, had correctly applied Marx's principles in the difficult and messy circumstances of a real-world revolution, but that the revolution had subsequently been betrayed by Stalin. A few (though for understandable reasons, not many of those who counted themselves as Marxism's friends), held that Joseph Stalin was the authentic inheritor of the practical and theoretical tradition of Marx and Lenin. Whichever one of these views one prefers, it is hard to argue that there is a single and monolithic Marxist view of the Soviet experience (see Callinicos, 1991).

That Marx's heritage should have been so widely contested is not perhaps very surprising. Marx's prodigious output, spanning the best part of fifty years in the middle of the nineteenth century and still not published in its entirety, simply does not yield an unambiguous account of what he *really* meant. Though Marx had a remarkable capacity to think in systemic terms, and though it is possible to identify elements of continuity across his lifetime, it is simply not possible to squeeze everything that he wrote into a single all-encompassing intellectual framework. Many of what are now regarded as Marx's most important writings (including much of what was written before 1845) were unavailable to the first two generations of Marxist thinkers. There simply is not, for all the pretenders to this title, one *authentic* Marxism and what we find, in practice, is a range of social and political arguments which seek to derive their authority from a reading of Marx. Nor is it clear that this diversity is something to be regretted. Even in the period of its greatest political and intellectual authority, the power of Marxist thinking lay quite as much in its dissenting as in its orthodox tradition. One suspects that much of this strength derives from the fact that Marx was perhaps quite as brilliant but almost certainly not as consistent as most of his admirers have imagined.

It follows that we cannot simply identify Marx with an undifferentiated Marxism, nor Marxism with the experience of the Soviet Union (nor, indeed, with any other state regime which claims to derive its authority from Marx). To this extent we may salvage Marx from the claim that he is obsolete *because* of the collapse of Soviet communism. This is not, however, an especially comforting outcome for the more general Marxist enterprise. Most academic Marxists in the West had long since dismissed the orthodoxies of the Soviet Union as cynical parodies of Marx's originally radical intent. In the wake of Soviet military intervention in Hungary (1956) and Czechoslovakia (1968), growing numbers of communists outside the immediate Soviet sphere came explicitly to abandon the model of the USSR and its satellites in Eastern Europe as even the most deformed expression of a socialism suited to the more advanced industrial societies. The Soviet Union remained an object of pained contemplation, but rarely of much admiration, for Marxists elsewhere. Much more important in the heartlands of advanced capitalism was the development of a broad current of *Western* Marxism, at once more critical, more (avowedly) theoretical and generally more pessimistic than its 'classical' forerunner. Its roots lay not in confident predictions of the coming collapse of capitalism but rather in explaining the *absence* of revolution in Western Europe in the aftermath of the First World War. Interest in this approach revived with the re-emergence of widespread industrial and political militancy in advanced Western capitalist societies from the late 1960s onwards. Coinciding with the dissemination of Marx's newly available early works and English translations of the writings of the interwar Italian Marxist, Antonio Gramsci, these developments contributed to a considerable renaissance in the more critical Marxist tradition. But this revival was to be comparatively short-lived and it is a position which, in recent years, has itself come under systematic intellectual assault.

The contemporary critics of Marx

Of course, criticism of Marxism from both the right and the left is nothing new. There are few vices of the twentieth century – from lax sexual morals to the rise of fascism – which *someone* has not attributed to Marx. Nor is the attempt to revise Marx 'sympathetically' to take account of 'flaws' in his original social theory or to reconcile his understanding with subsequent changes in the character of developed capitalism very new. Indeed, this is, very largely, what Western Marxism has been about. But in recent years Marxism in all its forms has come under an increasingly sustained attack from just those sorts of radical and critical thinkers who would once have been looked upon as its most natural supporters. Significantly, these are criticisms which are not plausibly confined to later 'perversions' of Marx's thought (as have been attacks upon the Leninist 'vanguard party' or Stalin's 'socialism in one country'). In as much as these criticisms are true, they are as true of Marx as of his later followers.

In this context, three sorts of criticism have been of especial importance. First, there has been the claim that Marx gave too much weight to the category of class, both as a determinant of people's broadly defined political interests and as a possible basis for their collective emancipation. It is suggested that by focusing exclusively upon class and the formal labour process, attention was directed away from other forms of exploitation and other forms of political mobilization, around for example, issues of gender or of national identity. Freedom for the wage-labourer alone could never constitute a final or 'truly human' emancipation. Secondly, ecological critics of Marx insist that his anticipated form of socialism premised upon the material base inherited from a hyper-industrialized capitalism would be no less environmentally destructive than the kinds of industrial capitalism it was to replace. What unites capitalism and Marxist socialism, upon this account, is a shared commitment to a super-industrialism which is ecologically unsustainable. The several subsequent attempts to marry these insights of ecologists or feminists or nationalists to the existing apparatus of Marxist theory have generally been regarded with acute suspicion (see, for example, Di Stefano, 1991).

A still more systematic attack upon the generic claims of Marx and of Marxism has come from the recent advocates of postmodernism. Postmodernism evades any straightforward classification (see Smart, 1993). At its simplest, it expresses a rejection of the claim, familiar from the time of the Enlightenment onwards, that the social world can be understood and thence re-formed in line with the dictates of objective, scientific thought or the application of Reason. Characteristically, modern modes of thought have been interventionist, promising to deliver progress, to sponsor greater human freedom and to give us control of our external environment. The tragedy of modernity is that the very ideas and practices which are supposed to produce this enhanced freedom and autonomy actually generate new and oppressive forms of social control. For postmodernist critics, this is abundantly true of Marxism.

Marx endorses the Enlightenment belief in the application of Reason to human affairs. His social theory recommends the replacement of myth and religion with scientific thought. He holds that the great expectations of reason and philosophy have now to be realized in day-to-day political practice. It is this grand theory or 'meta-narrative' of overall social change guided by the dictates of universal Reason which the postmodernists reject. They insist that the relationship between the practical application of Reason (seen as a unitary historical force) and emancipation is precisely the *opposite* of that promised by Marx. The meta-narratives of Reason and of modernity do not foster self-realization and Progress. They do not disclose but rather *mask* the exercise of power. The consequences of Marx's ambition for a wholesale transformation of the social world are dire. However well-intentioned may be the political intervention of Marxists, their ambition for social transformation in accord with the imperatives of a global reason will always tend towards totalitarian outcomes. The more rigorously and systematically do Marxists apply the presumptions of modernity, the more oppressive and distorting do the consequences prove to be. Marx promised universal human emancipation, but what we got in practice was genocide and the Gulag.

Post-Marx?

If Marx had *only* been a leading figure in the social philosophy of modernity, we should still have good reason to read him. But, of course, Marx's heritage has actually been one of the shaping forces of the 'short' twentieth century (1917–1991; see Hobsbawm, 1994). Following the successes of the Russian (1917) and Chinese (1949) Revolutions, and their subsequent empire-building, communist states came at one time to account for as much as a third of the world's population and more than 40 per cent of global industrial production (White et al., 1990, p. 3). In the period of the Cold War, Marxism, or more properly Marxism–Leninism, appeared as one of two great contending 'world views' and, it seemed at times, the one which might yet prevail. On both right and left, it has been argued that the coming of the Soviet Union and its advocacy of worldwide workers' revolution was a precipitating cause of the rise of fascism and with it of the great global war of 1939–45 and its incalculable consequences. More generally, Marx's social thought has had a pervasive influence upon almost every field of intellectual endeavour in the twentieth century (from aesthetics to zoology), and, even where an explicit debt to Marx is now denied, Marxian influences often lie unacknowledged in the origins of many contemporary disciplines, especially in the social sciences. Finally, the collapse of communism in 1989–90 has not so much ushered in an end to ideologies or a golden age of universal liberal democracy, but rather the global ascendancy of capitalism. Since this is a capitalism which appears increasingly unshackled from the moderating institutional restraints of the postwar 'mixed economy', it would be a strange time indeed to abandon our interest in capitalism's greatest critic.

Marx's Grand Synthesis

Lenin (1931, p. 11), echoing Engels, described Marx as 'the genius who continued and completed the three chief ideological currents of the nineteenth century: classical German philosophy, classical English political economy, and French socialism combined with French revolutionary doctrines'. Such a summary hardly does justice to the diversity and originality of Marx's thought (and the greatest representative of classical 'English' political economy, Adam Smith, was actually a Scot!). Nonetheless, it remains a useful starting point in making sense of Marx's work. This was, above all, a brilliant if flawed *synthesis*, drawing together elements from a remarkably broad reading of contemporary sources in social, political and economic thought. Although Marx's central concern with capitalism has often led to a focus upon his broadly economic writing (and his critique of British political economy), this only makes sense in terms of his encounter with (German) idealist philosophy and a (largely French) revolutionary tradition. All of these elements should become clear in reading the selections in this volume.

'Settling accounts' with Hegel

'Every beginning is difficult', Marx writes in the Preface to *Capital*, and this is certainly true of Marx's own earliest work (certainly down to 1844–5). These writings are dominated by Marx's critical engagement with German idealist philosophy. In the early 1840s, the intellectual climate in Germany was still dominated by the towering figure of G.W.F. Hegel, who had died in 1831 and whom Marx always regarded as the leading exponent of German Idealist philosophy. For Marx, the encounter with Hegel was mediated by the approach of the 'Young Hegelians', a group of younger thinkers who sought to radicalize Hegel's system of thought by 'inverting' it, that is by replacing his idealist assumptions with materialist ones.

At the heart of Hegel's thinking was a philosophy of history, the belief that through time humankind progressed through a number of distinct stages. Each of these stages embodied a higher expression of an ideal of self-consciousness or Reason which was itself the defining purpose of historical development. The End of History would come with the completion of this journey towards full self-knowledge or the final realization of the Ideal or the Absolute. Each of the historical stages that Hegel identified held within it the potential for transformation towards a still higher form. The transition from one stage to another, through the synthesis of the opposing elements inherent within it, Hegel described as *aufhebung*, a German word which conveys a sense of transformation but also of preservation-through-change. The power of the negative, of the potentiality for change, of the emergence within the present of the seeds of future transformation, Hegel called the *dialectic*.

At its simplest, the strategy of the most radical of the Young Hegelians (of whom Ludwig Feuerbach was, for Marx, clearly the most distinguished) was to retain much of the Hegelian philosophy of history and the dynamic and historicized conception of the dialectic, but to insist that the true subject of humanity's history was not the Ideal or Reason (or God) but humankind itself. Feuerbach's 'transformational criticism' of Hegel sought to invert subject and object and to insist that the *real* basis of humanity's history was this-worldly Man (sic). The world of ideas was but an alienated reflection of this mundane reality.

This critical engagement with Hegel had a profound effect upon the young Marx. In his *Contribution to the Critique of Hegel's 'Philosophy of Right'* (the *Introduction* to which is reproduced here), and in the essay *On the Jewish Question*, Marx works out his own inversion of the Hegelian system. Much of the Young Hegelian 'debate' with Hegel had been cast in the form and language of religious criticism. That chapter closes, so Marx supposes, with the recognition that '*Man makes religion*, religion does not make man'. The task now is to move forward from the critique of religion and the other-worldly and to disclose the nature of human self-estrangement *in this world*. Thus, Marx insists, 'the criticism of heaven turns into the criticism of the earth . . . the *criticism of theology* into the *criticism of politics*' (pp. 48–9 below).

It is characteristic of Marx's critical methodology that in making this move he does not simply *abandon* Hegel's world view, nor does he discount what he sees as the *real* basis underlying religious illusion. There is much in Hegel's analysis of the state which Marx endorses. Indeed, Marx supposes that Hegel, in identifying a division between the state and civil society (as the 'realm of needs' or the 'sphere of economic life'), has isolated what is probably the key institutional feature that marks off 'modern society' from its feudal forerunner. Hegel's mistake is to see the state as the dominant element in this relationship and to suppose that the profound divisions which he acknowledges to exist in civil society's 'realm of needs' are 'overcome' by the overarching presence of the state and its representative class, the bureaucracy. Having recognized the separation of civil and political life as a contradiction, Hegel claimed to find this opposition resolved in the form of the modern state. For Marx, by contrast, it was the *persistence* of this contradiction between political and civil society which *required* the modern state. Thus, the state was not the idealized representative of society. Rather, it was itself an expression of the continuing deep-seated contradictions within that society (leading to the supposition that a society 'without contradictions' would also be a society 'without need of a state'). Furthermore, it was the nature of the relationships *within civil society*, within the economic sphere, that tended to determine the form and character of the state (and not the other way around, as Hegel had supposed).

Echoing the Young Hegelians' critique of Hegel, in the essay *On the Jewish Question* Marx deploys a religious analogy to describe this relationship between civil society and the state. The individual in the 'modern world' lives a double life. Just as Christianity teaches us to expect inequality on earth but equality in heaven, so were people '*equal* in the heaven of their political world, though unequal in their earthly existence in *society*'. Continuing the religious analogy, Marx insists that 'the political state stands in the same opposition to civil society, and it prevails over the latter in the same way as religion prevails over the narrowness of the secular world, i.e. by likewise having always to acknowledge it, to restore it and allow itself to be dominated by it' (p. 35 below). He illustrates this by considering the long-standing contemporary case for the extension of full religious freedom to the Jewish population. Freedom *of* religion, Marx insists, is a very partial liberation because it simply translates religious differences into an aspect of private conduct (confined to civil society). *Fully human* emancipation would mean freedom *from* religion, that is liberation from the superstition and alienation that religion is seen, by Marx, to express. The purely political annulment of religion (as, by extension, of private property) consists only in declaring distinctions of religion/private property to be *non-political*, that is in confining these differences to civil society. But since civil society dominates over the political, these secular differences continue to dominate the political process from their 'purely private' locus in civil society. To take Marx's other example, abolishing the property limitation upon the franchise does not stop economic power from shaping the political process.

Characteristically, the individual in modern society is split into a *public* self, the citizen engaged in the exercise of political rights on a basis of equality with all other citizens, and a *private* self, in a world of profound economic inequality where the law is 'dog eat dog'. The political emancipation heralded in the slogans of the French Revolution promised to make political citizenship *really* universal and this, Marx acknowledges, was a significant advance. But such 'political emancipation' is strictly limited. What goes on in the heavenly world of political equality is actually determined by the grubby and selfish interests of individuals as economic agents in civil society. 'Truly human' emancipation, as Marx calls it, can only be achieved by overcoming the division between political society and civil society, by bringing public and private selves together and in the process eliminating the state and 'political life' as a separate sphere of human activity. For Marx this 'truly human' emancipation through the unity of civil and political life is what constitutes 'True Democracy'. At the same time, it describes that resolution of societal contradictions into a higher unity which Hegel saw at the end of history.

These earliest essays of Marx contain political ideas (about the dependence of the state upon society, the limitations of a 'purely political' emancipation and the need for the ultimate suppression of the state itself) which were to find echoes all the way down to the writings of the 1870s.

But, whilst they certainly show Marx to be severely critical of the egoism that characterizes economic relationships in civil society, they convey a rather limited sense that the study of *economic* relationships would be the key to understanding the processes of historical change. This awareness begins to emerge in the *Introduction to the Critique of Hegel's Doctrine of the State*, written at the very end of 1843. As well as lamenting the backward conditions of political life amongst the Germans, this work announces Marx's discovery of the emerging class of wage labourers, the *proletariat*, as the historical agent of revolutionary change. How is universal human emancipation in Germany possible?

> In the formation of a class with *radical chains*, a class of civil society which is not a class of civil society, an estate which is the dissolution of all estates, a sphere which has a universal character by its universal suffering ... a sphere, finally, which cannot emancipate itself without emancipating itself from all others spheres of society and thereby emancipating all other spheres of society, which in a word, is the complete loss of man and hence can win itself only through the complete rewinning of man. This dissolution of society as a particular estate is the proletariat.

What makes possible this historical transformation is the marriage of radical philosophy and revolutionary proletariat:

> The head of this emancipation is philosophy, its heart is the proletariat. Philosophy cannot be made a reality without the abolition of the proletariat, the proletariat cannot be abolished without philosophy being made a reality. (pp. 58–9 below)

Towards the critique of political economy

After a spell as a journalist in his native Rhineland, Marx moved to Paris in the autumn of 1843. Inspired by an article of the youthful Friedrich Engels on the 'Outlines of a Critique of Political Economy', Marx threw himself into a critical study of the classical political economists. The *Economic and Philosophical Manuscripts*, written in 1844, but lying unpublished until the 1930s, contain Marx's first sustained critical account of capitalism and his earliest elaboration of communism as its historical alternative and successor. For some, the *Manuscripts* set out the agenda which was to dominate the rest of Marx's working life.

Adopting the methodology which was to have its fullest flowering in *Capital*, Marx proceeds on the basis of a critique of political economy. The classical political economy of men such as Adam Smith and David Ricardo has considerable success in describing the workings of the capitalist economy. But its inability to understand the interrelationship of the several objects of its study and its own unacknowledged assumptions conceal from it the *true* nature of such an economy. For Marx, the character of the capitalist economy is condensed in the (untheorized) category of private property and in the still more fundamental role of *alienated labour*. In a key passage, Marx describes workers under capitalism as alienated from the product of their labour, from themselves, from their 'species-being' or 'social essence' and from other people. He insists that:

> On the basis of political economy itself, in its own words, we have shown that the worker sinks to the level of a commodity and becomes indeed the most wretched of commodities; that the wretchedness of the worker is in inverse proportion to the power and magnitude of his production; that the necessary result of competition is the accumulation of capital in a few hands, and thus the restoration of monopoly in a terrible form; and that finally the distinction between capitalist and land rentier, like that between the tiller of the soil and the factory worker, disappears and that the whole of society must fall into the two classes – the *property owners* and the propertyless *workers* . . . (pp. 60–1 below)

The alienation of labour can only be overcome through the supersession of private property, that is, by the transition to communism. Here Marx draws a distinction between what he calls 'crude communism' (the product of envy and levelling down) and the promise of communism as the *positive* transcendence of private property:

> This communism . . . is the *genuine* resolution of the conflict between man and nature and between man and man – the true resolution of the strife between existence and essence, between objectification and self-confirmation, between freedom and necessity, between the individual and the species. Communism is the riddle of history solved, and it knows itself to be this solution. (pp. 73–4 below)

The idea of a historical transformation which is inscribed in the contradictions of existing social and economic relations is still more explicitly drawn out in Marx and Engels' polemic, *The Holy Family*. In struggling to free itself, the proletariat is driven to overthrow the political economy of private property: 'the proletariat executes the sentence that private property pronounces on itself by producing the proletariat' (p. 88 below).

The German Ideology and the materialist conception of history

There is some disagreement about the status of *The German Ideology*, written jointly by Marx and Engels in 1845–6. Some have seen it as the last of the 'early' works, others as the first truly 'Marxist' text. It certainly occupies a pivotal position in Marx's own development, laying out the principles of the materialist conception of history within which virtually all of his subsequent work was to be located. At the core of Marx's treatment in *The German Ideology* (and amplified in the *Letter to Annenkov*) is the supposition that human history is above all constituted by the way in which human beings organize the production of the means of their subsistence:

> By producing their means of subsistence men are indirectly producing their actual material life ... This mode of production must not be considered simply as being the production of the physical existence of the individuals. Rather it is a definite form of activity of these individuals, a definite form of expressing their life, a definite *mode of life* ... What they are, therefore, coincides with their production, both with *what* they produce and with *how* they produce. (p. 95 below)

The character of the mode of production changes as increases in the human population generate a more developed division of labour and an ever greater productive capacity, whilst 'the existing stage in the division of labour determines ... the relations of individuals to one another with reference to the material, instrument, and product of labour' (p. 96 below). Thus the development of the division of labour gives rise to a succession of changing 'modes of production' with differing forms of property ownership, labour organization, customs, laws and so on. At this point, we can turn to Marx's own summary of the materialist conception of history (written in 1859), which outlines the position he had reached by the time of *The German Ideology* and which he identifies as the 'guiding principle' of all his work thereafter:

> In the social production of their life, men enter into definite relations, that are indispensable and independent of their will, relations of production which correspond to a definite stage of development of their material productive forces. The sum total of these relations of production constitutes the economic structure of society, the real foundation, on which rises a legal and political superstructure and to which correspond definite forms of social consciousness. The mode of production of material life conditions the social, political and intellectual life process in general. It is not the consciousness of men that determines their being, but, on the contrary, their social being

that determines their consciousness. At a certain stage of their development, the material productive forces of society come in conflict with the existing relations of production or – what is but a legal expression for the same thing – with the property relations within which they have been at work hitherto. From forms of development of the productive forces these relations turn into their fetters. Then begins an era of social revolution . . . In broad outlines Asiatic, ancient, feudal and modern bourgeois modes of production can be designated as progressive epochs in the economic formation of society. The bourgeois relations of production are the last antagonistic form of the social process of production . . . the productive forces developing in the womb of bourgeois society create the material conditions for the solution of that antagonism. This social formation brings, therefore, the prehistory of human society to a close. (pp. 119–20 below)

The true character of the historical materialism which Marx outlines here has always been fiercely contested. Did he really hold that the whole of social life could be explained in terms of developments in society's material (or economic) base and that human agency was, to this extent, irrelevant? Or did he believe that the action of human agents could make a difference, in a way that meant not everything was determined by the material base of society? Given Marx's condemnation at just this time (in the *Theses on Feuerbach*) of 'all previous materialism' which failed to grasp the centrality of 'sensuous human activity, practice', it seems unfair to depict him as the advocate of a mechanistic and deterministic materialism. The difficulty is that Marx sometimes wrote, in some fairly prominent places, as if he *did* indeed believe that material and above all economic relations drove forward the process of history unmindful of the wills and intentions of its human objects, as in the Preface to *Capital* (p. 204 below), where he speaks of 'the natural laws of capitalist production . . . working with iron necessity towards inevitable results'. At times, Marx sought to reconcile these two positions, as in the brilliant aphorism that 'men make their own history, but . . . they do not make it under circumstances chosen by themselves' (p. 156 below). In the end, however, and despite all the brilliant and banal things that have been said in between, it is perhaps best to treat Marx's views as internally inconsistent and the tension between the two principles of material determination and human agency as unresolved. Having said this, Marx's materialism could only ever be described as crude and unreflexive in a few exceptionally truncated or polemical statements.

The German Ideology also contains, in line with Marx's own recollections, perhaps the fullest discussion of successive historical modes of production culminating in capitalism, 'the last antagonistic form of the social process of production' and itself destined to be replaced by socialism's non-antagonistic arrangements. Followers of Marx, especially those beyond the 'heartlands' of the most advanced capitalism, were later to become increasingly vexed by the issue of whether these constituted 'necessary' historical stages through which all societies would have to pass. In particular, there was the question of whether societies which were still semi-feudal would have to pass through a 'capitalist phase' before they could hope to initiate a new and socialist order. This was to become one of the most fiercely contested aspects of Lenin's conduct in Russia (with his rival, Karl Kautsky, insisting that the Bolsheviks' attempt to make a socialist revolution in a backward and semi-feudal country was in defiance of Marx's teaching). In this context, considerable attention has been focused upon the (very few) things Marx had to say about this process (including the two *Letters on Russia* and the two *Articles on India* included here). His remarks on Russia do suggest that existing communal forms of property might afford a historical 'shortcut' to socialism. His comments on the oppression of the population of India, by contrast, seem to indicate that liberation here can only come 'when a great social revolution shall have mastered the results of the bourgeois epoch, the market of the world and the modern powers of production, and subjected them to the common control of the most advanced peoples' (*India*, p. 222). In fact, Marx's judgment is rather inconclusive. What his comments do suggest, however, was his general impatience with those who sought to apply his materialist conception of history too mechanically.

It is certainly possible to describe *The German Ideology* as completing the essential framework within which Marx was to develop the writings of his maturity. At one time, there was a very vigorous debate as to whether there was some sort of 'break' in Marx's thinking around 1845, relegating his work prior to this date to a rather lesser status as the precursor to a properly 'scientific' Marxism. Certainly, the fact that most of the early writings were unavailable during the formative years of Marxism itself (around the turn of the twentieth century) was enormously consequential. It is certainly possible to find important differences between the writings of the younger and the more mature Marx. Nonetheless, it now seems implausible to claim that it is discontinuity rather than continuity which best characterizes Marx's work before and after 1845. For example, the concept of *alienation*, so central to the *Economic and Philosophical Manuscripts*, re-appears in all but name (and in the case of *Grundrisse*, in name as well) in the writings of the later Marx. As late as 1873, he could still pay tribute to 'that mighty thinker' Hegel and to the dialectic which 'in its rational form [is] critical and revolutionary' (Marx, 1978, p. 302).

The *Manifesto* and the centrality of class struggle

The Communist Manifesto, written jointly by Marx and Engels, and first published in 1848, the year of revolutions, was a brilliant and polemical recapitulation of the key elements in the social theory that the authors had developed through the 1840s. Writing of the *Manifesto* nearly forty years later, Engels (1978b, p. 472) describes its 'basic thought' thus:

> that economic production and the structure of society of every historical epoch arising therefrom constitute the foundation for the political and intellectual history of that epoch; that consequently (ever since the dissolution of the primeval communal ownership of land) all history has been a history of class struggles, of struggles between exploited and exploiting, between dominated and dominating classes at various stages of social development; that this struggle, however, has now reached a stage where the exploited and oppressed class (the proletariat) can no longer emancipate itself from the class which exploits and oppresses it (the bourgeoisie) without at the same time forever freeing the whole of society from exploitation, oppression and class struggles.

The opening section of the *Manifesto* positively crackles with political invective. It remains a compelling and outraged *tour de force*, almost certainly the best known and most widely read document of revolutionary socialism. It is still probably the best point at which to start reading Marx, so long as one remembers that it is not only communist but also a manifesto. Although it had almost no effect upon the revolutionary events of 1848, it was intended as a call to arms in an emerging revolutionary situation and Marx's certainty about the imminent victory of proletarian forces and the defeat of the bourgeoisie, whilst real enough, should be read in this context.

The *Manifesto* also gives definitive expression to Marx's belief that politics was above all a struggle between classes. The first section – 'Bourgeois and proletarians' – opens with the declaration that 'the history of all hitherto existing society is the history of class struggles' and goes on to claim that what is distinctive about the present age is that 'it has simplified the class antagonisms: Society as a whole is more and more splitting up into two great hostile camps, into two great classes directly facing each other: Bourgeoisie and Proletariat' (p. 129 below). Even in the polemical context of the *Manifesto*, Marx recognizes the existence of other 'secondary' classes, but only to argue that these 'other classes decay and finally disappear' as the 'decisive hour' of confrontation between bourgeoisie and proletariat approaches. The fact that, to put it simply, capitalism never does quite resolve itself into two great contending classes and that the 'proletarian movement' never does quite come to constitute 'the self-conscious, independent movement of the immense majority, in the interest of the immense majority' presented enormous problems for subsequent generations of Marxists (and, indeed, for socialists more generally). But if we confine our attention to Marx alone, we find two other problems. First, the model of the 'two great contending classes' is only one of several accounts that Marx offers and, indeed, the more detailed and historical texts (rather than the grand schematic overviews) disclose quite diverse class formations (a tendency which is especially clear in Marx's detailed history of developments in France between 1848 and 1852). Secondly, Marx never furnishes a clear theoretical statement about the nature of classes. Notoriously, the 'Chapter on Classes' from volume 3 of *Capital* (included here) breaks off after one and a half pages. There is a voluminous literature detailing the ways in which all of Marx's scattered statements on class might somehow be 'resolved' into a single coherent account. But, once again, I think it is better simply to live with the diversity of Marx's theoretical and historical writings on class, rather than to pretend that this diversity can be usefully 'overcome'.

Marx's maturity: the critique of political economy

If settling accounts with German idealist philosophy was the most prominent theme of Marx's early writings, it is the critical analysis of capitalism that dominates the writings of his maturity. We have already seen this theme raised in the *Economic and Philosophical Manuscripts* and *The German Ideology*. It is the central topic of *Wage-Labour and Capital* (1847). With the general defeat of the revolutionary movements of 1848, Marx 'withdrew to the study' and he spent much of the 1850s and 1860s working through his critique of political economy in *Grundrisse*, in the three volumes of *Theories of Surplus Value* and, of course, definitively in *Capital*. In several places, including the Introduction to *Grundrisse* (pp. 191–2 below), Marx indicates that this critical analysis of capitalist production was to be but the first stage in a much more ambitious research programme. In the event, even this first stage was never fully realized and at his death Marx left many thousands of pages of work on the topic in a fragmentary and incomplete state. In this collection, Marx's account of the political economy of capitalism is represented by substantial selections from volume one of *Capital* and *Grundrisse* and by shorter selections from the third volume of *Capital* (compiled by Engels from Marx's notes after his death).

As indicated in the *Economic and Philosophical Manuscripts*, Marx's method in examining the capitalist mode of production was to proceed from the work of the classical political economists and to press what he saw as their authentic premises to radically new conclusions. Above all, he wished to show how two widely accepted assumptions of classical political economy, about labour as a source of value and the long-term tendency for the rate of profit to fall, once properly explicated or *demystified*, lead to the most radical political conclusions.

In *Capital*, analysis begins with the category of the commodity. Capitalism is a system of the production and exchange of commodities, where a commodity is anything which answers to a perceived need and may be bought and sold in the market. The *exchange* value of any commodity is given by the amount of labour power needed to produce it (by an average labourer working under normal conditions using the prevailing technology). The exchange value of any commodity is thus an expression of the labour power embodied in it. It is this characteristic which allows physically incommensurable objects (corn and iron, for example) to have a value which can be expressed in terms of each other or in terms of a third mediating medium, money. Under capitalism, commodities exchange at their values, which express the amount of socially necessary labour embodied in them. Yet, at the end of this exchange process the capitalist, the buyer of labour power, is sitting on a profit. In Marx's own sardonic words, 'our friend, Moneybags, must be so lucky as to find . . . in the market, a commodity, whose use-value possesses the peculiar property of being a source of value, whose actual consumption, therefore, is itself an embodiment of labour, and, consequently, a creation of value'. This 'special commodity' which generates a value in excess of its own value is *labour power*.

The value of this labour power (representing the capacity of the wage labourer to perform productive work) is, like any other commodity, given by the amount of socially necessary labour time embodied in its (re)production. Consequently, 'the value of labour-power is the value of the means of subsistence necessary for the maintenance of the labourer' (p. 228 below). The difference between the value of labour power and the value it is able to create, Marx called *surplus value*. If the capitalist hires a worker to work a ten-hour day for $10 (the value of the worker's labour power), yet the labourer manages to produce $10 of additional value in the first five hours of the shift, the value produced in the last five hours of the working day (let us say a further $10) is *surplus* value. This surplus value is the ultimate source of the capitalist's profit and, since Marx regards it as work which is unpaid, it expresses the relationship of capital to labour as one which is intrinsically exploitative. The ratio of surplus labour to necessary labour (in our example, five hours to five hours) gives the *rate of exploitation* (in this case, 100 per cent).

Marx believes that his analysis shows not only that capitalism is necessarily exploitative and antagonistic (built upon a division between the two classes of capitalists and wage-labourers) but also that the form of this exploitation is 'concealed' beneath what appears to be a 'free and equal' exchange. The 'mysterious' aspect of exploitation under capitalism (contrasting with the more 'open' process of exploitation in all previous class societies) is that 'the fetishism of commodities' makes it appear that the contractual relationship between owner and worker represents a 'free and equal exchange'. This does a great deal to make capitalistic private property and the labour contract appear legitimate. But, in fact, Marx insists, it only serves to conceal the appropriation of surplus value and with it the generalized exploitation of the wage labourer.

Thus far, Marx's analysis in *Capital* gives us a 'static' picture of the process of 'concealed' exploitation under capitalism. But, as we have already seen, Marx insisted (as the most radical lesson to be learned from Hegel) upon a sense of the *historicity* of any given social formation and of the inevitability of its change. Marx repeatedly chides the apologists of capitalism for presenting its economic 'laws of motion' as natural and immutable. The capitalist mode of production was, like all its historic predecessors, simply the product of a particular historical time and place. Like them, it was subject to a set of internal contradictions whose 'ripening' would precipitate the transition to a new form of economy and society. Marx's account of the 'dynamics' of capitalist development and of its maturing 'contradictions' are fashioned around a second radicalized principle drawn from classical political economy – the *tendency for the rate of profit to fall*.

For Marx, capitalism is history's most dynamic mode of production. In the *Manifesto*, he pays only half-ironic tribute to the transformation of the entire global order that the bourgeoisie in its historically progressive phase (as the revolutionary successor to feudalism) has wrought. Capitalism is unique as well in that expanded accumulation becomes an 'end in itself': 'the circulation of capital has ... no limits' (p. 223 below). Competition is the watchword of the capitalist mode of production, and competition exists not just between capital and labour but also, in the absence of countervailing co-operative forms of organization, *between* individual capitalists and *between* individual workers. Individual capitalists competing for a larger share of the available market (and profit) are constantly driven to seek greater labour productivity and to undercut the production costs of their competitors, by instituting technological innovation or implementing various 'economies of scale'. In so doing, they are likely to drive out many smaller capitalist enterprises and independent producers. They are also likely to 'release' redundant workers into an already crowded labour market. (Marx saw the existence of a 'reserve army' of unemployed workers as a necessary means of controlling those *in* work and exerting downward pressure on wages.) Any competitive advantage which an individual enterprise can derive from technological innovation is, however, likely to prove short-lived as competitors will take up the new cost-cutting technology leading to the establishment of a new equilibrium between (a smaller number of) competing firms.

The new equilibrium thus established differs from the old, however, in that it is potentially *less profitable*. This change relates to Marx's earlier argument about labour as the sole source of value. In volume one of *Capital*, Marx draws the distinction between *constant capital* (raw materials and the instruments of labour) which the capitalist must purchase but which do not add value in the process of production, and *variable capital* (labour power) which is the sole source of surplus value. The ratio between this constant and variable capital Marx calls the *organic composition* of capital (*Capital 1*, p. 612). Since it is only variable capital that creates surplus value (from which profit is derived), the higher the ratio of constant to variable capital, that is, the higher the organic composition of capital, the lower will be the rate of profit. The new equilibrium which follows upon a labour-saving technology will, however, be based upon a *higher organic composition* of capital (with variable capital as a smaller proportion of any given unit of capital) and thus a *lower rate of profit*. Marx makes it clear that he regards the rising organic composition of capital as an almost universal feature of the capitalist mode of production:

> This mode of production produces a progressive relative decrease of the variable capital compared to the constant capital, and consequently a continuously rising organic composition of the total capital. The immediate result of this is that the rate of surplus-value, at the same, or even a rising, degree of labour exploitation, is represented by a continually falling general rate of profit. *(Capital 1, pp. 212–3)*

A falling rate of profit need not, of course, lead to a fall in *absolute* levels of profit if the overall quantity of capital is growing sufficiently swiftly to offset the fall in the rate of profitability. In any case, Marx does not generally hold that capitalism experiences *actually* declining rates of profitability. Rather, he indicates that much of the dynamic of the development of the capitalist mode of production is given by the responses which are set in train to *counter* the *tendency* for the rate of profit to fall. These counteracting tendencies typically include increasing the intensity of exploitation (by either lengthening the working day or raising the rate of extraction of surplus value), cheapening the value of labour power (by, for example, reducing the costs of the labourers' reproduction through cheap imports of food and other essentials) or reducing the costs of some constituents of constant capital (*Capital 3*, pp. 232–40; p. 243 below). But the working through of these counter-tendencies accelerates the process of the concentration and centralization of capital (placing larger accumulations in fewer hands) and, at the same time, intensifies the burden of all the disadvantages of capitalism upon a growing pool of increasingly exploited wage-labourers. Through time, these developments intensify the 'socialization' of the forces of production. On the one hand, the organization of labour becomes increasingly social (with large concentrations of workers experiencing similar working conditions in large-scale production processes). On the other, the forms of capital (especially with the expansion of credit and the introduction of professional management) become themselves increasingly 'social', with the joint-stock company famously described by Marx as 'the abolition of capital as private property within the framework of capitalist production itself' (p. 244 below).

The belief that the internal contradictions of capitalism would lead to its demise, that eventually capitalist relations of production would become a barrier to the further development of society's productive forces and hence give way to a new (and socialist) mode of production, can be found in both the *Manifesto* and the *1859 Preface*. It is given its clearest summary statement in chapter 32 of Volume 1 of *Capital*:

> [The expropriation of the capitalist class] is accomplished by the action of the immanent laws of capitalist production itself, by the centralization of capital. One capitalist always kills many. Hand in hand with this centralization, or this expropriation of many capitalists by few, develop, on an ever extending scale, the co-operative form of the labour-process, the conscious technical application of science, the methodical cultivation of the soil, the transformation of the instruments of labour into instruments of labour only usable in common, the economising of all means of production by their use as the means of production of combined, socialised labour, the entanglement of all peoples in the net of the world-market, and with this, the international character of the capitalistic régime. Along with the constantly diminishing number of the magnates of capital who usurp and monopolise all advantages of this process of transformation, grows the mass of misery, oppression, slavery, degradation, exploitation; but with this too grows the revolt of the working-class, a class always increasing in numbers, and disciplined, united, organised by the very mechanism of the processes of capitalist production itself. The monopoly of capital becomes a fetter upon the mode of production, which has sprung up and flourished along with, and under it. Centralisation of the means of production and socialisation of labour at last reach a point where they become incompatible with their capitalist integument. This integument is burst asunder. The knell of capitalist private property sounds. The expropriators are expropriated. (p. 240 below)

Instructively, in both the *Preface* and in *Capital*, it is rather unclear who is to deliver this verdict of history and how they are to do it. If the agents of historical change are more clearly specified in the *Manifesto*, as the revolutionary working class, the mechanism of revolutionary change is still rather unclear. Certainly, Marx does not argue that capitalism will collapse 'automatically' under the weight of its own contradictions. In *Capital*, 'crisis' is typically a mechanism of systemic *adjustment* (albeit one that intensifies existing contradictions) rather than an embodiment of systemic *breakdown*. We may know who is to sound the death knell of capitalist private property, but how are the expropriators to be expropriated? To try to answer this question, we need to turn to the third schematic element in Marx's work, his account of politics and of revolution.

Marx's politics

Marx's political writings abound with ironies. At Marx's graveside, Engels described him as 'before all else a revolutionist' (Engels, 1978a, p. 682). Yet, as the great revolutionary dramas of the nineteenth century unfolded, Marx was generally left on the sidelines as an impassioned but disempowered commentator. His ambitions were above all else political, yet his most immediately political writings are scattered and comparatively unsystematic. He looked forward with confidence to the 'inevitable' victory of the proletariat, but found himself repeatedly writing, often with great subtlety and insight, about the 'temporary' successes of various 'forces of reaction'.

In fact, Marx's clearest engagement with an explicitly political object probably comes in his earliest essays of 1843. It is probably no coincidence that, after the 'discovery' of the materialist conception of history (around the time of *The German Ideology*), Marx hardly ever again addresses a 'purely' political object. In part, this is because in Marx's mature work politics was embraced within a critique of political economy which included both political and economic relationships. But it is also reasonable to argue that, from the time of *The German Ideology* onwards, Marx often wrote as if political relationships could, in however mediated a way, be *derived* from logically prior material or economic relationships. Politics was, above all, an expression of the clash of material interests reflected at the level of the state. According to *The German Ideology*, 'all struggles within the State are merely the illusory forms in which the real struggles of the different classes are fought out' (p. 103 below). In the similarly synoptic language of the *1859 Preface*:

> A distinction should always be made between the material transformation of the economic conditions of production, which can be determined with the precision of natural science, and the legal, political, religious, aesthetic or philosophic – in short, ideological forms in which men become conscious of this conflict and fight it out. (pp. 119–20 below)

In the *Communist Manifesto*, Marx gives particularly clear, if polemical, expression to these views in describing the political advance of the bourgeoisie. He writes that 'each step in the development of the bourgeoisie was accompanied by a corresponding political advance of that class [so that] in the modern representative State, [the bourgeoisie holds] exclusive political sway'. This leads on to Marx's famous conclusion that 'the executive of the modern State is but a committee for managing the common affairs of the whole bourgeoisie' (p. 130 below). Of course, this summary formulation does not mean that Marx became a simple and vulgar economic determinist, believing that all political struggles are simply a reflection of economic antagonisms. Given his stricture on all previous forms of materialism for neglecting the centrality of *practice*, how could it? But it is possible to argue that it encouraged Marx to give insufficient attention to politics as something other than a reflection of opinions and interests formed elsewhere. Certainly, as an old man, Engels (1978c, p. 766) was to regret the extent to which he and Marx had overemphasized 'the *derivation of the political* . . . from basic economic facts'.

The relatively autonomous state: France 1848–52

This view of the political process was probably the dominant (if often unarticulated) Marxian view of the political process. It certainly had the profoundest effect upon the propagators of 'orthodox Marxism' who wrote under the authority of Engels' popular version of this thesis in *Anti-Dühring* and without the benefit of access to Marx's early texts. But there is also a second view of state and politics in Marx's work. This less schematic and less deterministic approach is perhaps best represented by the articles collected as *The Class Struggles in France* and *The Eighteenth Brumaire of Louis Bonaparte*. Taken together, these two texts constitute Marx's detailed contemporary history of France from the defeated revolution of 1848 to the *coup d'état* of 1851 and its aftermath. Engels (1967, p. 641) later described *The Class Struggles* as 'Marx's first attempt to explain a section of contemporary history by means of the materialist conception'.

These commentaries are unlike anything in Marx's prior work. In contrast to the sweeping generalizations of the *Manifesto* or *The German Ideology*, they represent an attempt to apply materialist premises and class analysis to the minutiae of political life. Here there is much more of what we would normally recognize as the political process. Marx certainly gives due attention to the competition between a diversity of economic interests and seeks to show how what are apparently clashes of philosophical principle or dynastic preference may be reduced to differences of material interest. But he also analyses factions and in-fighting, the attempt to form coalitions, rhetorical excess, bungling, vanity – and even the occasional cock-up! As one might expect, Marx's commentary is not purely narrative. He persistently seeks to draw out from the apparent confusion of day-to-day events an explanation of the materialist premises underpinning French developments. In this process, the bold clear lines of the *Manifesto* disappear. In mid-century France, capitalism is as yet underdeveloped. Residues of earlier modes of production, and their classes, remain. Consequently, Marx's commentaries feature a rich variety of classes (of which the great landowners, peasants, bourgeoisie and workers are only the most important) and a diversity of fractions within these classes (most notably, a division between the financial and industrial fractions of the bourgeoisie). The peasantry, who have only a walk-on part in Marx's grander historical drama, emerge here as a central player (albeit without any lines of their own) in supporting the regime of the Emperor, Louis Bonaparte. Marx's ambition is to show how a political drama with many players, articulating a variety of ideological positions, can in the end be explained in terms of the underlying economic interests of a plurality of classes (and class fractions).

Consideration of the French counter-revolution also leads Marx towards a distinctive account of the state–society relationship, an account which echoes the condemnation of the state made in the earlier critique of Hegel. In *The Eighteenth Brumaire*, Marx explicitly abandons the idea that the state is, in any straightforward sense, the instrument of a single ruling class. He argues that the Bonapartist regime does indeed represent a class – 'the most numerous class of French society, the *small peasant proprietors*' – but the peasantry is not, in any sense, a ruling class. In the end, the state relies upon the capitalist economy for its revenues. To this extent, it shares with the bourgeoisie an interest in the continued exploitation of the working class. It is also complicit with the bourgeoisie in the exploitation of the peasantry through the imposition of a regime of high taxes and acute rural indebtedness. At the same time, it does enjoy a certain autonomy from the immediate interests of the bourgeoisie. Marx argues that the bourgeoisie, whose 'natural' political aspiration would be to govern under the form of a democratic republic, abandons this political ambition for fear that the working class would press for the democratic republic to become a *socialist* republic. Fearful of these further political consequences of securing its own political rule, the bourgeoisie 'hands over' its *political* power to a third and 'reactionary' force, the better to be able to protect its still more fundamental *economic* interests. In Marx's own words (1973, p. 190), 'the bourgeoisie confesses that its own interest requires its deliverance from the peril of its own self-government . . . that its political power must be broken in order to preserve its social power intact'. This judgement, that the bourgeoisie might fail to make its 'own' revolution for fear of the socialist revolution to which it might form a prelude, was one of the key lessons Marx drew from the failure of the revolutions of 1848. The strategic consequences, including the need for the proletariat to advance bourgeois-democratic ambitions but then to press forward to a socialist revolution, Marx outlined in his 'Address to the Communist League' of March 1850 (pp. 147–55 below). It was a lesson that was not to be lost upon Lenin and the Bolsheviks.

Under the Restoration monarchy (prior to 1848), the bureaucracy in France had seemed to act as 'the instrument of the ruling class'. Marx argues that 'only under the second Bonaparte does the state seem to have made itself *completely independent*' (p. 168 below). This state apparatus, now liberated from the 'control' of the bourgeoisie, appears as a 'specific oppression' of the society it is to administer:

> This executive power with its enormous bureaucratic and military organisa-
> tion, with its extensive and artificial state machinery, with a host of officials
> numbering half a million, this appalling parasitic body . . . enmeshes the body
> of French society like a net and chokes all its pores. (p. 167 below)

Marx was later to describe this seemingly autonomous and parasitic state of the Second Empire as a product of the unresolved balance of power between bourgeoisie and proletariat. It was, he argues, 'the only form of government possible at a time when the bourgeoisie had already lost, and the working class had not yet acquired, the faculty of ruling the nation' (p. 250 below).

The Paris Commune: 'political form of the social emancipation'

In the period 1848–51, Marx concluded that the French proletariat was, as yet, insufficiently developed to take power. Twenty years later, in a process reviewed in *The Civil War in France*, he found this immaturity overcome and a practical revolutionary strategy pioneered in the principles of the Paris Commune. The Commune had been established as a provisional form of government in the capital following a plebeian revolt against the prevailing governmental order. Though bloodily repressed, it represented to Marx 'the glorious harbinger of a new society' and it was not crushed before it had initiated a set of new governing principles which Marx identified as 'the political form . . . under which to work out the economic emancipation of labour'. It thus affords us what is probably Marx's fullest description of the anticipated form of a revolutionary working-class government.

Given the popular association of Marxism with an overmighty central-ized state, it is ironic that Marx, throughout forty years of active engagement with the political process, reserved his severest censure for the institutions of the state. Even the bourgeoisie had its redeeming features (eloquently championed in the *Manifesto*) but not, so it seemed, the state. Marx could hardly wait to be rid of it. On the other hand, at least in terms of revolutionary tactics, he was not an anarchist. He believed that on the morrow of the revolution, and perhaps for some considerable time thereafter, society would need a governing and administrative apparatus through which to manage its common affairs. This could not, however, be some *adaptation* of the existing state (which was, in its essence, an expression of a class-divided society) but had rather to be an *alternative* to it. Accordingly, the Commune, then, was 'a revolution not against this or that ... form of state power. It was a revolution against the *state* itself' (Marx, 1974, p. 249).

The most crucial part of *The Civil War in France* (reproduced here) describes this alternative Communard form of governance (or at least Marx's rather idealized rendering of it). Its unifying principle (which again goes back to the Marx of 1843 and 1844) is the overcoming of the division between state and society. The Commune is 'the reabsorption of the state power by society' (Marx, 1974, p. 250).

> The first decree of the Commune ... was the suppression of the standing army, and the substitution for it of the armed people. The Commune was formed of the municipal councillors, chosen by universal suffrage in the various wards of the town, responsible and revocable at short terms. The majority of its members were naturally working men ... The Commune was to be a working, not a parliamentary body, executive and legislative at the same time ... The police was at once stripped of all its political attributes, and turned into the responsible and at all times revocable agent of the Commune. So were the officials of all other branches of the Administration. From the members of the Commune downwards, the public service had to be done at *workmen's wages* ... judges and magistrates were to be elective, responsible, and revocable.
>
> The Commune made that catch-word of bourgeois revolutions, cheap government, a reality, by destroying the two greatest sources of expenditure – the standing army and State functionarism. (pp. 251–3 below)

The Commune itself was short-lived and it is not clear that, in practice, it corresponded in every particular to Marx's description of it (Edwards, 1973). It assumed great importance in the subsequent Marxist tradition both because it was one of the few places in which Marx described what 'the political form of the social emancipation' might look like and because it was to be taken up by Lenin in *State and Revolution* as a model for the soviets in making the Russian Revolution (Lenin, 1960). In this context, it is notable too that Engels (though not Marx) described the Paris Commune as 'the dictatorship of the proletariat' (Engels, 1962, p. 485).

'Dictatorship of the proletariat'

The phrase 'the dictatorship of the proletariat', used infrequently by Marx himself, was to assume an enormous significance in the subsequent history of Marxism, in the clash between Kautsky and Lenin and in forging the division between a communist and a social democratic left in Europe after the First World War. One of the most prominent places in which Marx uses the phrase is in his famous letter to Weydemeyer (written in 1852):

> as for myself, I do not claim to have discovered either the existence of classes in modern society or the struggle between them . . . My own contribution was: 1) to show that the *existence of classes* is merely bound up with *certain historical phases in the development of production*, 2) that the class struggle necessarily leads to the *dictatorship of the proletariat*, 3) that this dictatorship itself constitutes no more than a transition to the *abolition of all classes* and to *a classless society*. (p. 117 below)

The other prominent place in which Marx raises the spectre of proletarian dictatorship is in the *Critique of the Gotha Programme*, written in 1875. The *Critique* was Marx's commentary on the party programme adopted by the newly merged German Socialist Workers Party (SAPD). Marx condemned, in his usual combative style, all those elements of the new party programme which he felt issued from the undue influence of his sometime rival for the affection of the German workers, the 'opportunistic' Ferdinand Lassalle. He thought the Programme's economic premises were confused. He condemned both the suggestion of compromise with the existing German state and the claim that, in relation to the working class, 'all other classes are *only one reactionary mass*' (p. 268 below). But perhaps his most important comments were those which dealt with the transition to a post-capitalist social order.

Here, Marx writes, what we have to deal with is 'a communist society, not as it has *developed* on its own foundations, but, on the contrary, just as it *emerges* from capitalist society . . . still stamped with the birthmarks of the old society'. Although the private ownership of capital would have been abolished, this would still be a society and economy operating under the laws of exchange. It would still be a society of social and economic inequality. Only 'in a higher phase of communist society', with the further development of social labour and of the productive forces, could 'society inscribe on its banners: From each according to his ability, to each according to his needs!' (pp. 265, 267 below). He concludes that:

> Between capitalist and communist society lies the period of the revolutionary transformation of one into the other. There corresponds to this also a political transition period in which the state can be nothing but *the revolutionary dictatorship of the proletariat*. (p. 273 below)

This 'revolutionary dictatorship' has been subject to the most diverse interpretation. For some, it is an inconsequential aside, for others it describes an expansive and democratic form of government (on the model of the Commune), while a number of commentators, both sympathetic and hostile, identify in this formula the essence of Marx's commitment to a centralized state and coercive class-based rule. These disputes were always much more important in the subsequent history of institutionalized communist parties than they were for Marx. Marx was always much more concerned with the dictatorship of the bourgeoisie than the dictatorship of the proletariat! With the collapse of Leninist communist parties after 1989, this particular dispute is of much less interest. Three brief comments do seem in order, though. First, 'dictatorship' in the nineteenth century referred back to its classical usage (as a period of temporary extra-constitutional rule under exceptional circumstances) rather than forward to the 'totalitarian' dictatorships of the twentieth century. Second, given the aspiration of some to rehabilitate Marx as a good liberal democrat, it is clear that Marx did not shy away from extra-constitutional violence and coercion as necessary tools in the armoury of the revolutionary workers' struggle. Although there are a few brief passages in which Marx seems to concede the possibility of a peaceful and gradual transition to socialism, his general sentiment is closer to that with which he closes the opening section of *The German Ideology*: 'revolution is necessary . . . not only because the *ruling* class cannot be overthrown in any other way, but also because the class *overthrowing* it can only in a revolution succeed in ridding itself of all the muck of ages and become fitted to found society anew' (*GI*, p. 95). Third, and having said this, it is clear that he expected the repressive function of the transitional workers' state would be much reduced from its imperialist bourgeois predecessor and increasingly confined to the containment of 'slaveholder's rebellions'.

Conclusion

I began by considering the consequences of the collapse of the Soviet Empire for the reading of Marx. Critics of Marx have had great fun pointing to the irony that, in the face of his confident expectations, history seems in fact to run *from* socialism *to* capitalism, with the latter overcoming the contradictions of the former. But this is not the only possible response to the dramatic transformations of 1989–91 (and to the much more ambiguous developments of the subsequent period). At the end of the twentieth century, we can hardly avoid reading Marx through the prism of the subsequent history of Marxism. But the death of the 'official' Soviet variant of Marxism may allow more of an opportunity for Marx to speak to us 'in his own voice'. At the very least, he should not be drowned out by the barrage of distorting noise thrown up by his partisan interpreters. We no longer have to contend with the debilitating view that all of Marx's work (indeed, all of the work of both Marx and Engels) somehow constitutes a single, seamless and flawless account of the 'inner workings' of capitalism whose political judgements remain unchallenged by a century's further social development. Gone, too (or so we may fervently hope), is the belief that contemporary political problems can somehow be resolved by trawling through Marx's works for an appropriately authoritative pronouncement.

In fact, what Marx had to say is of much more than purely historic interest. It is true that Marx was, aside from a few ritual denunciations of the hypocrisy of the bourgeois institution of marriage, quite silent on questions of gender and generally unmindful of the ecological limits to growth (though not of the environmentally destructive aspects of capitalism). It is true that many of his economic conceptions, including the nature of value and the character of exploitation, now look rather outmoded. His confidence about the demise of capitalism, once every proviso and qualification has been made, now looks quite misplaced. In his confidence in the promise of natural science and of Progress and in his expectation that the future belonged to the 'toiling masses', he looks very much a man of his own time (a 'fault' much less freely attributed to other nineteenth-century social thinkers).

Yet, whilst there is much in Marx that is archaic, and some things which it would be simplest to discount as plainly wrong, there is also a sense in which (as the critique of the postmodernists actually suggests) he remains a figure for our own times. We are still actively engaged with the ambiguities of modernity. Although it is seldom put this way, we are still, we are perhaps *increasingly* concerned with the social, political and economic consequences of living with capitalism. Indeed, were it not for the spectacular failings of socialist regimes (and the consequent sense that we lack any alternatives), we might have noticed that many of those things that have always made global capitalism unattractive and irrational remain. After all, the last time we were promised an *end of ideology* this was premised upon the unparalleled growth and prosperity which the West enjoyed in the twenty-five years following the Second World War. We now have societies with sluggish growth, permanent mass unemployment, growing income inequality, social exclusion, impoverished public services and chronic, long-term environmental problems. Seemingly commonplace expectations of only a generation ago – about employment opportunities, income maintenance and trade union rights – have disappeared under a newly 'leaner and meaner' global capitalism. It is no longer plausible to look to Marx to furnish the 'answers' to the problems which capitalism presents. But so long as we are still tangling with capitalism, we should probably keep struggling with Marx.

References

Callinicos, A. 1991: *The Revenge of History*. Cambridge: Polity.

Di Stefano, C. 1991: Masculine Marx. In M.L. Shanley and C. Pateman (eds), *Feminist Interpretations and Political Theory*. Cambridge: Polity, 146–63.

Edwards, S. 1973: *The Paris Commune 1871*. New York: Quadrangle.

Engels, F. 1962: Introduction to the *Civil War in France*. In K. Marx and F. Engels, *Selected Works*, Vol. 1, London: Lawrence and Wishart, 473–85.

Engels, F. 1967: Introduction to 1895 edition of *The Class Struggles in France*. In *Selected Writings*. Harmondsworth: Penguin.

Engels, F. 1978a: Speech at the graveside of Karl Marx. In R.C. Tucker (ed.), *The Marx–Engels Reader*, 2nd ed., London: Norton, 681–2.

Engels, F. 1978b: Preface to the German edition of the *Communist Manifesto* of 1883. In R.C. Tucker (ed.), *The Marx–Engels Reader*, 2nd edn. London: Norton, 472.

Engels, F. 1978c: Letter to Franz Mehring. In R.C. Tucker (ed.), *The Marx–Engels Reader*, 2nd edn., London: Norton. 765–7.

Fukuyama, F 1992: *The End of History and the Last Man*. New York: Free Press.

Hobsbawm, E.J. 1994: *Age of Extremes: the Short Twentieth Century 1914–1991*. London: Michael Joseph.

Lenin, V.I. 1931: *The Teaching of Karl Marx*. London: Lawrence and Wishart.

Lenin, V.I. 1960: State and revolution. In *Collected Works*, 25, London: Lawrence and Wishart, 385–497.

Marx, K. 1973: *The Eighteenth Brumaire*. In D. Fernbach (ed.), *Surveys from Exile*, Harmondsworth: Penguin, 143–249.

Marx, K. 1974: First draft of the *Civil War in France*. In D. Fernbach (ed.), *The First International and After*, Harmondsworth: Penguin, 236–68.

Marx, K. 1978: Afterword to the second German edition of *Capital*. In R.C. Tucker (ed.), *The Marx–Engels Reader*, 2nd edn. London: Norton, 299–302.

Smart, B. 1993: *Postmodernity*. London: Routledge.

White, S., Pravda, A. and Gitelman, Z.Y. 1990: *Developments in Soviet Politics*, Basingstoke: Macmillan.

2

On the Jewish Question

In this early critical commentary on Bruno Bauer's book The Jewish Question, *Marx moves from the issue of Jewish emancipation towards a much broader critique of the state and of the limited nature of political liberty. He focuses in particular upon the limitations of a 'purely political' emancipation, the continuing divisions between political and civil society and the persistence of the state as an expression of underlying societal contradictions. In the modern world, people are formally equal as citizens, but substantively and radically unequal in their economic status. Although the state declares that these economic inequalities are politically irrelevant, they still dominate the formal political process. Only with the reintegration of civil and political life – and the consequent disappearance of the state – can 'truly human' emancipation be realized.*

[. . .]

We must emancipate ourselves before we can emancipate others.

The most rigid form of the opposition between the Jew and the Christian is the *religious* opposition. How is an opposition resolved? By making it impossible. How is *religious* opposition made impossible? By *abolishing religion*. As soon as Jew and Christian recognise that their respective religions are no more than *different stages in the development of the human mind*, different snake skins cast off by *history*, and that *man* is the snake who sloughed them, the relation of Jew and Christian is no longer religious but is only a critical, *scientific* and human relation. *Science* then constitutes their unity. But contradictions in science are resolved by science itself.

The *German* Jew in particular is confronted by the general absence of political emancipation and the strongly marked Christian character of the state. In Bauer's conception, however, the Jewish question has a universal significance, independent of specifically German conditions. It is the question of the relation of religion to the state, of the *contradiction between religious constraint and political emancipation*. Emancipation from religion is laid down as a condition, both to the Jew who wants to be emancipated politically, and to the state which is to effect emancipation and is itself to be emancipated.

> Very well, it is said, and the Jew himself says it, the Jew is to become emancipated not as a Jew, not because he is a Jew, not because he possesses such an excellent, universally human principle of morality; on the contrary, the *Jew* will retreat behind the *citizen* and be a *citizen*, although he is a Jew and is to remain a Jew. That is to say, he is and remains a *Jew*, although he is a *citizen* and lives in universally human conditions: his Jewish and restricted nature triumphs always in the end over his human and political obligations. The *prejudice* remains in spite of being outstripped by *general* principles. But if it remains, then, on the contrary, it outstrips everything else. Only sophistically, only apparently, would the Jew be able to remain a Jew in the life of the state. Hence, if he wanted to remain a Jew, the mere appearance would become the essential and would triumph; that is to say, his *life in the state* would be only a semblance or only a temporary exception to the essential and the rule. ('The Capacity of Present-Day Jews and Christians to Become Free'; *(Einundzwanzig Bogen*, p. 57*)*

Let us hear, on the other hand, how Bauer presents the task of the state.

> France . . . has recently shown us (Proceedings of the Chamber of Deputies, December 26, 1840) in connection with the Jewish question – just as it has continually done in all other *political* questions – the spectacle of a life which is free, but which revokes its freedom by law, hence declaring it to be an appearance, and on the other hand contradicting its free laws by its action. (*The Jewish Question*, p. 64)
>
> In France, universal freedom is not yet the law, the *Jewish question too* has *not* yet been solved, because legal freedom – the fact that all citizens are equal – is restricted in actual life, which is still dominated and divided by religious privileges, and this lack of freedom in actual life reacts on law and compels the latter to sanction the division of the citizens, who as such are free, into oppressed and oppressors. (p. 65)

When, therefore, would the Jewish question be solved for France?

> The Jew, for example, would have ceased to be a Jew if he did not allow himself to be prevented by his laws from fulfilling his duty to the state and his fellow citizens, that is, for example, if on the Sabbath he attended the Chamber of Deputies and took part in the official proceedings. Every *religious privilege*, and therefore also the monopoly of a privileged church, would have been abolished altogether, and if some or many persons, or *even the overwhelming majority, still believed themselves bound to fulfil religious*

duties, this fulfilment ought to be left to *them* as a *purely private matter*. (p. 65) There is no longer any religion when there is no longer any privileged religion. Take from religion its exclusive power and it will no longer exist. (p. 66) Just as M. Martin du Nord saw the proposal to omit mention of Sunday in the law as a motion to declare that Christianity has ceased to exist, with equal reason (and this reason is very well founded) the declaration that the law of the Sabbath is no longer binding on the Jew would be a proclamation abolishing Judaism. (p. 71)

Bauer therefore demands, on the one hand, that the Jew should renounce Judaism, and that mankind in general should renounce religion, in order to achieve *civic* emancipation. On the other hand, he quite consistently regards the *political* abolition of religion as the abolition of religion as such. The state which presupposes religion is not yet a true, real state.

Of course, the religious notion affords security to the state. But to what state? *To what kind of state?* (p. 97)

At this point the *one-sided* formulation of the Jewish question becomes evident.

It was by no means sufficient to investigate: Who is to emancipate? Who is to be emancipated? Criticism had to investigate a third point. It had to inquire: *What kind of emancipation* is in question? What conditions follow from the very nature of the emancipation that is demanded? Only the criticism of *political emancipation* itself would have been the conclusive criticism of the Jewish question and its real merging in the *'general question of the time'*.

Because Bauer does not raise the question to this level, he becomes entangled in contradictions. He puts forward conditions which are not based on the nature of *political* emancipation itself. He raises questions which are not part of his problem, and he solves problems which leave his question unanswered. When Bauer says of the opponents of Jewish emancipation: 'Their error was only that they assumed the Christian state to be the only true one and did not subject it to the same criticism that they applied to Judaism' (op. cit., p. 3), we find that his error lies in the fact that he subjects to criticism *only* the 'Christian state', not the 'state as such', that he does not investigate *the relation of political emancipation to human emancipation* and therefore puts forward conditions which can be explained only by uncritical confusion of political emancipation with general human emancipation. If Bauer asks the Jews: Have you from your standpoint the right to want *political emancipation*? we ask the converse question: Does the standpoint of *political* emancipation give the right to demand from the Jew the abolition of Judaism and from man the abolition of religion?

The Jewish question acquires a different form depending on the state in which the Jew lives. In Germany, where there is no political state, no state as such, the Jewish question is a purely *theological* one. The Jew finds himself in *religious* opposition to the state, which recognises Christianity as its basis. This state is a theologian *ex professo*. Criticism here is criticism of theology, a double-edged criticism, criticism of Christian theology and of Jewish theology. Hence, we continue to operate in the sphere of theology, however much we may operate *critically* within it.

In France, a *constitutional* state, the Jewish question is a question of constitutionalism, the question of the *incompleteness of political emancipation*. Since the *semblance* of a state religion is retained here, although in a meaningless and self-contradictory formula, that of a *religion of the majority*, the relation of the Jew to the state retains the *semblance* of a religious, theological opposition.

Only in the North American states – at least in some of them – does the Jewish question lose its *theological* significance and become a really *secular* question. Only where the political state exists in its completely developed form can the relation of the Jew, and of the religious man in general, to the political state, and therefore the relation of religion to the state, show itself in its specific character, in its purity. The criticism of this relation ceases to be theological criticism as soon as the state ceases to adopt a *theological* attitude towards religion, as soon as it behaves towards religion as a state, i.e., *politically*. Criticism then becomes *criticism of the political state*. At this point, where the question ceases to be *theological*, Bauer's criticism ceases to be critical.

> In the United States there is neither a state religion nor a religion declared to be that of the majority, nor the predominance of one cult over another. The state stands aloof from all cults. ... Indeed, there are some North American states where the constitution does not impose any religious belief or religious practice as a condition of political rights. Nevertheless, in the United States people do not believe that a man without religion could be an honest man.

Nevertheless, North America is pre-eminently the country of religiosity, as Beaumont, Tocqueville and the Englishman Hamilton unanimously assure us. The North American states, however, serve us only as an example. The question is: What is the relation of *complete* political emancipation to religion? If we find that even in the country of complete political emancipation, religion not only *exists*, but displays a *fresh and vigorous vitality*, that is proof that the existence of religion is not in contradiction to the perfection of the state. Since, however, the existence of religion is the existence of a defect, the source of this defect can only be sought in the *nature* of the state itself. We no longer regard religion as the *cause*, but only as the *manifestation* of secular narrowness. Therefore we explain the religious limitations of the free citizens by their secular limitations. We do not assert that they must overcome their religious narrowness in order to get rid of their secular restrictions, we assert that they will overcome their religious narrowness once they get rid of their secular restrictions. We do not turn secular questions into theological questions. We turn theological questions into secular ones. History has long enough been merged in superstition, we now merge superstition in history. The question of the *relation of political emancipation to religion* becomes for us the question of the *relation of political emancipation to human emancipation*. We criticise the religious weakness of the political state by criticising the political state in its *secular* form, *apart* from its weaknesses as regards religion. The contradiction between the state and a *particular religion*, for instance *Judaism*, is given by us a human form as the contradiction between the state and *particular secular* elements; the contradiction between the state and *religion in general* as the contradiction between the state and its *presuppositions* in general.

The *political* emancipation of the Jew, the Christian, and in general of *religious* man is the *emancipation of the state* from Judaism, from Christianity, from *religion* in general. In its own form, in the manner characteristic of its nature, the state as a *state* emancipates itself from religion by emancipating itself from the *state religion*, that is to say, by the state as a state not professing any religion, but, on the contrary, asserting itself as a state. The *political* emancipation from religion is not a religious emancipation that has been carried through to completion and is free from contradiction, because political emancipation is not a form of *human* emancipation which has been carried through to completion and is free from contradiction.

The limits of political emancipation are evident at once from the fact that the *state* can free itself from a restriction without man being *really* free from this restriction, that the state can be a *free state* without man being a *free man*. Bauer himself tacitly admits this when he lays down the following condition for political emancipation:

> Every religious privilege, and therefore also the monopoly of a privileged church, would have been abolished altogether, and if some or many persons, or even the *overwhelming majority, still believed themselves bound to fulfil religious duties*, this fulfilment ought to be left to them as a *purely private matter*. (*Bruno Bauer, The Jewish Question*, p. 65)

It is possible, therefore, for the *state* to have emancipated itself from religion even if the *overwhelming majority* is still religious. And the overwhelming majority does not cease to be religious through being religious *in private*.

But the attitude of the state, and of the *republic* in particular, to religion is after all only the attitude to religion of the *men* who compose the state. It follows from this that man frees himself through the *medium of the state*, that he frees himself *politically* from a limitation when, in contradiction with himself, he raises himself above this limitation in an *abstract, limited*, and partial way. It follows further that, by freeing himself *politically*, man frees himself in a *roundabout way*, through an *intermediary*, although an *essential intermediary*. It follows, finally, that man, even if he proclaims himself an atheist through the medium of the state, that is, if he proclaims the state to be atheist, still remains in the grip of religion, precisely because he acknowledges himself only by a roundabout route, only through an intermediary. Religion is precisely the recognition of man in a roundabout way, through an *intermediary*. The state is the intermediary between man and man's freedom. Just as Christ is the intermediary to whom man transfers the burden of all his divinity, all his *religious constraint*, so the state is the intermediary to whom man transfers all his non-divinity and *all his human unconstraint*.

The *political* elevation of man above religion shares all the defects and all the advantages of political elevation in general. The state as a state annuls, for instance, *private property*, man declares by *political* means that private property is *abolished* as soon as the *property qualification* for the right to elect or be elected is abolished, as has occurred in many states of North America. *Hamilton* quite correctly interprets this fact from a political point of view as meaning: '*the masses have won a victory over the property owners and financial wealth*'. Is not private property abolished in idea if the non-property owner has become the legislator for the property owner? The *property qualification* for the suffrage is the last *political* form of giving recognition to private property.

Nevertheless the political annulment of private property not only fails to abolish private property but even presupposes it. The state abolishes, in its own way, distinctions of *birth, social rank, education, occupation*, when it declares that birth, social rank, education, occupation, are *non-political* distinctions, when it proclaims, without regard to these distinctions, that every member of the nation is an *equal* participant in national sovereignty, when it treats all elements of the real life of the nation from the standpoint of the state. Nevertheless, the state allows private property, education, occupation, to *act* in *their* way, i.e., as private property, as education, as occupation, and to exert the influence of their *special* nature. Far from abolishing these *real* distinctions, the state only exists on the presupposition of their existence; it feels itself to be a *political state* and asserts its *universality* only in opposition to these elements of its being. *Hegel* therefore defines the relation of the *political state* to religion quite correctly when he says:

In order [. . .] that the state should come into existence as the *self-knowing*, *moral reality* of the mind, its *distinction* from the form of authority and faith is essential. But this distinction emerges only insofar as the ecclesiastical aspect arrives at a *separation* within itself. It is *only* in this way that the state, *above* the *particular* churches, has achieved and brought into existence *universality* of thought, which is the principle of its form. (Hegel's *Philosophy of Right*)

Of course! Only in this way, *above* the *particular* elements, does the state constitute itself as universality.

The perfect political state is, by its nature, man's *species-life*, as *opposed* to his material life. All the preconditions of this egoistic life *continue* to exist in *civil society outside* the sphere of the state, but as qualities of civil society. Where the political state has attained its true development, man – not only in thought, in consciousness, but in *reality*, in *life* – leads a twofold life, a heavenly and an earthly life: life in the *political community*, in which he considers himself a *communal being*, and life in *civil society*, in which he acts as a *private individual*, regards other men as a means, degrades himself into a means, and becomes the plaything of alien powers. The relation of the political state to civil society is just as spiritual as the relation of heaven to earth. The political state stands in the same opposition to civil society, and it prevails over the latter in the same way as religion prevails over the narrowness of the secular world, i.e., by likewise having always to acknowledge it, to restore it, and allow itself to be dominated by it. In his *most immediate* reality, in civil society, man is a secular being. Here, where he regards himself as a real individual, and is so regarded by others, he is a *fictitious* phenomenon. In the state, on the other hand, where man is regarded as a species-being, he is the imaginary member of an illusory sovereignty, is deprived of his real individual life and endowed with an unreal universality.

Man, as the adherent of a *particular* religion, finds himself in conflict with his citizenship and with other men as members of the community. This conflict reduces itself to the *secular* division between the *political* state and *civil society*. For man as a *bourgeois*, 'life in the state' is 'only a semblance or a temporary exception to the essential and the rule'. Of course, the *bourgeois*, like the Jew, remains only sophistically in the sphere of political life, just as the *citoyen* only sophistically remains a Jew or a *bourgeois*. But this sophistry is not personal. It is the *sophistry of the political state* itself. The difference between the religious man and the citizen is the difference between the merchant and the citizen, between the day-labourer and the citizen, between the landowner and the citizen, between the *living individual* and the *citizen*. The contradiction in which the religious man finds himself with the political man is the same contradiction in which the *bourgeois* finds himself with the *citoyen*, and the member of civil society with his *political lion's skin*.

This secular conflict, to which the Jewish question ultimately reduces itself, the relation between the political state and its preconditions, whether these are material elements, such as private property, etc., or spiritual elements, such as culture or religion, the conflict between the *general interest* and *private interest*, the schism between the *political state* and *civil society* – these secular antitheses Bauer allows to persist, whereas he conducts a polemic against their *religious* expression.

> It is precisely the basis of *civil society*, the need that ensures the continuance of this society and *guarantees its necessity*, which exposes its existence to continual dangers, maintains in it an element of uncertainty, and produces that continually changing mixture of poverty and riches, of distress and prosperity, and brings about change in general. (p. 8)

Compare the whole section: 'Civil Society' (pp. 8–9), which has been drawn up along the basic lines of Hegel's philosophy of law. Civil society, in its opposition to the political state, is recognised as necessary, because the political state is recognised as necessary.

Political emancipation is, of course, a big step forward. True, it is not the final form of human emancipation in general, but it is the final form of human emancipation *within* the hitherto existing world order. It goes without saying that we are speaking here of real, practical emancipation.

Man emancipates himself *politically* from religion by banishing it from the sphere of public law to that of private law. Religion is no longer the spirit of the *state*, in which man behaves – although in a limited way, in a particular form, and in a particular sphere – as a species-being, in community with other men. Religion has become the spirit of *civil society*, of the sphere of egoism, of *bellum omnium contra omnes*. It is no longer the essence of *community*, but the essence of *difference*. It has become the expression of man's *separation* from his *community*, from himself and from other men – as it was *originally*. It is only the abstract avowal of specific perversity, *private whimsy*, and arbitrariness. The endless fragmentation of religion in North America, for example, gives it even *externally* the form of a purely individual affair. It has been thrust among the multitude of private interests and ejected from the community as such. But one should be under no illusion about the limits of political emancipation. The division of the human being into a *public man* and a *private man*, the *displacement* of religion from the state into civil society, this is not a stage of political emancipation but its *completion*; this emancipation therefore neither abolishes the *real* religiousness of man, nor strives to do so.

The *decomposition* of man into Jew and citizen, Protestant and citizen, religious man and citizen, is neither a deception directed *against* citizenhood, nor is it a circumvention of political emancipation, it is *political emancipation itself*, the *political* method of emancipating oneself from religion. Of course, in periods when the political state as such is born violently out of civil society, when political liberation is the form in which men strive to achieve their liberation, the state can and must go as far as the *abolition* of *religion*, the *destruction* of religion. But it can do so only in the same way that it proceeds to the abolition of private property, to the maximum, to confiscation, to progressive taxation, just as it goes as far as the abolition of life, the *guillotine*. At times of special self-confidence, political life seeks to suppress its prerequisite, civil society and the elements composing this society, and to constitute itself as the real species-life of man devoid of contradictions. But it can achieve this only by coming into *violent* contradiction with its own conditions of life, only by declaring the revolution to be *permanent*, and therefore the political drama necessarily ends with the re-establishment of religion, private property, and all elements of civil society, just as war ends with peace.

Indeed, the perfect Christian state is not the so-called *Christian* state, which acknowledges Christianity as its basis, as the state religion, and therefore adopts an exclusive attitude towards other religions. On the contrary, the perfect Christian state is the *atheistic* state, the *democratic* state, the state which relegates religion to a place among the other elements of civil society. The state which is still theological, which still officially professes Christianity as its creed, which still does not dare to proclaim itself *as a state*, has, in its *reality* as a state, not yet succeeded in expressing the *human* basis – of which Christianity is the high-flown expression – in a *secular, human* form. The so-called Christian state is simply nothing more than a *non-state*, since it is not Christianity as a religion, but only the *human background* of the Christian religion, which can find its expression in actual human creations.

The so-called Christian state is the Christian negation of the state, but by no means the political realisation of Christianity. The state which still professes Christianity in the form of religion, does not yet profess it in the form appropriate to the state, for it still has a religious attitude towards religion, that is to say, it is not the *true implementation* of the human basis of religion, because it still relies on the *unreal, imaginary* form of this human core. The so-called Christian state is the *imperfect* state, and the Christian religion is regarded by it as the *supplementation* and *sanctification* of its imperfection. For the Christian state, therefore, religion necessarily becomes a *means*; hence it is a *hypocritical* state. It makes a great difference whether the *complete* state, because of the defect inherent in the general *nature* of the state, counts religion among its *presuppositions*, or whether the *incomplete* state, because of the defect inherent in its *particular existence* as a defective state, declares that religion is its *basis*. In the latter case, religion becomes *imperfect politics*. In the former case, the imperfection even of consummate *politics* becomes evident in religion. The so-called

Christian state needs the Christian religion in order to complete itself *as a state*. The democratic state, the real state, does not need religion for its political completion. On the contrary, it can disregard religion because in it the human basis of religion is realised in a secular manner. The so-called Christian state, on the other hand, has a political attitude to religion and a religious attitude to politics. By degrading the forms of the state to mere semblance, it equally degrades religion to mere semblance.

In order to make this contradiction clearer, let us consider Bauer's projection of the Christian state, a projection based on his observation of the Christian-German state.

> Recently . . . in order to prove the *impossibility* or *non-existence* of a Christian state, reference has frequently been made to those sayings in the Gospel with which the [present-day] state *not only does not* comply, but *cannot possibly comply, if it does not want to dissolve itself completely* [as a state]. But the matter cannot be disposed of so easily. What do these Gospel sayings demand? Supernatural renunciation of self, submission to the authority of revelation, a turning-away from the state, the abolition of secular conditions. Well, the Christian state demands and accomplishes all that. It has assimilated the *spirit of the Gospel*, and if it does not reproduce this spirit in the same terms as the Gospel, that occurs only because it expresses this spirit in political forms, i.e., in forms which, it is true, are taken from the political system in this world, but which in the religious rebirth that they have to undergo become degraded to a mere semblance. This is a turning-away from the state while making use of political forms for its realisation. (p. 55)

Bauer then explains that the people of a Christian state is only a non-people, no longer having a will of its own, but whose true existence lies in the leader to whom it is subjected, although this leader by his origin and nature is alien to it, i.e., given by God and imposed on the people without any co-operation on its part. Bauer declares that the laws of such a people are not its own creation, but are actual revelations, that its supreme chief needs privileged intermediaries with the people in the strict sense, with the masses, and that the masses themselves are divided into a multitude of particular groupings which are formed and determined by chance, which are differentiated by their interests, their particular passions and prejudices, and obtain permission, as a privilege, to isolate themselves from one another, etc. (p. 56.)

However, Bauer himself says:

> Politics, if it is to be nothing but religion, ought not to be politics, just as the cleaning of saucepans, if it is to be accepted as a religious matter, ought not to be regarded as a matter of domestic economy. (p. 108)

In the Christian–German state, however, religion is an 'economic matter' just as 'economic matters' belong to the sphere of religion. The domination of religion in the Christian–German state is the religion of domination.

The separation of the 'spirit of the Gospel' from the 'letter of the Gospel' is an *irreligious* act. A state which makes the Gospel speak in the language of politics, that is, in another language than that of the Holy Ghost, commits sacrilege, if not in human eyes, then in the eyes of its own religion. The state which acknowledges Christianity as its supreme criterion and the *Bible* as its *Charter*, must be confronted with the *words* of Holy Scripture, for every word of Scripture is holy. This state, as well as the *human rubbish* on which it is based, is caught in a painful contradiction that is insoluble from the standpoint of religious consciousness when it is referred to those sayings of the Gospel with which it 'not only does not comply, but *cannot possibly comply, if it does not want to dissolve itself completely as a state'*. And why does it not want to dissolve itself completely? The state itself cannot give an answer either to itself or to others. In its *own consciousness* the official Christian state is an *imperative*, the realisation of which is unattainable, the state can assert the *reality* of its existence only by lying to itself, and therefore always remains in its own eyes an object of doubt, an unreliable, problematic object. Criticism is therefore fully justified in forcing the state that relies on the Bible into a mental derangement in which it no longer knows whether it is an *illusion* or a *reality*, and in which the infamy of its *secular* aims, for which religion serves as a cloak, comes into insoluble conflict with the sincerity of its *religious* consciousness, for which religion appears as the aim of the world. This state can only save itself from its inner torment if it becomes the *police agent* of the Catholic Church. In relation to the church, which declares the secular power to be its servant, the state is powerless, the *secular* power which claims to be the rule of the religious spirit is powerless.

It is indeed *estrangement* which matters in the so-called Christian state, but not *man*. The only man who counts, the *king*, is a being specifically different from other men, and is moreover a religious being, directly linked with heaven, with God. The relationships which prevail here are still relationships dependent on *faith*. The religious spirit, therefore, is still not really secularised.

But, furthermore, the religious spirit cannot be *really* secularised, for what is it in itself but the *non-secular* form of a stage in the development of the human mind? The religious spirit can only be secularised insofar as the stage of development of the human mind of which it is the religious expression makes its appearance and becomes constituted in its *secular* form. This takes place in the *democratic* state. Not Christianity, but the *human basis* of Christianity is the basis of this state. Religion remains the ideal, non-secular consciousness of its members, because religion is the ideal form of the *stage of human development* achieved in this state.

The members of the political state are religious owing to the dualism between individual life and species-life, between the life of civil society and political life. They are religious because men treat the political life of the state, an area beyond their real individuality, as if it were their true life. They are religious insofar as religion here is the spirit of civil society, expressing the separation and remoteness of man from man. Political democracy is Christian since in it man, not merely one man but every man, ranks as *sovereign*, as the highest being, but it is man in his uncivilised, unsocial form, man in his fortuitous existence, man just as he is, man as he has been corrupted by the whole organisation of our society, who has lost himself, been alienated, and handed over to the rule of inhuman conditions and elements – in short, man who is not yet a *real* species-being. That which is a creation of fantasy, a dream, a postulate of Christianity, i.e., the sovereignty of man – but man as an alien being different from the real man – becomes in democracy tangible reality, present existence, and secular principle.

In the perfect democracy, the religious and theological consciousness itself is in its own eyes the more religious and the more theological because it is apparently without political significance, without worldly aims, the concern of a disposition that shuns the world, the expression of intellectual narrow-mindedness, the product of arbitrariness and fantasy, and because it is a life that is really of the other world. Christianity attains here the *practical* expression of its universal-religious significance in that the most diverse world outlooks are grouped alongside one another in the form of Christianity and still more because it does not require other people to profess Christianity, but only religion in general, any kind of religion . . . The religious consciousness revels in the wealth of religious contradictions and religious diversity.

We have thus shown that political emancipation from religion leaves religion in existence, although not a privileged religion. The contradiction in which the adherent of a particular religion finds himself involved in relation to his citizenship is only *one aspect* of the universal *secular contradiction between the political state and civil society*. The consummation of the Christian state is the state which acknowledges itself as a state and disregards the religion of its members. The emancipation of the state from religion is not the emancipation of the real man from religion.

Therefore we do not say to the Jews as Bauer does: You cannot be emancipated politically without emancipating yourselves radically from Judaism. On the contrary, we tell them: Because you can be emancipated politically without renouncing Judaism completely and incontrovertibly, *political emancipation* itself is not *human* emancipation. If you Jews want to be emancipated politically without emancipating yourselves humanly, the half-hearted approach and contradiction is not in you alone, it is inherent in the *nature* and *category* of political emancipation. If you find yourself within the confines of this category, you share in a general confinement. Just as the state *evangelises* when, although it is a state, it adopts a Christian attitude towards the Jews, so the Jew *acts politically* when, although a Jew, he demands civic rights.

But if a man, although a Jew, can be emancipated politically and receive civic rights, can he lay claim to the so-called *rights of man* and receive them? Bauer *denies* it.

> The question is whether the Jew as such, that is, the Jew who himself admits that he is compelled by his true nature to live permanently in separation from other men, is capable of receiving the *universal rights of man* and of conceding them to others.
>
> For the Christian world, the idea of the rights of man was only discovered in the last century. It is not innate in men; on the contrary, it is gained only in a struggle against the historical traditions in which hitherto man was brought up. Thus the rights of man are not a gift of nature, not a legacy from past history, but the reward of the struggle against the accident of birth and against the privileges which up to now have been handed down by history from generation to generation. These rights are the result of culture, and only one who has earned and deserved them can possess them.
>
> Can the Jew really take possession of them? As long as he is a Jew, the restricted nature which makes him a Jew is bound to triumph over the human nature which should link him as a man with other men, and will separate him from non-Jews. He declares by this separation that the particular nature which makes him a Jew is his true, highest nature, before which human nature has to give way.
>
> Similarly, the Christian as a Christian cannot grant the rights of man. (pp. 19, 20)

According to Bauer, man has to sacrifice the '*privilege of faith*' to be able to receive the universal rights of man. Let us examine for a moment the so-called rights of man, to be precise, the rights of man in their authentic form, in the form which they have among those who *discovered* them, the North Americans and the French. These rights of man are in part *political* rights, rights which can only be exercised in a community with others. Their content is *participation* in the *community*, and specifically in the *political* community, in the *life of the state*. They come within the category of *political freedom*, the category of *civic rights*, which, as we have seen, in no way presuppose the incontrovertible and positive abolition of religion, nor therefore of Judaism. There remains to be examined the other part of the rights of man, the rights of man insofar as these differ from the rights of the citizen.

Included among them is freedom of conscience, the right to practise any religion one chooses. The *privilege of faith* is expressly recognised either as a *right of man* or as the consequence of a right of man, that of liberty.

> *Declaration of the Rights of Man and of the Citizen*, 1791, Article 10: 'No one is to be subjected to annoyance because of his opinions, even *religious* opinions.' 'The freedom of every man to practise the religion of which he is an adherent' is guaranteed as a right of man in section 1 of the Constitution of 1791.
>
> *The Declaration of the Rights of Man*, etc., 1793, includes among the rights of man, Article 7: 'The free exercise of religion'. Indeed, in regard to man's right to express his thoughts and opinions, to hold meetings, and to exercise his religion it is even stated: 'The necessity of proclaiming these *rights* presupposes either the existence or the recent memory of despotism.' Compare the constitution of 1795, section XIV, Article 354.
>
> *Constitution of Pennsylvania*, Article 9, § 3: 'All men have received from nature the imprescriptible *right* to worship the Almighty according to the dictates of their conscience, and no one can be legally compelled to follow, establish or support against his will any religion or religious ministry. No human authority can, in any circumstances, intervene in a matter of conscience or control the forces of the soul.'
>
> *Constitution of New Hampshire*, Articles 5 and 6: 'Among these natural rights some are by nature inalienable since nothing can replace them. The *rights* of conscience are among them.'

Incompatibility between religion and the rights of man is to such a degree absent from the concept of the rights of man that, on the contrary, a man's *right to be religious* in any way he chooses, to practise his own particular religion, is expressly included among the rights of man. The *privilege of faith* is a *universal right of man.*

The rights of man, are as *such* distinct from the rights of the citizen. Who is man as distinct from citizen? None other than the *member of civil society.* Why is the member of civil society called 'man', simply man; why are his rights called the *rights of man*? How is this fact to be explained? From the relationship between the political state and civil society, from the nature of political emancipation.

Above all, we note the fact that the so-called *rights of man*, (as distinct from the rights of the citizen) are nothing but the rights of a *member of civil society*, i.e., the rights of egoistic man, of man separated from other men and from the community. Let us hear what the most radical Constitution, the Constitution of 1793, has to say:

> *Declaration of the Rights of Man and of the Citizen.* Article 2. 'These rights, etc., (the natural and imprescriptible rights) are: *equality, liberty, security, property.*'

What constitutes *liberty*?

Article 6. 'Liberty is the power which man has to do everything that does not harm the rights of others', or . . . 'Liberty consists in being able to do everything which does not harm others.'

Liberty, therefore, is the right to do everything that harms no one else. The limits within which anyone can act *without harming* someone else are defined by law, just as the boundary between two fields is determined by a boundary post. It is a question of the liberty of man as an isolated monad, withdrawn into himself. Why is the Jew, according to Bauer, incapable of acquiring the rights of man?

As long as he is a Jew, the restricted nature which makes him a Jew is bound to triumph over the human nature which should link him as a man with other men, and will separate him from non-Jews.

But the right of man to liberty is based not on the association of man with man, but on the separation of man from man. It is the *right* of this separation, the right of the *restricted* individual, withdrawn into himself.

The practical application of man's right to liberty is man's right to *private property*.

What constitutes man's right to private property?

Article 16 (Constitution of 1793): The right of *property* is that which every citizen has of enjoying and of disposing *at his discretion* of his goods and income, of the fruits of his labour and industry.

The right of man to private property is, therefore, the right to enjoy one's property and to dispose of it at one's discretion . . . without regard to other men, independently of society, the right of self-interest. This individual liberty and its application form the basis of civil society. It makes every man see in other men not the *realisation* of his own freedom, but the *barrier* to it. But, above all, it proclaims the right of man 'of enjoying and of disposing *at his discretion* of his goods and income, of the fruits of his labour and industry'.

There remain the other rights of man: equality and security. Equality, used here in its non-political sense, is nothing but the equality of the liberty described above, namely: each man is to the same extent regarded as such a self-sufficient monad. The Constitution of 1795 defines the concept of this equality, in accordance with its significance, as follows:

Article 3 (Constitution of 1795): Equality consists in the law being the same for all, whether it protects or punishes.

And security?

Article 8 (Constitution of 1793): Security consists in the protection afforded by society to each of its members for the preservation of his person, his rights, and his property.

Security is the highest social concept of civil society, the concept of *police*, expressing the fact that the whole of society exists only in order to guarantee to each of its members the preservation of his person, his rights, and his property. It is in this sense that Hegel calls civil society 'the state of need and reason'.

The concept of security does not raise civil society above its egoism. On the contrary, security is the *insurance* of its egoism.

None of the so-called rights of man, therefore, go beyond egoistic man, beyond man as a member of civil society, that is, an individual withdrawn into himself, into the confines of his private interests and private caprice, and separated from the community. In the rights of man, he is far from being conceived as a species-being; on the contrary, species-life itself, society, appears as a framework external to the individuals, as a restriction of their original independence. The sole bond holding them together is natural necessity, need and private interest, the preservation of their property and their egoistic selves.

It is puzzling enough that a people which is just beginning to liberate itself, to tear down all the barriers between its various sections, and to establish a political community, that such a people solemnly proclaims (Declaration of 1791) the rights of egoistic man separated from his fellow men and from the community, and that indeed it repeats this proclamation at a moment when only the most heroic devotion can save the nation, and is therefore imperatively called for, at a moment when the sacrifice of all the interests of civil society must be the order of the day, and egoism must be punished as a crime. (Declaration of the Rights of Man, etc., of 1793.) This fact becomes still more puzzling when we see that the political emancipators go so far as to reduce citizenship, and the *political community*, to a mere *means* for maintaining these so-called rights of man, that therefore the citizen is declared to be the servant of egoistic man, that the sphere in which man acts as a communal being is degraded to a level below the sphere in which he acts as a partial being, and that, finally, it is not man as citizen, but man as *bourgeois* who is considered to be the *essential* and *true* man.

The *aim* of all *political association* is the *preservation* of the natural and imprescriptible rights of man. *(Declaration of the Rights, etc., of 1791, Article 2.) Government* is instituted in order to guarantee man the enjoyment of his natural and imprescriptible rights. *(Declaration, etc., of 1793, Article 1.)*

Hence even in moments when its enthusiasm still has the freshness of youth and is intensified to an extreme degree by the force of circumstances, political life declares itself to be a mere *means*, whose purpose is the life of civil society. It is true that its revolutionary practice is in flagrant contradiction with its theory. Whereas, for example, security is declared one of the rights of man, violation of the privacy of correspondence is openly declared to be the order of the day. Whereas the '*unlimited* freedom of the press' (Constitution of 1793, Article 122) is guaranteed as a consequence of the right of man to individual liberty, freedom of the press is totally destroyed, because 'Freedom of the press should not be permitted when it endangers public liberty'. (Robespierre jeune, *Histoire parlementaire de la Révolution française* par Buchez et Roux, T. 28, p. 159). That is to say, therefore: The right of man to liberty ceases to be a right as soon as it comes into conflict with *political* life, whereas in theory political life is only the guarantee of human rights, the rights of the individual, and therefore must be abandoned as soon as it comes into contradiction with its *aim*, with these rights of man. But practice is merely the exception, theory is the rule. But even if one were to regard revolutionary practice as the correct presentation of the relationship, there would still remain the puzzle of why the relationship is turned upside-down in the minds of the political emancipators and the aim appears as the means, while the means appears as the aim. This optical illusion of their consciousness would still remain a puzzle, although now a psychological, a theoretical puzzle.

The puzzle is easily solved.

Political emancipation is at the same time the *dissolution* of the old society on which the state alienated from the people, the sovereign power, is based. Political revolution is a revolution of civil society. What was the character of the old society? It can be described in one word – *feudalism*. The character of the old civil society was *directly political*, that is to say, the elements of civil life, for example, property, or the family, or the mode of labour, were raised to the level of elements of political life in the form of seigniory, estates, and corporations. In this form they determined the relation of the individual to the *state as a whole*, i.e., his *political* relation, that is, his relation of separation and exclusion from the other components of society. For that organisation of national life did not raise property or labour to the level of social elements; on the contrary, it completed their *separation* from the state as a whole and constituted them as *discrete* societies within society. Thus, the vital functions and conditions of life of civil society remained nevertheless political, although political in the feudal sense, that is to say, they secluded the individual from the state as a whole and they converted the *particular* relation of his corporation to the state as a whole into his general relation to the life of the nation, just as they converted his particular civil activity and situation into his general activity and situation. As a result of this organisation, the unity of the state, and also the consciousness, will and activity of this unity, the general power of the state, are likewise bound to appear as the *particular* affair of a ruler isolated from the people, and of his servants.

The political revolution which overthrew this sovereign power and raised state affairs to become affairs of the people, which constituted the political state as a matter of *general* concern, that is, as a real state, necessarily smashed all estates, corporations, guilds, and privileges, since they were all manifestations of the separation of the people from the community. The political revolution thereby *abolished* the *political character of civil society*. It broke up civil society into its simple component parts; on the one hand, the *individuals*; on the other hand, the *material* and *spiritual elements* constituting the content of the life and social position of these individuals. It set free the political spirit, which had been, as it were, split up, partitioned and dispersed in the various blind alleys of feudal society. It gathered the dispersed parts of the political spirit, freed it from its intermixture with civil life, and established it as the sphere of the community, the *general* concern of the nation, ideally independent of those *particular* elements of civil life. A person's *distinct* activity and distinct situation in life were reduced to a merely individual significance. They no longer constituted the general relation of the individual to the state as a whole. Public affairs as such, on the other hand, became the general affair of each individual, and the political function became the individual's general function.

But the completion of the idealism of the state was at the same time the completion of the materialism of civil society. Throwing off the political yoke meant at the same time throwing off the bonds which restrained the egoistic spirit of civil society. Political emancipation was at the same time the emancipation of civil society from politics, from having even the *semblance* of a universal content.

Feudal society was resolved into its basic element – *man*, but man as he really formed its basis – *egoistic* man.

This *man*, the member of civil society, is thus the basis, the precondition, of the *political* state. He is recognised as such by this state in the rights of man.

The liberty of egoistic man and the recognition of this liberty, however, is rather the recognition of the *unrestrained* movement of the spiritual and material elements which form the content of his life.

Hence man was not freed from religion, he received religious freedom. He was not freed from property, he received freedom to own property. He was not freed from the egoism of business, he received freedom to engage in business.

The *establishment of the political state* and the dissolution of civil society into independent *individuals* – whose relations with one another depend on *law*, just as the relations of men in the system of estates and guilds depended on *privilege* – is accomplished by *one and the same act*. Man as a member of civil society, *unpolitical* man, inevitably appears, however, as the *natural* man. The rights of man appear as natural rights, because *conscious activity* is concentrated on the *political act*. *Egoistic* man is the *passive* result of the dissolved society, a result that is simply *found in existence*, an object of *immediate certainty*, therefore a *natural* object. The *political revolution* resolves civil life into its component parts, without *revolutionising* these components themselves or subjecting them to criticism. It regards civil society, the world of needs, labour, private interests, civil law, as the *basis of its existence*, as a *precondition* not requiring further substantiation and therefore as its *natural basis*. Finally, man as a member of civil society is held to be man *in the proper sense*, man as distinct from the citizen, because he is man in his sensuous, individual, *immediate* existence, whereas *political* man is only abstract, artificial man, man as an *allegorical, juridical* person. The real man is recognised only in the shape of the *egoistic* individual, the *true* man is recognised only in the shape of the *abstract* citizen.

Therefore Rousseau correctly describes the abstract idea of political man as follows:

> Whoever dares undertake to establish a people's institutions must feel himself capable of *changing*, as it were, *human nature*, of *transforming* each individual, who by himself is a complete and solitary whole, into a *part* of a larger whole, from which, in a sense, the individual receives his life and his being, of substituting a *limited* and *mental existence* for the physical and independent existence. He has to take from *man his own powers*, and give him in exchange alien powers which he cannot employ without the help of other men.

All emancipation is a *reduction* of the human world and relationships to *man himself*.

Political emancipation is the reduction of man, on the one hand, to a member of civil society, to an *egoistic, independent* individual, and, on the other hand, to a *citizen*, a juridical person.

Only when the real, individual man re-absorbs in himself the abstract citizen, and as an individual human being has become a *species-being* in his everyday life, in his particular work, and in his particular situation, only when man has recognised and organised his own powers as *social* forces, and consequently no longer separates social power from himself in the shape of *political* power, only then will human emancipation have been accomplished.

From: *Collected Works*, Vol. 3, pp. 147–68

3

Introduction to a Contribution to the Critique of Hegel's Doctrine of the State

In this article, written at the very end of 1843, Marx insists upon the necessity of moving from 'the criticism of religion' to 'the criticism of politics'. In its closing pages, Marx identifies the proletariat as the historical agent of revolutionary change and announces the marriage of radical philosophy and revolutionary proletariat. 'The head of [revolutionary] emancipation is philosophy, its heart is the proletariat'.

For Germany the *criticism of religion* is in the main complete, and criticism of religion is the premise of all criticism.

The *profane* existence of error is discredited after its *heavenly oratio pro aris et focis* [Speech for the altars and hearths] has been disproved. Man, who looked for a superhuman being in the fantastic reality of heaven and found nothing there but the *reflection* of himself, will no longer be disposed to find but the *semblance* of himself, only an inhuman being, where he seeks and must seek his true reality.

The basis of irreligious criticism is: *Man makes religion*, religion does not make man. Religion is the self-consciousness and self-esteem of man who has either not yet found himself or has already lost himself again. But *man* is no abstract being encamped outside the world. Man is *the world of man*, the state, society. This state, this society, produce religion, an *inverted world-consciousness*, because they are an *inverted world*. Religion is the general theory of that world, its encyclopaedic compendium, its logic in a popular form, its spiritualistic *point d'honneur*, its enthusiasm, its moral sanction, its solemn complement, its universal source of consolation and justification. It is the *fantastic realisation* of the human essence because the *human essence* has no true reality. The struggle against religion is therefore indirectly a fight against *the world* of which religion is the spiritual *aroma*.

Religious distress is at the same time the *expression* of real distress and also the *protest* against real distress. Religion is the sigh of the oppressed creature, the heart of a heartless world, just as it is the spirit of spiritless conditions. It is the *opium* of the people.

To abolish religion as the *illusory* happiness of the people is to demand their *real* happiness. The demand to give up illusions about the existing state of affairs is the *demand to give up a state of affairs which needs illusions*. The criticism of religion is therefore in *embryo the criticism of the vale of tears*, the *halo* of which is religion.

Criticism has torn up the imaginary flowers from the chain not so that man shall wear the unadorned, bleak chain but so that he will shake off the chain and pluck the living flower. The criticism of religion disillusions man to make him think and act and shape his reality like a man who has been disillusioned and has come to reason, so that he will revolve round himself and therefore round his true sun. Religion is only the illusory sun which revolves round man as long as he does not revolve round himself.

The *task of history*, therefore, once the *world beyond the truth* has disappeared, is to establish the *truth of this world*. The immediate *task of philosophy*, which is at the service of history, once the *holy form* of human self-estrangement has been unmasked, is to unmask self-estrangement in its *unholy forms*. Thus the criticism of heaven turns into the criticism of the earth, the *criticism of religion* into the *criticism of law* and the *criticism of theology* into the *criticism of politics*.

The following exposition – a contribution to that task – deals immediately not with the original, but with a copy, the German *philosophy* of state and of law, for no other reason than that it deals with *Germany*.

If one wanted to proceed from the *status quo* itself in Germany, even in the only appropriate way, i.e., negatively, the result would still be an *anachronism*. Even the negation of our political present is a reality already covered with dust in the historical lumber-room of modern nations. If I negate powdered pigtails, I am still left with unpowdered pigtails. If I negate the German state of affairs in 1843, then, according to the French computation of time, I am hardly in the year 1789, and still less in the focus of the present.

Yes, German history flatters itself with a movement which no people in the firmament of history went through before it or will go through after it. For we shared the restorations of the modern nations although we had not shared their revolutions. We underwent a restoration, first because other nations dared to carry out a revolution and second because other nations suffered a counter-revolution, the first time because our rulers were afraid, and the second because our rulers were not afraid. We – and our shepherds first and foremost – never found ourselves in the company of freedom except once – on the *day of its burial*.

A school which legitimates the baseness of today by the baseness of yesterday, a school that declares rebellious every cry of the serf against the knout once that knout is a time-honoured, ancestral, historical one, a school to which history only shows its *posterior* as the God of Israel did to his servant Moses – the *historical school of law* – would hence have invented German history had it not been an invention of German history. For every pound of flesh cut from the heart of the people the historical school of law – Shylock, but Shylock the bondsman – swears on its bond, its historical bond, its Christian-Germanic bond.

Good-natured enthusiasts, Germanomaniacs by extraction and free-thinkers by reflection, on the contrary, seek our history of freedom beyond our history in the primeval Teutonic forests. But what difference is there between the history of our freedom and the history of the boar's freedom if it can be found only in the forests? Besides, it is common knowledge that the forest echoes back what you shout into it. So let us leave the ancient Teutonic forests in peace!

War on the German conditions! By all means! They are *below the level of history, beneath any criticism*, but they are still an object of criticism like the criminal who is below the level of humanity but still an object for the *executioner*. In the struggle against those conditions criticism is no passion of the head, it is the head of passion. It is not a lancet, it is a weapon. Its object is its *enemy*, which it wants not to refute but to *exterminate*. For the spirit of those conditions is refuted. In themselves they are not objects *worthy of thought*, but *phenomena* which are as despicable as they are despised. Criticism does not need to make things clear to itself as regards this subject-matter, for it has already dealt with it. Criticism appears no longer as an *end in itself*, but only as a *means*. Its essential sentiment is *indignation*, its essential activity is *denunciation*.

It is a case of describing the dull reciprocal pressure of all social spheres on one another, a general inactive ill humour, a limitedness which recognises itself as much as it misjudges itself, within the frame of a government system which, living on the preservation of all wretchedness, is itself nothing but *wretchedness in office*.

What a sight! This infinitely proceeding division of society into the most manifold races opposed to one another by petty antipathies, uneasy consciences and brutal mediocrity, and which, precisely because of their reciprocal ambiguous and distrustful attitude, are all, without exception although with various formalities, treated by their *rulers as licensed existences*. And they must recognise and acknowledge as a *concession of heaven* the very fact that they are *mastered, ruled, possessed!* On the other side are the rulers themselves, whose greatness is in inverse proportion to their number!

Criticism dealing with this content is criticism in *hand-to-hand combat*, and in such a fight the point is not whether the opponent is a noble, equal, *interesting* opponent, the point is to *strike* him. The point is not to allow the Germans a minute for self-deception and resignation. The actual pressure must be made more pressing by adding to it consciousness of pressure, the shame must be made more shameful by publicising it. Every sphere of German society must be shown as the Shame of German society; these petrified relations must be forced to dance by singing their own tune to them! The people must be taught to be *terrified* at itself in order to give it *courage*. This will be fulfilling an imperative need of the German nation, and needs of the nations are in themselves the ultimate reason for their satisfaction.

This struggle against the limited content of the German *status quo* cannot be without interest even for the *modern* nations, for the German *status quo* is the *open completion of the ancien régime*, and the *ancien régime* is the *concealed deficiency of the modern state*. The struggle against the German political present is the struggle against the past of the modern nations, and they are still troubled by reminders of that past. It is instructive for them to see the *ancien régime*, which has been through its *tragedy* with them, playing its *comedy* as a German ghost. *Tragic* indeed was the history of the *ancien régime* so long as it was the pre-existing power of the world, and freedom, on the other hand, was a personal notion, i.e., as long as this regime believed and had to believe in its own justification. As long as the *ancien régime*, as an existing world order, struggled against a world that was only coming into being, there was on its side a historical error, not a personal one. That is why its downfall was tragic.

On the other hand, the present German regime, an anachronism, a flagrant contradiction of generally recognised axioms, the nothingness of the *ancien régime* exhibited to the world, only imagines that it believes in itself and demands that the world should imagine the same thing. If it believed in its own *essence*, would it try to hide that essence under the *semblance* of an alien essence and seek refuge in hypocrisy and sophism? The modern *ancien régime* is only the *comedian* of a world order whose *true heroes* are dead. History is thorough and goes through many phases when carrying an old form to the grave. The last phase of a world-historical form is its *comedy*. The gods of Greece, already tragically wounded to death in Aeschylus' *Prometheus Bound*, had to re-die a comic death in Lucian's *Dialogues*. Why this course of history? So that humanity should part with its past *cheerfully*. This *cheerful* historical destiny is what we vindicate for the political authorities of Germany.

However, once *modern* politico-social reality itself is subjected to criticism, once criticism rises to truly human problems, it finds itself outside the German *status quo* or else it would reach out for its object *below* its object. An example. The relation of industry, of the world of wealth generally, to the political world is one of the major problems of modern times. In what form is this problem beginning to engage the attention of the Germans? In the form of *protective duties*, of the *prohibitive system*, of *national economy*. Germanomania has passed out of man into matter, and thus one morning our cotton barons and iron champions saw themselves turned into patriots. People are therefore beginning in Germany to acknowledge the sovereignty of monopoly within the country by lending it *sovereignty abroad*. People are thus about to begin in Germany with what people in France and England are about to end. The old corrupt condition against which these countries are rebelling in theory and which they only bear as one bears chains is greeted in Germany as the dawn of a beautiful future which still hardly dares to pass from *cunning* theory to the most ruthless practice. Whereas the problem in France and England is: *Political economy* or the *rule of society over wealth*, in Germany it is: *National economy* or the *mastery of private property over nationality*. In France and England, then, it is a case of abolishing monopoly that has proceeded to its last consequences; in Germany it is a case of proceeding to the last consequences of monopoly. There it is a case of solution, here as yet a case of collision. This is an adequate example of the *German* form of modern problems, an example of how our history, like a clumsy recruit, still has to do extra drill in matters that are old and hackneyed in history.

If therefore the *whole* German development did not exceed the German *political* development, a German could at the most participate in the problems of the present to the same extent as a *Russian* can. But, if the separate individual is not bound by the limitations of the nation, still less is the nation as a whole liberated by the liberation of one individual. The fact that Greece had a Scythian among its philosophers did not help the Scythians to make a single step towards Greek culture.

Luckily we Germans are not Scythians.

As the ancient peoples went through their pre-history in imagination, in *mythology*, so we Germans have gone through our post-history in thought, in *philosophy*. We are *philosophical* contemporaries of the present without being its *historical* contemporaries. German philosophy is the *ideal prolongation* of German history. If therefore, instead of the *œuvres incomplètes* of our real history, we criticise the *œuvres posthumes* of our ideal history, *philosophy*, our criticism is among the questions of which the present says: *That is the question*. What in advanced nations is a *practical* break with modern political conditions, is in Germany, where even those conditions do not yet exist, at first a *critical* break with the philosophical reflection of those conditions.

German philosophy of law and state is the only *German history* which is *al pari* with the *official* modern reality. The German nation must therefore take into account not only its present conditions but also its dream-history, and subject to criticism not only these existing conditions but at the same time their abstract continuation. Its future cannot be *limited* either to the immediate negation of its real conditions of state and law or to the immediate implementation of its ideal state and legal conditions, for it has the immediate negation of its real conditions in its ideal conditions, and it has almost *outlived* the immediate implementation of its ideal conditions in the contemplation of neighbouring nations. Hence it is with good reason that the *practical* political party in Germany demands the *negation of philosophy*. It is wrong, not in its demand, but in stopping at the demand, which it neither seriously implements nor can implement. It believes that it implements that negation by turning its back on philosophy and with averted face muttering a few trite and angry phrases about it. Owing to the limitation of its outlook it does not include philosophy in the circle of *German* reality or it even fancies it is *beneath* German practice and the theories that serve it. You demand that *real living germs* be made the starting point but you forget that the real living germ of the German nation has grown so far only inside its *cranium*. In a word – *you cannot supersede philosophy without making it a reality.*

The same mistake, but with the factors *reversed*, was made by the *theoretical* political party originating from philosophy.

In the present struggle it saw *only the critical struggle of philosophy against the German world*; it did not give a thought to the fact that the *hitherto prevailing philosophy* itself belongs to this world and is its *complement*, although an ideal one. Critical towards its adversary, it was uncritical towards itself when, proceeding from the *premises* of philosophy, it either stopped at the results given by philosophy or passed off demands and results from somewhere else as immediate demands and results of philosophy, although these, provided they are justified, can be obtained only by the *negation of hitherto existing philosophy*, of philosophy as such. We reserve ourselves the right to a more detailed description of this party. Its basic deficiency may be reduced to the following: *It thought it could make philosophy a reality without superseding it.*

The criticism of the *German philosophy of state and law*, which attained its most consistent, richest and final formulation through *Hegel*, is both a critical analysis of the modern state and of the reality connected with it, and the resolute negation of the whole *German political and legal consciousness* as *practised* hitherto, the most distinguished, most universal expression of which, raised to the level of a *science*, is the *speculative philosophy of law* itself. If the speculative philosophy of law, that abstract extravagant *thinking* on the modern state, the reality of which remains a thing of the beyond, if only beyond the Rhine, was possible only in Germany, inversely the *German* thought-image of the modern state which disregards *real man* was possible only because and insofar as the modern state itself disregards *real man* or satisfies the *whole* of man only in imagination. In politics the Germans *thought* what other nations *did*. Germany was their *theoretical consciousness*. The abstraction and conceit of its thought always kept in step with the one-sidedness and stumpiness of its reality. If therefore the *status quo of German statehood* expresses the *perfection of the ancien régime*, the perfection of the thorn in the flesh of the modern state, the *status quo of German political theory* expresses the *imperfection of the modern state*, the defectiveness of its flesh itself.

Even as the resolute opponent of the previous form of *German* political consciousness the criticism of speculative philosophy of law turns, not towards itself, but towards *problems* which can only be solved by one means – *practice*.

It is asked: can Germany attain a practice *à la hauteur des principes*, i.e., a *revolution* which will raise it not only to the *official level* of the modern nations but to the *height of humanity* which will be the near future of those nations?

The weapon of criticism cannot, of course, replace criticism by weapons, material force must be overthrown by material force; but theory also becomes a material force as soon as it has gripped the masses. Theory is capable of gripping the masses as soon as it demonstrates *ad hominem*, and it demonstrates *ad hominem* as soon as it becomes radical. To be radical is to grasp the root of the matter. But for man the root is man himself. The evident proof of the radicalism of German theory, and hence of its practical energy, is that it proceeds from a resolute *positive* abolition of religion. The criticism of religion ends with the teaching that *man is the highest being for man*, hence with the *categorical imperative to overthrow all relations* in which man is a debased, enslaved, forsaken, despicable being, relations which cannot be better described than by the exclamation of a Frenchman when it was planned to introduce a tax on dogs: Poor dogs! They want to treat you like human beings!

Even historically, theoretical emancipation has specific practical significance for Germany. For Germany's *revolutionary* past is theoretical, it is the *Reformation*. As the revolution then began in the brain of the *monk*, so now it begins in the brain of the *philosopher*.

Luther, we grant, overcame the bondage of *piety* by replacing it by the bondage of *conviction*. He shattered faith in authority because he restored the authority of faith. He turned priests into laymen because he turned laymen into priests. He freed man from outer religiosity because he made religiosity the inner man. He freed the body from chains because he enchained the heart.

But if Protestantism was not the true solution it was at least the true setting of the problem. It was no longer a case of the layman's struggle against the *priest outside himself* but of his struggle against his *own priest inside himself*, his *priestly nature*. And if the Protestant transformation of the German laymen into priests emancipated the lay popes, the *princes*, with the whole of their priestly clique, the privileged and philistines, the philosophical transformation of priestly Germans into men will emancipate the *people*. But *secularisation* will not stop at the *pillaging of churches* practised mainly by hypocritical Prussia any more than emancipation stops at princes. The Peasant War, the most radical fact of German history, came to grief because of theology. Today, when theology itself has come to grief, the most unfree fact of German history, our *status quo*, will be shattered against philosophy. On the eve of the Reformation official Germany was the most unconditional slave of Rome. On the eve of its revolution it is the unconditional slave of less than Rome, of Prussia and Austria, of country squires and philistines.

A major difficulty, however, seems to stand in the way of a *radical* German revolution.

For revolutions require a *passive* element, a *material* basis. Theory can be realised in a people only insofar as it is the realisation of the needs of that people. But will the enormous discrepancy between the demands of German thought and the answers of German reality be matched by a corresponding discrepancy between civil society and the state and between civil society and itself? Will the theoretical needs be immediate practical needs? It is not enough for thought to strive for realisation, reality must itself strive towards thought.

But Germany did not go through the intermediary stages of political emancipation at the same time as the modern nations. It has not even reached in practice the stages which it has overtaken in theory. How can it do a *somersault*, not only over its own limitations, but at the same time over the limitations of the modern nations, over limitations which in reality it must feel and strive for as bringing emancipation from its real limitations? Only a revolution of radical needs can be a radical revolution and it seems that for this the preconditions and ground are lacking.

If however Germany has accompanied the development of the modern nations only with the abstract activity of thought without playing an effective role in the real struggle of that development, it has, on the other hand, shared the *sufferings* of that development, without sharing in its enjoyment or its partial satisfaction. To abstract activity on the one hand corresponds abstract suffering on the other. That is why Germany will one day find itself on the level of European decadence before ever having been on the level of European emancipation. It will be comparable to a *fetish worshipper* pining away with the diseases of Christianity.

If we now consider the *German governments* we find that because of the existing state of affairs, because of Germany's condition, because of the standpoint of German education and finally under the impulse of their own fortunate instinct, they are driven to combine the *civilised shortcomings of the modern political world*, the advantages of which we do not enjoy, with the *barbaric deficiencies of the ancien régime*, which we enjoy in full; hence Germany must share more and more, if not in the reasonableness, at least in the unreasonableness of those state formations which are beyond the bounds of its *status quo*. Is there in the world, for example, a country which shares so naively in all the illusions of the constitutional state without sharing in its realities as so-called constitutional Germany? And was it not perforce a German government's idea to combine the tortures of censorship with the tortures of the French September laws which presuppose freedom of the press? As you could find the *gods* of all nations in the Roman Pantheon, so you will find in the Germans' Holy Roman Empire all the *sins* of all political forms. That this eclecticism will reach a height never dreamt of before is guaranteed in particular by the *political-aesthetic gourmandising* of a German king who intends to play all the roles of monarchy, whether feudal or bureaucratic, absolute or constitutional, autocratic or democratic, if not in the person of the people, at least in his *own* person, and if not for the people, at least for *himself. Germany, as the deficiency of the political present constituted as a particular world*, will not be able to throw down the specific German limitations without throwing down the general limitation of the political present.

It is not the *radical* revolution, not the *general human* emancipation which is a utopian dream for Germany, but rather the partial, the *merely* political revolution, the revolution which leaves the pillars of the house standing. On what is a partial, a merely political revolution based? On the fact that *part of civil society* emancipates itself and attains *general* domination; on the fact that a definite class, proceeding from its *particular situation*, undertakes the general emancipation of society. This class emancipates the whole of society but only provided the whole of society is in the same situation as this class, e.g., possesses money and education or can acquire them at will.

No class of civil society can play this role without arousing a moment of enthusiasm in itself and in the masses, a moment in which it fraternises and merges with society in general, becomes confused with it and is perceived and acknowledged as its *general representative*; a moment in which its demands and rights are truly the rights and demands of society itself; a moment in which it is truly the social head and the social heart.

Only in the name of the general rights of society can a particular class lay claim to general domination. For the storming of this emancipatory position, and hence for the political exploitation of all spheres of society in the interests of its own sphere, revolutionary energy and intellectual self-confidence alone are not sufficient. For the *revolution of a nation* and the *emancipation of a particular class* of civil society to coincide, for *one* estate to be acknowledged as the estate of the whole society, all the defects of society must conversely be concentrated in another class, a particular estate must be the general stumbling-block, the incorporation of the general limitation, a particular social sphere must be looked upon as the *notorious crime* of the whole of society, so that liberation from that sphere appears as general self-liberation. For *one* estate to be *par excellence* the estate of liberation, another estate must conversely be the obvious estate of oppression. The negative general significance of the French nobility and the French clergy determined the positive general significance of the immediately adjacent and opposed class of the *bourgeoisie*.

But no particular class in Germany has the consistency, the severity, the courage or the ruthlessness that could mark it out as the negative representative of society. No more has any estate the breadth of soul that identifies itself, even for a moment, with the soul of the nation, the genius that inspires material might to political violence, or that revolutionary audacity which flings at the adversary the defiant words: *I am nothing and I should be everything.* The main stem of German morals and honesty, of the classes as well as of individuals, is rather that *modest egoism* which asserts its limitedness and allows it to be asserted against itself. The relation of the various sections of German society is therefore not dramatic but epic. Each of them begins to be aware of itself and to settle down beside the others with all its particular claims not as soon as it is oppressed, but as soon as the circumstances of the time, without the section's own participation, create a social substratum on which it can in turn exert pressure. Even the *moral self-confidence of the German middle class* rests only on the consciousness that it is the general representative of the philistine mediocrity of all the other classes. It is therefore not only the German kings who accede to the throne *mal à propos*; every section of civil society goes through a defeat before it has celebrated victory, develops its own limitations before it has overcome the limitations facing it and asserts its narrow-hearted essence before it has been able to assert its magnanimous essence. Thus the very opportunity of a great role has on every occasion passed away before it is to hand, thus every class, once it begins the struggle against the class above it, is involved in the struggle against the class below it. Hence the princes are struggling against the monarchy, the bureaucrats against the nobility, and the bourgeois against them all, while the proletariat is already beginning to struggle against the bourgeoisie. No sooner does the middle class dare to think of emancipation from its own standpoint than the development of the social conditions and the progress of political theory pronounce that standpoint antiquated or at least problematic.

In France it is enough for somebody to be something for him to want to be everything; in Germany one has to be nothing if one is not to forego everything; In France partial emancipation is the basis of universal emancipation; in Germany universal emancipation is the *conditio sine qua non* of any partial emancipation. In France it is the reality of gradual liberation, in Germany the impossibility of gradual liberation, that must give birth to complete freedom. In France every class is *politically idealistic* and becomes aware of itself at first not as a particular class but as the representative of social requirements generally. The role of *emancipator* therefore passes in dramatic motion to the various classes of the French nation one after the other until it finally comes to the class which implements social freedom no longer on the basis of certain conditions lying outside man and yet created by human society, but rather organises all conditions of human existence on the presupposition of social freedom. In Germany, on the contrary, where practical life is as spiritless as spiritual life is unpractical, no class in civil society has any need or capacity for general emancipation until it is forced by its *immediate* condition, by *material* necessity, by its *very chains*.

Where, then, is the *positive* possibility of a German emancipation?

Answer: In the formation of a class with *radical chains*, a class of civil society which is not a class of civil society, an estate which is the dissolution of all estates, a sphere which has a universal character by its universal suffering and claims no *particular right* because no *particular wrong* but *wrong generally* is perpetrated against it; which can no longer invoke a *historical* but only a *human* title; which does not stand in any one-sided antithesis to the consequences but in an all-round antithesis to the premises of the German state; a sphere, finally, which cannot emancipate itself without emancipating itself from all other spheres of society and thereby emancipating all other spheres of society, which, in a word, is the *complete loss* of man and hence can win itself only through the *complete rewinning of man*. This dissolution of society as a particular estate is the *proletariat*.

The proletariat is coming into being in Germany only as a result of the rising *industrial* development. For it is not the *naturally arising* poor but the *artificially impoverished*, not the human masses mechanically oppressed by the gravity of society but the masses resulting from the *drastic dissolution* of society, mainly of the middle estate, that form the proletariat, although it is obvious that gradually the naturally arising poor and the Christian-Germanic serfs also join its ranks.

By proclaiming the *dissolution of the hitherto existing world order* the proletariat merely states the *secret of its own existence*, for it *is in fact* the dissolution of that world order. By demanding the *negation of private property*, the proletariat merely raises to the rank of a *principle of society* what society has made the principle of the *proletariat*, what, without its own co-operation, is already incorporated in *it* as the negative result of society. In regard to the world which is coming into being the proletarian then finds himself possessing the same right as the *German king* in regard to the world which has come into being when he calls the people *his* people as he calls the horse *his* horse. By declaring the people his private property the king simply states that the property owner is king.

As philosophy finds its *material* weapons in the proletariat, so the proletariat finds its *spiritual* weapons in philosophy. And once the lightning of thought has squarely struck this ingenuous soil of the people the emancipation of the *Germans* into *human beings* will take place.

Let us sum up the result:

The only *practically* possible liberation of Germany is liberation that proceeds from the standpoint of *the* theory which proclaims man to be the highest being for man. In Germany emancipation from the *Middle Ages* is possible only as emancipation from the *partial* victories over the Middle Ages as well. In Germany *no* kind of bondage can be broken without breaking *every* kind of bondage. The *thorough* Germany cannot make a revolution without making a *thoroughgoing* revolution. The *emancipation of the German* is the *emancipation of the human being*. The *head* of this emancipation is *philosophy*, its *heart* is the *proletariat*. Philosophy cannot be made a reality without the abolition of the proletariat, the proletariat cannot be abolished without philosophy being made a reality.

When all inner requisites are fulfilled the *day of German resurrection* will be proclaimed by the *ringing call of the Gallic cock*.

From: *Collected Works*, Vol. 3, pp. 175– 87

4

Economic and Philosophical Manuscripts

Many commentators consider the notes collected as the Economic and Philosophical Manuscripts *(written in the summer months of 1844 though not published until the 1930s) as perhaps the most original and important of all Marx's early writings. In them, Marx develops his first sustained and critical account of the political economy of capitalism. He concentrates upon the crucial category of 'alienated labour' and relates this to the character of an economy premised upon private property. He contrasts 'crude communism' (based on envy and levelling down) with his own preference for 'Communism as the positive transcendence of private property'. The critique of political economy was, of course, to be the central concern of Marx's mature writings.*

[. . .]

[Alienated labour]

We have proceeded from the premises of political economy. We have accepted its language and its laws. We presupposed private property, the separation of labour, capital and land, and of wages, profit of capital and rent of land – likewise division of labour, competition, the concept of exchange-value, etc. On the basis of political economy itself, in its own words, we have shown that the worker sinks to the level of a commodity and becomes indeed the most wretched of commodities; that the wretchedness of the worker is in inverse proportion to the power and magnitude of his production; that the necessary result of competition is the accumulation of capital in a few hands, and thus the restoration of monopoly in a more terrible form; and that finally the distinction between capitalist and land rentier, like that between the tiller of the soil and the factory worker, disappears and that the whole of society must fall apart into the two classes – the *property owners* and the propertyless *workers.*

Political economy starts with the fact of private property; it does not explain it to us. It expresses in general, abstract formulas the *material* process through which private property actually passes, and these formulas it then takes for *laws*. It does not *comprehend* these laws, i.e., it does not demonstrate how they arise from the very nature of private property. Political economy throws no light on the cause of the division between labour and capital, and between capital and land. When, for example, it defines the relationship of wages to profit, it takes the interest of the capitalists to be the ultimate cause, i.e., it takes for granted what it is supposed to explain. Similarly, competition comes in everywhere. It is explained from external circumstances. As to how far these external and apparently accidental circumstances are but the expression of a necessary course of development, political economy teaches us nothing. We have seen how exchange itself appears to it as an accidental fact. The only wheels which political economy sets in motion are *greed* and the *war amongst the greedy – competition.*

Precisely because political economy does not grasp the way the movement is connected, it was possible to oppose, for instance, the doctrine of competition to the doctrine of monopoly, the doctrine of the freedom of the crafts to the doctrine of the guild, the doctrine of the division of landed property to the doctrine of the big estate – for competition, freedom of the crafts and the division of landed property were explained and comprehended only as accidental, premeditated and violent consequences of monopoly, of the guild system, and of feudal property, not as their necessary, inevitable and natural consequences.

Now, therefore, we have to grasp the intrinsic connection between private property, avarice, the separation of labour, capital and landed property; the connection of exchange and competition, of value and the devaluation of men, of monopoly and competition, etc. – we have to grasp this whole estrangement connected with the *money* system.

Do not let us go back to a fictitious primordial condition as the political economist does, when he tries to explain. Such a primordial condition explains nothing; it merely pushes the question away into a grey nebulous distance. The economist assumes in the form of a fact, of an event, what he is supposed to deduce – namely, the necessary relationship between two things – between, for example, division of labour and exchange. Thus the theologian explains the origin of evil by the fall of man; that is, he assumes as a fact, in historical form, what has to be explained.

We proceed from an *actual* economic fact.

The worker becomes all the poorer the more wealth he produces, the more his production increases in power and size. The worker becomes an ever cheaper commodity the more commodities he creates. The *devaluation* of the world of men is in direct proportion to the *increasing value* of the world of things. Labour produces not only commodities: it produces itself and the worker as a *commodity* – and this at the same rate at which it produces commodities in general.

This fact expresses merely that the object which labour produces – labour's product – confronts it as *something alien*, as a *power independent* of the producer. The product of labour is labour which has been embodied in an object, which has become material: it is the *objectification* of labour. Labour's realisation is its objectification. Under these economic conditions this realisation of labour appears as *loss of realisation* for the workers; objectification as *loss of the object and bondage to it*; appropriation as *estrangement*, as *alienation*.

So much does labour's realisation appear as loss of realisation that the worker loses realisation to the point of starving to death. So much does objectification appear as loss of the object that the worker is robbed of the objects most necessary not only for his life but for his work. Indeed, labour itself becomes an object which he can obtain only with the greatest effort and with the most irregular interruptions. So much does the appropriation of the object appear as estrangement that the more objects the worker produces the less he can possess and the more he falls under the sway of his product, capital.

All these consequences are implied in the statement that the worker is related to the *product of his labour* as to an *alien* object. For on this premise it is clear that the more the worker spends himself, the more powerful becomes the alien world of objects which he creates over and against himself, the poorer he himself – his inner world – becomes, the less belongs to him as his own. It is the same in religion. The more man puts into God, the less he retains in himself. The worker puts his life into the object; but now his life no longer belongs to him but to the object. Hence, the greater this activity, the more the worker lacks objects. Whatever the product of his labour is, he is not. Therefore the greater this product, the less is he himself. The *alienation* of the worker in his product means not only that his labour becomes an object, an *external* existence, but that it exists *outside him*, independently, as something alien to him, and that it becomes a power on its own confronting him. It means that the life which he has conferred on the object confronts him as something hostile and alien.

Let us now look more closely at the *objectification*, at the production of the worker; and in it at the *estrangement*, the *loss* of the object, of his product.

The worker can create nothing without *nature*, without the *sensuous external world*. It is the material on which his labour is realised, in which it is active, from which and by means of which it produces.

But just as nature provides labour with [the] *means of life* in the sense that labour cannot *live* without objects on which to operate, on the other hand, it also provides the *means of life* in the more restricted sense, i.e., the means for the physical subsistence of the *worker* himself.

Thus the more the worker by his labour *appropriates* the external world, sensuous nature, the more he deprives himself of *means of life* in two respects: first, in that the sensuous external world more and more ceases to be an object belonging to his labour – to be his labour's *means of life*; and secondly, in that it more and more ceases to be *means of life* in the immediate sense, means for the physical subsistence of the worker.

In both respects, therefore, the worker becomes a servant of his object, first, in that he receives an *object of labour*, i.e., in that he receives *work*; and secondly, in that he receives *means of subsistence*. This enables him to exist, first, as a *worker*; and, second, as a *physical subject*. The height of this servitude is that it is only as a *worker* that he can maintain himself as a *physical subject*, and that it is only as a *physical subject* that he is a worker.

(According to the economic laws the estrangement of the worker in his object is expressed thus: the more the worker produces, the less he has to consume; the more values he creates, the more valueless, the more unworthy he becomes; the better formed his product, the more deformed becomes the worker; the more civilised his object, the more barbarous becomes the worker; the more powerful labour becomes, the more powerless becomes the worker; the more ingenious labour becomes, the less ingenious becomes the worker and the more he becomes nature's servant.)

Political economy conceals the estrangement inherent in the nature of labour by not considering the **direct** *relationship between the* **worker** (labour) *and production*. It is true that labour produces wonderful things for the rich – but for the worker it produces privation. It produces palaces – but for the worker, hovels. It produces beauty – but for the worker, deformity. It replaces labour by machines, but it throws one section of the workers back to a barbarous type of labour, and it turns the other section into a machine. It produces intelligence – but for the worker, stupidity, cretinism.

The direct relationship of labour to its products is the relationship of the worker to the objects of his production. The relationship of the man of means to the objects of production and to production itself is only a *consequence* of this first relationship – and confirms it. We shall consider this other aspect later. When we ask, then, what is the essential relationship of labour we are asking about the relationship of the *worker* to production.

Till now we have been considering the estrangement; the alienation of the worker only in one of its aspects, i.e., the worker's *relationship to the products of his labour*. But the estrangement is manifested not only in the result but in the *act of production*, within the *producing activity* itself. How could the worker come to face the product of his activity as a stranger, were it not that in the very act of production he was estranging himself from himself? The product is after all but the summary of the activity, of production. If then the product of labour is alienation, production itself must be active alienation, the alienation of activity, the activity of alienation. In the estrangement of the object of labour is merely summarised the estrangement, the alienation, in the activity of labour itself.

What, then, constitutes the alienation of labour?

First, the fact that labour is *external* to the worker, i.e., it does not belong to his intrinsic nature; that in his work, therefore, he does not affirm himself but denies himself, does not feel content but unhappy, does not develop freely his physical and mental energy but mortifies his body and ruins his mind. The worker therefore only feels himself outside his work, and in his work feels outside himself. He feels at home when he is not working, and when he is working he does not feel at home. His labour is therefore not voluntary, but coerced; it is *forced labour*. It is therefore not the satisfaction of a need; it is merely a *means* to satisfy needs external to it. Its alien character emerges clearly in the fact that as soon as no physical or other compulsion exists, labour is shunned like the plague. External labour, labour in which man alienates himself, is a labour of self-sacrifice, of mortification. Lastly, the external character of labour for the worker appears in the fact that it is not his own, but someone else's, that it does not belong to him, that in it he belongs, not to himself, but to another. Just as in religion the spontaneous activity of the human imagination, of the human brain and the human heart, operates on the individual independently of him – that is, operates as an alien, divine or diabolical activity – so is the worker's activity not his spontaneous activity. It belongs to another; it is the loss of his self.

As a result, therefore, man (the worker) only feels himself freely active in his animal functions – eating, drinking, procreating, or at most in his dwelling and in dressing-up, etc.; and in his human functions he no longer feels himself to be anything but an animal. What is animal becomes human and what is human becomes animal.

Certainly eating, drinking, procreating, etc., are also genuinely human functions. But taken abstractly, separated from the sphere of all other human activity and turned into sole and ultimate ends, they are animal functions.

We have considered the act of estranging practical human activity, labour, in two of its aspects. (1) The relation of the worker to the *product of labour* as an alien object exercising power over him. This relation is at the same time the relation to the sensuous external world, to the objects of nature, as an alien world inimically opposed to him. (2) The relation of labour to the *act of production* within the *labour* process. This relation is the relation of the worker to his own activity as an alien activity not belonging to him; it is activity as suffering, strength as weakness, begetting as emasculating, the worker's *own* physical and mental energy, his personal life – for what is life but activity? – as an activity which is turned against him, independent of him and not belonging to him. Here we have *self-estrangement*, as previously we had the estrangement of the *thing*.

We have still a third aspect of *estranged labour* to deduce from the two already considered.

Man is a species-being, not only because in practice and in theory he adopts the species (his own as well as those of other things) as his object, but – and this is only another way of expressing it – also because he treats himself as the actual, living species; because he treats himself as a *universal* and therefore a free being.

The life of the species, both in man and in animals, consists physically in the fact that man (like the animal) lives on inorganic nature; and the more universal man (or the animal) is, the more universal is the sphere of inorganic nature on which he lives. Just as plants, animals, stones, air, light, etc., constitute theoretically a part of human consciousness, partly as objects of natural science, partly as objects of art – his spiritual inorganic nature, spiritual nourishment which he must first prepare to make palatable and digestible – so also in the realm of practice they constitute a part of human life and human activity. Physically man lives only on these products of nature, whether they appear in the form of food, heating, clothes, a dwelling, etc. The universality of man appears in practice precisely in the universality which makes all nature his *inorganic* body – both inasmuch as nature is (1) his direct means of life, and (2) the material, the object, and the instrument of his life activity. Nature is man's *inorganic body* – nature, that is, insofar as it is not itself human body. Man *lives* on nature – means that nature is his *body*, with which he must remain in continuous interchange if he is not to die. That man's physical and spiritual life is linked to nature means simply that nature is linked to itself, for man is a part of nature.

In estranging from man (1) nature, and (2) himself, his own active functions, his life activity, estranged labour estranges the *species* from man. It changes for him the *life of the species* into a means of individual life. First it estranges the life of the species and individual life, and secondly it makes individual life in its abstract form the purpose of the life of the species, likewise in its abstract and estranged form.

For labour, *life activity, productive life* itself, appears to man in the first place merely as a *means* of satisfying a need – the need to maintain physical existence. Yet the productive life is the life of the species. It is life-engendering life. The whole character of a species – its species-character – is contained in the character of its life activity; and free, conscious activity is man's species-character. Life itself appears only as a *means to life*.

The animal is immediately one with its life activity. It does not distinguish itself from it. It is *its life activity*. Man makes his life activity itself the object of his will and of his consciousness. He has conscious life activity. It is not a determination with which he directly merges. Conscious life activity distinguishes man immediately from animal life activity. It is just because of this that he is a species-being. Or it is only because he is a species-being that he is a conscious being, i.e., that his own life is an object for him. Only because of that is his activity free activity. Estranged labour reverses this relationship, so that it is just because man is a conscious being that he makes his life activity, his *essential being*, a mere means to his *existence*.

In creating a *world of objects* by his practical activity, in his *work upon* inorganic nature, man proves himself a conscious species-being, i.e., as a being that treats the species as its own essential being, or that treats itself as a species-being. Admittedly animals also produce. They build themselves nests, dwellings, like the bees, beavers, ants, etc. But an animal only produces what it immediately needs for itself or its young. It produces one-sidedly, whilst man produces universally. It produces only under the dominion of immediate physical need, whilst man produces even when he is free from physical need and only truly produces in freedom therefrom. An animal produces only itself, whilst man reproduces the whole of nature. An animal's product belongs immediately to its physical body, whilst man freely confronts his product. An animal forms objects only in accordance with the standard and the need of the species to which it belongs, whilst man knows how to produce in accordance with the standard of every species, and knows how to apply everywhere the inherent standard to the object. Man therefore also forms objects in accordance with the laws of beauty.

It is just in his work upon the objective world, therefore, that man really proves himself to be a *species-being*. This production is his active species-life. Through this production, nature appears as *his* work and his reality. The object of labour is, therefore, the *objectification of man's species-life*: for he duplicates himself not only, as in consciousness, intellectually, but also actively, in reality, and therefore he sees himself in a world that he has created. In tearing away from man the object of his production, therefore, estranged labour tears from him his *species-life*, his real objectivity as a member of the species, and transforms his advantage over animals into the disadvantage that his inorganic body, nature, is taken away from him.

Similarly, in degrading spontaneous, free activity to a means, estranged labour makes man's species-life a means to his physical existence.

The consciousness which man has of his species is thus transformed by estrangement in such a way that species [-life] becomes for him a means.

Estranged labour turns thus:

(3) *Man's species-being*, both nature and his spiritual species-property, into a being *alien* to him, into a *means* for his *individual existence*. It estranges from man his own body, as well as external nature and his spiritual aspect, his *human* aspect.

(4) An immediate consequence of the fact that man is estranged from the product of his labour, from his life activity, from his species-being is the *estrangement of man* from *man*. When man confronts himself, he confronts the *other* man. What applies to a man's relation to his work, to the product of his labour and to himself, also holds of a man's relation to the other man, and to the other man's labour and object of labour.

In fact, the proposition that man's species-nature is estranged from him means that one man is estranged from the other, as each of them is from man's essential nature.

The estrangement of man, and in fact every relationship in which man [stands] to himself, is realised and expressed only in the relationship in which a man stands to other men.

Hence within the relationship of estranged labour each man views the other in accordance with the standard and the relationship in which he finds himself as a worker.

We took our departure from a fact of political economy – the estrangement of the worker and his product. We have formulated this fact in conceptual terms as *estranged, alienated* labour. We have analysed this concept – hence analysing merely a fact of political economy.

Let us now see, further, how the concept of estranged, alienated labour must express and present itself in real life.

If the product of labour is alien to me, if it confronts me as an alien power, to whom, then, does it belong?

If my own activity does not belong to me, if it is an alien, a coerced activity, to whom, then, does it belong?

To a being *other* than myself.

Who is this being?

The *gods*? To be sure, in the earliest times the principal production (for example, the building of temples, etc., in Egypt, India and Mexico) appears to be in the service of the gods, and the product belongs to the gods. However, the gods on their own were never the lords of labour. No more was *nature*. And what a contradiction it would be if, the more man subjugated nature by his labour and the more the miracles of the gods were rendered superfluous by the miracles of industry, the more man were to renounce the joy of production and the enjoyment of the product to please these powers.

The *alien* being, to whom labour and the product of labour belongs, in whose service labour is done and for whose benefit the product of labour is provided, can only be *man* himself.

If the product of labour does not belong to the worker, if it confronts him as an alien power, then this can only be because it belongs to some *other man than the worker*. If the worker's activity is a torment to him, to another it must give *satisfaction* and pleasure. Not the gods, not nature, but only man himself can be this alien power over man.

We must bear in mind the previous proposition that man's relation to himself only becomes for him *objective* and *actual* through his relation to the other man. Thus, if the product of his labour, his labour objectified, is for him an *alien, hostile,* powerful object independent of him, then his position towards it is such that someone else is master of this object, someone who is alien, hostile, powerful, and independent of him. If he treats his own activity as an unfree activity, then he treats it as an activity performed in the service, under the dominion, the coercion, and the yoke of another man.

Every self-estrangement of man, from himself and from nature, appears in the relation in which he places himself and nature to men other than and differentiated from himself. For this reason religious self-estrangement necessarily appears in the relationship of the layman to the priest, or again to a mediator, etc., since we are here dealing with the intellectual world. In the real practical world self-estrangement can only become manifest through the real practical relationship to other men. The medium through which estrangement takes place is itself *practical.* Thus through estranged labour man not only creates his relationship to the object and to the act of production as to powers[1] that are alien and hostile to him; he also creates the relationship in which other men stand to his production and to his product, and the relationship in which he stands to these other men. Just as he creates his own production as the loss of his reality, as his punishment; his own product as a loss, as a product not belonging to him; so he creates the domination of the person who does not produce over production and over the product. Just as he estranges his own activity from himself, so he confers upon the stranger an activity which is not his own.

We have until now considered this relationship only from the standpoint of the worker and later we shall be considering it also from the standpoint of the non-worker.

Through *estranged, alienated labour,* then, the worker produces the relationship to this labour of a man alien to labour and standing outside it. The relationship of the worker to labour creates the relation to it of the capitalist (or whatever one chooses to call the master of labour). *Private property* is thus the product, the result, the necessary consequence, of *alienated labour*, of the external relation of the worker to nature and to himself.

Private property thus results by analysis from the concept of *alienated labour*, i.e., of *alienated man*, of estranged labour, of estranged life, of *estranged* man.

True, it is as a result of the *movement of private property* that we have obtained the concept of *alienated labour* (*of alienated life*) in political economy. But analysis of this concept shows that though private property appears to be the reason, the cause of alienated labour, it is rather its consequence, just as the gods are *originally* not the cause but the effect of man's intellectual confusion. Later this relationship becomes reciprocal.

Only at the culmination of the development of private property does this, its secret, appear again, namely, that on the one hand it is the *product* of alienated labour, and that on the other it is the *means* by which labour alienates itself, the *realisation of this alienation*.

This exposition immediately sheds light on various hitherto unsolved conflicts.

1 Political economy starts from labour as the real soul of production; yet to labour it gives nothing, and to private property everything. Confronting this contradiction, Proudhon has decided in favour of labour against private property. We understand, however, that this apparent contradiction is the contradiction of *estranged labour* with itself, and that political economy has merely formulated the laws of estranged labour.

We also understand, therefore, that *wages* and *private property* are identical. Indeed, where the product, as the object of labour, pays for labour itself, there the wage is but a necessary consequence of labour's estrangement. Likewise, in the wage of labour, labour does not appear as an end in itself but as the servant of the wage. We shall develop this point later, and meanwhile will only draw some conclusions.

An enforced *increase of wages* (disregarding all other difficulties, including the fact that it would only be by force, too, that such an increase, being an anomaly, could be maintained) would therefore be nothing but better *payment for the slave*, and would not win either for the worker or for labour their human status and dignity.

Indeed, even the *equality of wages*, as demanded by Proudhon, only transforms the relationship of the present-day worker to his labour into the relationship of all men to labour. Society is then conceived as an abstract capitalist.

Wages are a direct consequence of estranged labour, and estranged labour is the direct cause of private property. The downfall of the one must therefore involve the downfall of the other.

2 From the relationship of estranged labour to private property it follows further that the emancipation of society from private property, etc., from servitude, is expressed in the *political* form of the *emancipation of the workers*; not that *their* emancipation alone is at stake, but because the emancipation of the workers contains universal human emancipation – and it contains this, because the whole of human servitude is involved in the relation of the worker to production, and all relations of servitude are but modifications and consequences of this relation.

Just as we have derived the concept of *private property* from the concept of *estranged, alienated labour* by *analysis*, so we can develop every *category* of political economy with the help of these two factors; and we shall find again in each category, e.g., trade, competition, capital, money, only a *particular* and *developed expression* of these first elements.

Before considering this phenomenon, however, let us try to solve two other problems.

1 To define the general *nature of private property*, as it has arisen as a result of estranged labour, in its relation to *truly human* and *social property*.
2 We have accepted the *estrangement of labour*, its *alienation*, as a fact, and we have analysed this fact. How, we now ask, does *man* come to *alienate*, to estrange, his *labour*? How is this estrangement rooted in the nature of human development? We have already gone a long way to the solution of this problem by *transforming* the question of the *origin of private property* into the question of the relation of *alienated labour* to the course of humanity's development. For when one speaks of *private property*, one thinks of dealing with something external to man. When one speaks of labour, one is directly dealing with man himself. This new formulation of the question already contains its solution.

As to (1): The general nature of private property and its relation to truly human property.

Alienated labour has resolved itself for us into two components which depend on one another, or which are but different expressions of one and the same relationship. *Appropriation* appears as *estrangement*, as *alienation*; and *alienation* appears as *appropriation, estrangement* as truly *becoming a citizen*.

We have considered the one side – *alienated* labour in relation to the worker himself, i.e., the *relation of alienated labour to itself*. The product, the necessary outcome of this relationship, as we have seen, is the *property relation of the non-worker to the worker and to labour*. Private property, as the material, summary expression of alienated labour, embraces both relations – the *relation of the worker to labour and to the product of his labour and to the non-worker*, and the relation of the *non-worker to the worker and to the product of his labour*.

Having seen that in relation to the worker who *appropriates* nature by means of his labour, this appropriation appears as estrangement, his own spontaneous activity as activity for another and as activity of another, vitality as a sacrifice of life, production of the object as loss of the object to an alien power, to an *alien* person – we shall now consider the relation to the worker, to labour and its object of this person who is *alien* to labour and the worker.

First it has to be noted that everything which appears in the worker as an *activity of alienation, of estrangement*, appears in the non-worker as a *state of alienation, of estrangement*.

Secondly, that the worker's *real, practical attitude* in production and to the product (as a state of mind) appears in the non-worker confronting him as a *theoretical* attitude.

Thirdly, the non-worker does everything against the worker which the worker does against himself; but he does not do against himself what he does against the worker.

[. . .]

[Private property and communism]

The antithesis between *lack of property* and *property*, so long as it is not comprehended as the antithesis of *labour* and *capital*, still remains an indifferent antithesis, not grasped in its *active connection*, in its *internal* relation, not yet grasped as a *contradiction*. It can find expression in this *first* form even without the advanced development of private property (as in ancient Rome, Turkey, etc.). It does not yet *appear* as having been established by private property itself. But labour, the subjective essence of private property as exclusion of property, and capital, objective labour as exclusion of labour, constitute *private property* as its developed state of contradiction – hence a dynamic relationship driving towards resolution.

. . . The transcendence of self-estrangement follows the same course as self-estrangement. *Private property* is first considered only in its objective aspect – but nevertheless with labour as its essence. Its form of existence is therefore *capital*, which is to be annulled 'as such' (Proudhon). Or a *particular form* of labour – labour levelled down, fragmented, and therefore unfree – is conceived as the source of private property's *perniciousness* and of its existence in estrangement from men. For instance, *Fourier*, who, like the Physiocrats, also conceives *agricultural labour* to be at least the *exemplary* type, whereas *Saint-Simon* declares in contrast that *industrial labour* as such is the essence, and accordingly aspires to the *exclusive* rule of the industrialists and the improvement of the workers' condition. Finally, *communism* is the *positive* expression of annulled private property – at first as *universal* private property. By embracing this relation as a *whole*, communism is:

(1) In its first form only a *generalisation* and *consummation* of it [of this relation]. As such it appears in a twofold form: on the one hand, the dominion of *material* property bulks so large that it wants to destroy *everything* which is not capable of being possessed by all as *private property*. It wants to disregard talent, etc., in an *arbitrary* manner. For it the sole purpose of life and existence is direct, physical *possession*. The category of the *worker* is not done away with, but extended to all men. The relationship of private property persists as the relationship of the community to the world of things. Finally, this movement of opposing universal private property to private property finds expression in the brutish form of opposing to *marriage* (certainly a *form of exclusive private property*) the *community of women*, in which a woman becomes a piece of *communal* and *common* property. It may be said that this idea of the *community of women gives away the secret* of this as yet completely crude and thoughtless communism. Just as woman passes from marriage to general prostitution,[2] so the entire world of wealth (that is, of man's objective substance) passes from the relationship of exclusive marriage with the owner of private property to a state of universal prostitution with the community. This type of communism – since it negates the *personality* of man in every sphere – is but the logical expression of private property, which is this negation. General *envy* constituting itself as a power is the disguise in which *greed* re-establishes itself and satisfies itself, only in *another* way. The thought of every piece of private property as such is *at least* turned against *wealthier* private property in the form of envy and the urge to reduce things to a common level, so that this envy and urge even constitute the essence of competition. Crude communism is only the culmination of this envy and of this levelling-down proceeding from the *preconceived* minimum. It has a *definite, limited* standard. How little this annulment of private property is really an appropriation is in fact proved by the abstract negation of the entire world of culture and civilisation, the regression to the *unnatural* simplicity of the *poor* and crude man who has few needs and who has not only failed to go beyond private property, but has not yet even reached it.

The community is only a community of *labour*, and equality of *wages* paid out by communal capital – by the *community* as the universal capitalist. Both sides of the relationship are raised to an *imagined* universality – *labour* as the category in which every person is placed, and *capital* as the acknowledged universality and power of the community.

In the approach to *woman* as the *spoil* and handmaid of communal lust is expressed the infinite degradation in which man exists for himself, for the secret of this approach has its *unambiguous*, decisive, *plain* and undisguised expression in the relation of *man* to *woman* and in the manner in which the *direct* and *natural* species-relationship is conceived. The direct, natural, and necessary relation of person to person is the *relation of man to woman*. In this *natural* species-relationship man's relation to nature is immediately his relation to man, just as his relation to man is immediately his relation to nature – his own *natural* destination. In this relationship, therefore, is *sensuously manifested*, reduced to an observable *fact*, the extent to which the human essence has become nature to man, or to which nature to him has become the human essence of man. From this relationship one can therefore judge man's whole level of development. From the character of this relationship follows how much *man as a species-being*, as *man*, has come to be himself and to comprehend himself; the relation of man to woman is the *most natural* relation of human being to human being. It therefore reveals the extent to which man's *natural* behaviour has become *human*, or the extent to which the *human* essence in him has become a *natural* essence – the extent to which his *human nature* has come to be *natural* to him. This relationship also reveals the extent to which man's *need* has become a *human* need; the extent to which, therefore, the *other* person as a person has become for him a need – the extent to which he in his individual existence is at the same time a social being.

The first positive annulment of private property – *crude* communism – is thus merely a *manifestation* of the vileness of private property, which wants to set itself up as the *positive community system*.

(2) Communism (a) still political in nature – democratic or despotic; (b) with the abolition of the state, yet still incomplete, and being still affected by private property, i.e., by the estrangement of man. In both forms communism already is aware of being reintegration or return of man to himself, the transcendence of human self-estrangement; but since it has not yet grasped the positive essence of private property, and just as little the *human* nature of need, it remains captive to it and infected by it. It has, indeed, grasped its concept, but not its essence.

(3) *Communism* as the *positive* transcendence of *private property* as *human self-estrangement*, and therefore as the real *appropriation* of the *human* essence by and for man; communism therefore as the complete return of man to himself as a *social* (i.e., human) being – a return accomplished consciously and embracing the entire wealth of previous development. This communism, as fully developed naturalism, equals humanism, and as fully developed humanism equals naturalism; it is the *genuine* resolution of the conflict between man and nature and between man and man – the true resolution of the strife between existence and

essence, between objectification and self-confirmation, between freedom and necessity, between the individual and the species. Communism is the riddle of history solved, and it knows itself to be this solution.

The entire movement of history, just as its [communism's] *actual* act of genesis – the birth act of its empirical existence – is, therefore, also for its thinking consciousness the *comprehended* and *known* process of its *becoming*. Whereas the still immature communism seeks an *historical* proof for itself – a proof in the realm of what already exists – among disconnected historical phenomena opposed to private property, tearing single phases from the historical process and focusing attention on them as proofs of its historical pedigree (a hobby-horse ridden hard especially by Cabet, Villegardelle, etc.). By so doing it simply makes clear that by far the greater part of this process contradicts its own claim, and that, if it has ever existed, precisely its being in the *past* refutes its pretension to *reality*.

It is easy to see that the entire revolutionary movement necessarily finds both its empirical and its theoretical basis in the movement of *private property* – more precisely, in that of the economy.

This *material*, immediately *perceptible* private property is the material perceptible expression of *estranged human* life. Its movement – production and consumption – is the *perceptible* revelation of the movement of all production until now, i.e., the realisation or the reality of man. Religion, family, state, law, morality, science, art, etc., are only *particular* modes of production, and fall under its general law. The positive transcendence of *private property*, as the appropriation of *human* life, is therefore the positive transcendence of all estrangement – that is to say, the return of man from religion, family, state, etc., to his *human*, i.e., *social*, existence. Religious estrangement as such occurs only in the realm of *consciousness*, of man's inner life, but economic estrangement is that of *real life*; its transcendence therefore embraces both aspects. It is evident that the *initial* stage of the movement amongst the various peoples depends on whether the true *recognised* life of the people manifests itself more in consciousness or in the external world – is more ideal or real. Communism begins from the outset (*Owen*) with atheism; but atheism is at first far from being *communism*; indeed, that atheism is still mostly an abstraction.

The philanthropy of atheism is therefore at first only *philosophical*, abstract philanthropy, and that of communism is at once *real* and directly bent on *action*.

We have seen how on the assumption of positively annulled private property man produces man – himself and the other man; how the object, being the direct manifestation of his individuality, is simultaneously his own existence for the other man, the existence of the other man, and that existence for him. Likewise, however, both the material of labour and man as the subject, are the point of departure as well as the result of the movement (and precisely in this fact, that they must constitute the *point of departure*, lies the historical *necessity* of private property). Thus the *social* character is the general character of the whole movement: *just as* society itself produces *man as man*, so is society *produced* by him. Activity and enjoyment, both in their content and in their *mode of existence*, are *social: social*[3] activity and *social* enjoyment. The *human* aspect of nature exists only for *social* man; for only then does nature exist for him as a *bond* with *man* – as his existence for the other and the other's existence for him – and as the life-element of human reality. Only then does nature exist as the *foundation* of his own *human* existence. Only here has what is to him his *natural* existence become his *human* existence, and nature become man for him. Thus *society* is the complete unity of man with nature – the true resurrection of nature – the accomplished naturalism of man and the accomplished humanism of nature.

Social activity and social enjoyment exist by no means *only* in the form of some *directly* communal activity and directly *communal* enjoyment, although *communal* activity and *communal* enjoyment – i.e., activity and enjoyment which are manifested and affirmed in *actual* direct *association* with other men – will occur wherever such a *direct* expression of sociability stems from the true character of the activity's content and is appropriate to the nature of the enjoyment.

But also when I am active *scientifically*, etc. – an activity which I can seldom perform in direct community with others – then my activity is *social*, because I perform it as a *man*. Not only is the material of my activity given to me as a social product (as is even the language in which the thinker is active): my *own* existence *is* social activity, and therefore that which I make of myself, I make of myself for society and with the consciousness of myself as a social being.

My *general* consciousness is only the *theoretical* shape of that of which the *living* shape is the *real* community, the social fabric, although at the present day *general* consciousness is an abstraction from real life and as such confronts it with hostility. The *activity* of my general consciousness, as an activity, is therefore also my *theoretical* existence as a social being.

Above all we must avoid postulating 'society' again as an abstraction *vis-à-vis* the individual. The individual *is the social being*. His manifestations of life – even if they may not appear in the direct form of *communal* manifestations of life carried out in association with others – *are* therefore an expression and confirmation of *social life*. Man's individual and species-life are not *different*, however much – and this is inevitable – the mode of existence of the individual is a more *particular* or more *general* mode of the life of the species, or the life of the species is a more *particular* or more *general* individual life.

In his *consciousness of species* man confirms his real *social life* and simply repeats his real existence in thought, just as conversely the being of the species confirms itself in species consciousness and exists for itself in its generality as a thinking being.

Man, much as he may therefore be a *particular* individual (and it is precisely his particularity which makes him an individual, and a real *individual* social being), is just as much the *totality* – the ideal totality – the subjective existence of imagined and experienced society for itself; just as he exists also in the real world both as awareness and real enjoyment of social existence, and as a totality of human manifestation of life.

Thinking and being are thus certainly *distinct*, but at the same time they are in *unity* with each other.

Death seems to be a harsh victory of the species over the *particular* individual and to contradict their unity. But the particular individual is only a *particular species-being*, and as such mortal.

(4) Just as *private property* is only the perceptible expression of the fact that man becomes *objective* for himself and at the same time becomes to himself a strange and inhuman object; just as it expresses the fact that the manifestation of his life is the alienation of his life, that his realisation is his loss of reality, is an *alien* reality: so, the positive transcendence of private property – i.e., the *perceptible* appropriation for and by man of the human essence and of human life, of objective man, of human *achievements* – should not be conceived merely in the sense of *immediate*, one-sided *enjoyment*, merely in the sense of *possessing*, of *having*. Man appropriates his comprehensive essence in a comprehensive manner, that is to say, as a whole man. Each of his *human* relations to the world – seeing, hearing, smelling, tasting, feeling, thinking, observing, experiencing, wanting, acting, loving – in short, all the organs of his individual being, like those organs which are directly social in their form, are in their *objective* orientation, or in their *orientation to the object*, the appropriation of the object, the appropriation of *human* reality. Their orientation to the object is the *manifestation of the human reality*,[4] it is human *activity* and human *suffering*, for suffering, humanly considered, is a kind of self-enjoyment of man.

Private property has made us so stupid and one-sided that an object is only *ours* when we have it – when it exists for us as capital, or when it is directly possessed, eaten, drunk, worn, inhabited, etc., – in short, when it is *used* by us. Although private property itself again conceives all these direct realisations of possession only as *means of life*, and the life which they serve as means is the *life of private property* – labour and conversion into capital.

In the place of *all* physical and mental senses there has therefore come the sheer estrangement of *all* these senses, the sense of *having*. The human being had to be reduced to this absolute poverty in order that he might yield his inner wealth to the outer world . . .

The abolition of private property is therefore the complete *emancipation* of all human senses and qualities, but it is this emancipation precisely because these senses and attributes have become, subjectively and objectively, *human*. The eye has become a *human* eye, just as its *object* has become a social, *human* object – an object made by man for man. The *senses* have therefore become directly in their practice *theoreticians*. They relate themselves to the *thing* for the sake of the thing, but the thing itself is an *objective human* relation to itself and to man, and vice versa. Need or enjoyment has consequently lost its *egotistical* nature, and nature has lost its mere *utility* by use becoming *human* use.

In the same way, the senses and enjoyment of other men have become my *own* appropriation. Besides these direct organs, therefore, *social* organs develop in the *form* of society; thus, for instance, activity in direct association with others, etc., has become an organ for *expressing* my own *life*, and a mode of appropriating *human* life.

It is obvious that the *human* eye enjoys things in a way different from the crude, non-human eye; the human *ear* different from the crude ear, etc.

We have seen that man does not lose himself in his object only when the object becomes for him a *human* object or objective man. This is possible only when the object becomes for him a *social* object, he himself for himself a social being, just as society becomes a being for him in this object.

On the one hand, therefore, it is only when the objective world becomes everywhere for man in society the world of man's essential powers – human reality, and for that reason the reality of his *own* essential powers – that all *objects* become for him the *objectification* of himself, become objects which confirm and realise his individuality, become *his* objects: that is, *man himself* becomes the object. The *manner* in which they become *his* depends on the *nature of the objects* and on the nature of the *essential power* corresponding to *it*; for it is precisely the *determinate nature* of this relationship which shapes the particular, *real* mode of affirmation. To the *eye* an object comes to be other than it is to the *ear*, and the object of the eye *is* another object than the object of the *ear*. The specific character of each essential power is precisely its *specific essence*, and therefore also the specific mode of its objectification, of its *objectively actual*, living *being*. Thus man is affirmed in the objective world not only in the act of thinking, but with *all* his senses.

On the other hand, let us look at this in its subjective aspect. Just as only music awakens in man the sense of music, and just as the most beautiful music has *no* sense for the unmusical ear – is [no] object for it, because my object can only be the confirmation of one of my essential powers – it can therefore only exist for me insofar as my essential power exists for itself as a subjective capacity; because the meaning of an object for me goes only so far as *my* sense goes (has only a meaning for a sense corresponding to that object) – for this reason the *senses* of the social man *differ* from those of the non-social man. Only through the objectively unfolded richness of man's essential being is the richness of subjective *human* sensibility (a musical ear, an eye for beauty of form – in short, *senses* capable of human gratification, senses affirming themselves as essential powers of *man*) either cultivated or brought into being. For not only the five senses but also the so-called mental senses, the practical senses (will, love, etc.), in a word, *human* sense, the human nature of the senses, comes to be by virtue of *its* object, by virtue of *humanised* nature. The *forming* of the five senses is a labour of the entire history of the world down to the present. The *sense* caught up in crude practical need has only a *restricted* sense. For the starving man, it is not the human form of food that exists, but only its abstract existence as food. It could just as well be there in its crudest form, and it would be impossible to say wherein this feeding activity differs from that of *animals.* The care-burdened, poverty-stricken man has no *sense* for the finest play; the dealer in minerals sees only the commercial value but not the beauty and the specific character of the mineral: he has no mineralogical sense. Thus, the objectification of the human essence, both in its theoretical and practical aspects, is required to make man's *sense human*, as well as to create the *human sense* corresponding to the entire wealth of human and natural substance.

Just as through the movement of *private property*, of its wealth as well as its poverty – of its material and spiritual wealth and poverty – the budding society finds at hand all the material for this *development*, so *established* society produces man in this entire richness of his being – produces the *rich* man *profoundly endowed with all the senses* – as its enduring reality.

We see how subjectivity and objectivity, spirituality and materiality, activity and suffering, lose their antithetical character, and thus their existence as such antitheses only within the framework of society; we see how the resolution of the *theoretical* antitheses is *only* possible in a *practical* way, by virtue of the practical energy of man. Their resolution is therefore by no means merely a problem of understanding, but a *real* problem of life, which *philosophy* could not solve precisely because it conceived this problem as *merely* a theoretical one.

We see how the history of *industry* and the established *objective* existence of industry are the *open* book of *man's essential powers*, the perceptibly existing human *psychology.* Hitherto this was not conceived in its connection with man's *essential being*, but only in an external relation of utility, because, moving in the realm of estrangement, people could only think of man's general mode of being – religion or history in its abstract-general character as politics, art, literature, etc. – as the reality of man's essential powers and *man's species-activity*. We have before us the *objectified essential powers* of man in the form of *sensuous, alien, useful objects*, in the form of estrangement, displayed in *ordinary material industry* (which can be conceived either as a part of that general movement, or that movement can be conceived as a *particular* part of industry, since all human activity hitherto has been labour – that is, industry – activity estranged from itself).

A *psychology* for which this book, the part of history existing in the most perceptible and accessible form, remains a closed book, cannot become a genuine, comprehensive and *real* science. What indeed are we to think of a science which *airily* abstracts from this large part of human labour and which fails to feel its own incompleteness, while such a wealth of human endeavour, unfolded before it, means nothing more to it than, perhaps, what can be expressed in one word – '*need*', '*vulgar need*'?

The *natural sciences* have developed an enormous activity and have accumulated an ever-growing mass of material. Philosophy, however, has remained just as alien to them as they remain to philosophy. Their momentary unity was only a *chimerical illusion*. The will was there, but the power was lacking. Historiography itself pays regard to natural science only occasionally, as a factor of enlightenment, utility, and of some special great discoveries. But natural science has invaded and transformed human life all the more *practically* through the medium of industry; and has prepared human emancipation, although its immediate effect had to be the furthering of the dehumanisation of man. *Industry* is the *actual*, historical relationship of nature, and therefore of natural science, to man. If, therefore, industry is conceived as the *exoteric* revelation of man's *essential powers*, we also gain an understanding of the *human* essence of nature or the *natural* essence of man. In consequence, natural science will lose its abstractly material – or rather, its idealistic – tendency, and will become the basis of *human* science, as it has already become – albeit in an estranged form – the basis of actual human life, and to assume *one* basis for life and a different basis for *science* is as a matter of course a lie. The nature which develops in human history – the genesis of human society – is man's *real* nature; hence nature as it develops through industry, even though in an *estranged* form, is true *anthropological* nature.

Sense-perception (see Feuerbach) must be the basis of all science. Only when it proceeds from sense-perception in the twofold form of *sensuous* consciousness and *sensuous* need – that is, only when science proceeds from nature – is it *true* science. All history is the history of preparing and developing '*man*' to become the object of *sensuous* consciousness, and turning the requirements of 'man as man' into his needs. History itself is a *real* part of *natural history* – of nature developing into man. Natural science will in time incorporate into itself the science of man, just as the science of man will incorporate into itself natural science: there will be *one* science.

Man is the immediate object of natural science; for immediate, *sensuous nature* for man is, immediately, human sensuousness (the expressions are identical) – presented immediately in the form of the *other* man sensuously present for him. Indeed, his own sense-perception first exists as human sensuousness for himself through the *other* man. But *nature* is the immediate object of the *science of man*: the first object of man – man – is nature, sensuousness; and the particular human sensuous essential powers can only find their self-understanding in the science of the natural world in general, just as they can find their objective realisation only in *natural* objects. The element of thought itself – the element of thought's living expression – *language* – is of a sensuous nature. The *social* reality of nature, and *human* natural science, or the *natural science of man*, are identical terms.

It will be seen how in place of the *wealth* and *poverty* of political economy come the *rich human being* and the rich *human* need. The *rich* human being is simultaneously the human being *in need of* a totality of human manifestations of life – the man in whom his own realisation exists as an inner necessity, as *need*. Not only *wealth*, but likewise the *poverty* of man – under the assumption of socialism – receives in equal measure a *human* and therefore social significance. Poverty is the passive bond which causes the human being to experience the need of the greatest wealth – the *other* human being. The dominion of the objective being in me, the sensuous outburst of my life activity, is *passion*, which thus becomes here the *activity* of my being.

(5) A *being* only considers himself independent when he stands on his own feet; and he only stands on his own feet when he owes his *existence* to himself. A man who lives by the grace of another regards himself as a dependent being. But I live completely by the grace of another if I owe him not only the maintenance of my life, but if he has, moreover, *created* my *life* – if he is the *source* of my life. When it is not of my own creation, my life has necessarily a source of this kind outside of it. The *Creation* is therefore an idea very difficult to dislodge from popular consciousness. The fact that nature and man exist on their own account is *incomprehensible* to it, because it contradicts everything *tangible* in practical life.

The creation of the *earth* has received a mighty blow from *geognosy* – i.e., from the science which presents the formation of the earth, the development of the earth, as a process, as a self-generation. *Spontaneous generation* is the only practical refutation of the theory of creation.

Now it is certainly easy to say to the single individual what Aristotle has already said: You have been begotten by your father and your mother;

therefore in you the mating of two human beings – a species-act of human beings – has produced the human being. You see, therefore, that even physically man owes his existence to man. Therefore you must not only keep sight of the *one* aspect – the *infinite* progression which leads you further to inquire: Who begot my father? Who his grandfather? etc. You must also hold on to the *circular movement* sensuously perceptible in that progress by which man repeats himself in procreation, *man* thus always remaining the subject. You will reply, however: I grant you this circular movement; now grant me the progress which drives me ever further until I ask: Who begot the first man, and nature as a whole? I can only answer you: Your question is itself a product of abstraction. Ask yourself how you arrived at that question. Ask yourself whether your question is not posed from a standpoint to which I cannot reply, because it is wrongly put. Ask yourself whether that progress as such exists for a reasonable mind. When you ask about the creation of nature and man, you are abstracting, in so doing, from man and nature. You postulate them as *non-existent*, and yet you want me to prove them to you as *existing*. Now I say to you: Give up your abstraction and you will also give up your question. Or if you want to hold on to your abstraction, then be consistent, and if you think of man and nature as *non-existent*, then think of yourself as non-existent, for you too are surely nature and man. Don't think, don't ask me, for as soon as you think and ask, your *abstraction* from the existence of nature and man has no meaning. Or are you such an egotist that you conceive everything as nothing, and yet want yourself to exist?

You can reply: I do not want to postulate the nothingness of nature, etc. I ask you about its *genesis*, just as I ask the anatomist about the formation of bones, etc.

But since for the socialist man the *entire so-called history of the world* is nothing but the creation of man through human labour, nothing but the emergence of nature for man, so he has the visible, irrefutable proof of his *birth* through himself, of his *genesis*. Since the *real existence* of man and nature has become evident in practice, through sense experience, because man has thus become evident for man as the being of nature, and nature for man as the being of man, the question about an *alien* being, about a being above nature and man – a question which implies the admission of the unreality of nature and of man – has become impossible in practice. *Atheism*, as the denial of this unreality, has no longer any meaning, for atheism is a *negation of God*, and postulates the *existence of man* through this negation; but socialism as socialism no longer stands in any need of such a mediation. It proceeds from the *theoretically and practically sensuous consciousness* of man and of nature as the *essence*. Socialism is man's *positive self-consciousness*, no longer mediated through the abolition of religion, just as *real life* is man's positive reality, no longer mediated through the abolition of private property, through *communism*. Communism is the position as the negation of the negation, and is hence the *actual* phase necessary for the next stage of historical development in the process of human emancipation and rehabilitation. *Communism* is the necessary form and the dynamic principle of the immediate future, but communism as such is not the goal of human development, the form of human society.

[Human requirements and division of labour under the rule of private property]

(7)   We have seen what significance, given socialism, the *wealth* of human needs acquires, and what significance, therefore, both a *new mode of production* and a new *object* of production obtain: a new manifestation of the forces of *human* nature and a new enrichment of *human* nature. Under private property their significance is reversed: every person speculates on creating a *new* need in another, so as to drive him to fresh sacrifice, to place him in a new dependence and to seduce him into a new mode of *enjoyment* and therefore economic ruin. Each tries to establish over the other an *alien* power, so as thereby to find satisfaction of his own selfish need. The increase in the quantity of objects is therefore accompanied by an extension of the realm of the alien powers to which man is subjected, and every new product represents a new *potentiality* of mutual swindling and mutual plundering. Man becomes ever poorer as man, his need for *money* becomes ever greater if he wants to master the hostile power. The power of his *money* declines in inverse proportion to the increase in the volume of production: that is, his neediness grows as the *power* of money increases.

The need for money is therefore the true need produced by the economic system, and it is the only need which the latter produces. The *quantity* of money becomes to an ever greater degree its sole *effective* quality. Just as it reduces everything to its abstract form, so it reduces itself in the course of its own movement to *quantitative* being. *Excess* and *intemperance* come to be its true norm.

Subjectively, this appears partly in the fact that the extension of products and needs becomes a *contriving* and ever-*calculating* subservience to inhuman, sophisticated, unnatural and *imaginary* appetites. Private property does not know how to change crude need into *human* need. Its *idealism* is *fantasy, caprice* and *whim*; and no eunuch flatters his despot more basely or uses more despicable means to stimulate his dulled capacity for pleasure in order to sneak a favour for himself than does the industrial eunuch – the producer – in order to sneak for himself a few pieces of silver, in order to charm the golden birds out of the pockets of his dearly beloved neighbours in Christ. He puts himself at the service of the other's most depraved fancies, plays the pimp between him and his need, excites in him morbid appetites, lies in wait for each of his weaknesses – all so that he can then demand the cash for this service of love. (Every product is a bait with which to seduce away the other's very being, his money; every real and possible need is a weakness which will lead the fly to the glue-pot. General exploitation of communal human nature, just as every imperfection in man, is a bond with heaven – an avenue giving the priest access to his heart; every need is an opportunity to approach one's neighbour under the guise of the utmost amiability and to say to him: Dear friend, I give you what you need, but you know the *conditio sine qua non*; you know the ink in which you have to sign yourself over to me; in providing for your pleasure, I fleece you.)

This estrangement manifests itself in part in that the sophistication of needs and of the means [of their satisfaction] on the one side produces a bestial barbarisation, a complete, crude, abstract simplicity of need, on the other; or rather in that it merely reproduces itself in its opposite. Even the need for fresh air ceases to be a need for the worker. Man returns to a cave dwelling, which is now, however, contaminated with the pestilential breath of civilisation, and which he continues to occupy only *precariously*, it being for him an alien habitation which can be withdrawn from him any day – a place from which, if he does not pay, he can be thrown out any day. For this mortuary he has to *pay*. A dwelling in the *light*, which Prometheus in Aeschylus designated as one of the greatest boons, by means of which he made the savage into a human being, ceases to exist for the worker. Light, air, etc. – the simplest *animal* cleanliness – ceases to be a need for man. *Filth*, this stagnation and putrefaction of man – the *sewage* of civilisation (speaking quite literally) – comes to be the *element of life* for him. Utter, *unnatural* depravation, putrefied nature, comes to be his *life-element*. None of his senses exist any longer, and [each has ceased to function] not only in its human fashion, but in an *inhuman* fashion, so that it does not exist even in an animal fashion. The crudest *methods* (and *instruments*) of human labour are coming back: the *treadmill* of the Roman slaves, for instance, is the means of production, the means of existence, of many English workers. It is not only that man has no human needs – even his *animal* needs cease to exist. The Irishman no longer knows any need now but the need to *eat*, and indeed only the need to eat *potatoes* – and *scabby potatoes* at that, the worst kind of potatoes. But in each of their industrial towns England and France have already a *little* Ireland. The savage and the animal have at least the need to hunt, to roam, etc. – the need of companionship. The simplification of the machine, of labour is used to make a worker out of the human being still in the making, the completely immature human being, the *child* – whilst the worker has become a neglected child. The machine accommodates itself to the *weakness* of the human being in order to make the *weak* human being into a machine.

How the multiplication of needs and of the means [of their satisfaction] breeds the absence of needs and of means is demonstrated by the political economist (and by the capitalist: in general it is always *empirical* businessmen we are talking about when we refer to political economists, [who represent] their *scientific* creed and form of existence) as follows:

(1) By reducing the worker's need to the barest and most miserable level of physical subsistence, and by reducing his activity to the most abstract mechanical movement; thus he says: Man has no other need either of activity or of enjoyment. For he declares that this life, *too*, is *human* life and existence.

(2) By *counting* the most *meagre* form of life (existence) as the standard, indeed, as the general standard – general because it is applicable to the mass of men. He turns the worker into an insensible being lacking all needs, just as he changes his activity into a pure abstraction from all activity. To him, therefore, every *luxury* of the worker seems to be reprehensible, and everything that goes beyond the most abstract need – be it in the realm of passive enjoyment, or a manifestation of activity – seems to him a luxury. Political economy, this science of *wealth*, is therefore simultaneously the science of renunciation, of want, of *saving* – and it actually reaches the point where it *spares* man the *need* of either fresh *air* or physical *exercise*. This science of marvellous industry is simultaneously the science of *asceticism*, and its true ideal is the *ascetic* but *extortionate* miser and the *ascetic* but *productive* slave. Its moral ideal is the *worker* who takes part of his wages to the savings-bank, and it has even found ready-made a servile *art* which embodies this pet idea: it has been presented, bathed in sentimentality, on the stage. Thus political economy – despite its wordly and voluptuous appearance – is a true moral science, the most moral of all the sciences. Self-renunciation, the renunciation of life and of all human needs, is its principal thesis. The less you eat, drink and buy books; the less you go to the theatre, the dance hall, the public house; the less you think, love, theorise, sing, paint, fence, etc., the more you *save* – the *greater* becomes your treasure which neither moths nor rust will devour – your *capital*. The less you *are*, the less you express your own life, the more you *have*, i.e., the greater is your *alienated* life, the greater is the store of your estranged being. Everything which the political economist takes from you in life and in humanity, he replaces for you in *money* and in *wealth*; and all the things which you cannot do, your money can do. It can eat and drink, go to the dance hall and the theatre; it can travel, it can appropriate art, learning, the treasures of the past, political power – all this it *can* appropriate for you – it can buy all this: it is true *endowment*. Yet being all this, it *wants* to do nothing but create itself, buy itself; for everything else is after all its servant, and when I have the master I have the servant and do not need

his servant. All passions and all activity must therefore be submerged in *avarice*. The worker may only have enough for him to want to live, and may only want to live in order to have that.

[. . .]

From: Collected Works, *Vol. 3, pp. 270–82, 293–309*

Notes

1 In the manuscript *Menschen* (men) instead of *Mächte* (powers). (*Ed.*)
2 Prostitution is only a *specific* expression of the *general* prostitution of the *labourer*, and since it is a relationship in which falls not the prostitute alone, but also the one who prostitutes – and the latter's abomination is still greater – the capitalist, etc., also comes under this head. (*Note by Marx*)
3 This word is crossed out in the manuscript. (*Ed.*)
4 For this reason it is just as highly varied as the *determinations* of human *essence* and *activities*. (*Note by Marx*)

5

The Holy Family

Co-authored by Marx and Engels in the autumn of 1844, much of The Holy Family *is taken up with Marx's rather heavy-handed attack on German 'Critical Criticism' and is of limited interest. Included here are a number of short passages in which Marx develops his account of the proletariat as the agent of revolutionary transformation and reinforces his insistence upon the material basis of historical change. Also included is a very brief passage in which Marx addresses the emancipation of women. In contrast to Engels, Marx wrote very little about the social status of women (another of the brief passages in which this issue is raised is included in the selection from the* Communist Manifesto *below). Almost half of this fragment is a quotation from Fourier!*

[. . .]

Hitherto political economy proceeded from *wealth*, which the movement of private property supposedly creates for the *nations*, to its considerations which are an apology for private property. Proudhon proceeds from the opposite side, which political economy sophistically conceals, from the poverty bred by the movement of private property to his considerations which negate private property. The first criticism of private property proceeds, of course, from the fact in which its contradictory essence appears in the form that is most perceptible and most glaring and most directly arouses man's indignation – from the fact of poverty, of misery.

> Criticism, on the other hand, joins the two facts, poverty and property, in a single unity, grasps the inner link between them and makes them a single whole, which it investigates as such to find the preconditions for its existence.

Criticism, which has hitherto understood nothing of the facts of property and of poverty, uses, 'on the other hand', the deed which it has accomplished in its imagination as an argument against Proudhon's real deed. It unites the *two* facts in a *single* one, and having made *one* out of *two*, grasps the inner link between the *two*. Criticism cannot deny that Proudhon, too, is aware of an inner link between the facts of poverty and of property, since because of that very link he abolishes property in order to abolish poverty. Proudhon did even more. He proved in detail *how* the movement of capital produces poverty. But Critical Criticism does not bother with such trifles. It recognises that poverty and private property are *opposites* – a rather widespread recognition. It *makes* poverty and wealth *a single whole*, which it 'investigates *as such* to find the preconditions for its existence'; an investigation which is all the more superfluous since it has just *made* 'the whole as such' and therefore its *making* is in itself the precondition for the existence of this whole.

By investigating 'the whole as such' to find the preconditions for its existence, Critical Criticism is searching in the genuine theological manner *outside* the 'whole' for the preconditions for its existence. Critical speculation operates outside the object which it pretends to deal with. Whereas the *whole antithesis* is nothing but the *movement of both its sides*, and the precondition for the existence of the whole lies in the very nature of the two sides. But Critical Criticism dispenses with the study of this real movement which forms the whole in order to be able to declare that it, Critical Criticism as the tranquillity of knowledge, is above both extremes of the antithesis, and that its activity, which has made 'the whole as such', is now alone in a position to abolish the abstraction of which it is the maker.

Proletariat and wealth are opposites; as such they form a single whole. They are both creations of the world of private property. The question is exactly what place each occupies in the antithesis. It is not sufficient to declare them two sides of a single whole.

Private property as private property, as wealth, is compelled to maintain *itself*, and thereby its opposite, the proletariat, in *existence*. That is the *positive* side of the antithesis, self-satisfied private property.

The proletariat, on the contrary, is compelled as proletariat to abolish itself and thereby its opposite, private property, which determines its existence, and which makes it proletariat. It is the *negative* side of the antithesis, its restlessness within its very self, dissolved and self-dissolving private property.

The propertied class and the class of the proletariat present the same human self-estrangement. But the former class feels at ease and strengthened in this self-estrangement, it recognises estrangement as *its own power* and has in it the *semblance* of a human existence. The latter feels annihilated in estrangement; it sees in it its own powerlessness and the reality of an inhuman existence. It is, to use an expression of Hegel, in its abasement the *indignation* at that abasement, an indignation to which it is necessarily driven by the contradiction between its human *nature* and its condition of life, which is the outright, resolute and comprehensive negation of that nature.

Within this antithesis the private property-owner is therefore the *conservative* side, the proletarian the *destructive* side. From the former arises the action of preserving the antithesis, from the latter the action of annihilating it.

Indeed private property drives itself in its economic movement towards its own dissolution, but only through a development which does not depend on it, which is unconscious and which takes place against the will of private property by the very nature of things, only inasmuch as it produces the proletariat *as* proletariat, poverty which is conscious of its spiritual and physical poverty, dehumanisation which is conscious of its dehumanisation, and therefore self-abolishing. The proletariat executes the sentence that private property pronounces on itself by producing the proletariat, just as it executes the sentence that wage-labour pronounces on itself by producing wealth for others and poverty for itself. When the proletariat is victorious, it by no means becomes the absolute side of society, for it is victorious only by abolishing itself and its opposite. Then the proletariat disappears as well as the opposite which determines it, private property.

When socialist writers ascribe this world-historic role to the proletariat, it is not at all, as Critical Criticism pretends to believe, because they regard the proletarians as *gods*. Rather the contrary. Since in the fully-formed proletariat the abstraction of all humanity, even of the *semblance* of humanity, is practically complete; since the conditions of life of the proletariat sum up all the conditions of life of society today in their most inhuman form; since man has lost himself in the proletariat, yet at the same time has not only gained theoretical consciousness of that loss, but through urgent, no longer removable, no longer disguisable, absolutely imperative *need* – the practical expression of *necessity* – is driven directly to revolt against this inhumanity, it follows that the proletariat can and must emancipate itself. But it cannot emancipate itself without abolishing the conditions of its own life. It cannot abolish the conditions of its own life without abolishing *all* the inhuman conditions of life of society today which are summed up in its own situation. Not in vain does it go through the stern but steeling school of *labour*. It is not a question of what this or that proletarian, or even the whole proletariat, at the moment *regards* as its aim. It is a question of *what the proletariat is*, and what, in accordance with this *being*, it will historically be compelled to do. Its aim and historical action is visibly and irrevocably foreshadowed in its own life situation as well as in the whole organisation of bourgeois society today. There is no need to explain here that a large part of the English and French proletariat is already *conscious* of its historic task and is constantly working to develop that consciousness into complete clarity.

[. . .]

Absolute Criticism [. . .] rejects *mass-type* history to replace it by *Critical* history. [. . .] According to previous *un-Critical* history, i.e., history not conceived in the sense of Absolute Criticism, it must further be precisely distinguished to what extent the *mass* was '*interested*' in aims and to what extent it was '*enthusiastic*' over them. The '*idea*' always disgraced itself insofar as it differed from the '*interest*'. On the other hand, it is easy to understand that every mass-type '*interest*' that asserts itself historically goes far beyond its real limits in the '*idea*' or '*imagination*' when it first comes on the scene and is confused with *human* interest in general. This *illusion* constitutes what *Fourier* calls the *tone* of each historical epoch. The *interest* of the bourgeoisie in the 1789 Revolution, far from having been a '*failure*', '*won*' everything and had '*most effective success*', however much its '*pathos*' has evaporated and the '*enthusiastic*' flowers with which that interest adorned its cradle have faded. That *interest* was so powerful that it was victorious over the pen of Marat, the guillotine of the Terror and the sword of Napoleon as well as the crucifix and the blue blood of the Bourbons. The Revolution was a 'failure' only for the mass which did not have in the *political* 'idea' the idea of its real '*interest*', i.e., whose true life-principle did not coincide with the life-principle of the Revolution, the mass whose real conditions for emancipation were essentially different from the conditions within which the bourgeoisie could emancipate itself and society. If the Revolution, which can exemplify all great historical 'actions', was a failure, it was so because the mass within whose living conditions it essentially came to a stop, was an *exclusive, limited* mass, not an all-embracing one. If the Revolution was a failure it was not because the mass was '*enthusiastic*' over it and '*interested*' in it, but because the most numerous part of the mass, the part distinct from the bourgeoisie, did not have its *real* interest in the principle of the Revolution, did not have a revolutionary principle of its *own*, but *only* an 'idea', and hence only an object of momentary *enthusiasm* and only seeming *uplift*.

[. . .]

But to rise it is not enough to do so in *thought* and to leave hanging over one's *real sensuously perceptible* head the *real sensuously perceptible* yoke that cannot be subtilised away with ideas.

[. . .]

Does Critical Criticism believe that it has reached even the *beginning* of a knowledge of historical reality so long as it excludes *from* the historical movement the theoretical and practical relation of man to nature, i.e., natural science and industry? Or does it think that it actually knows any period without knowing, for example, the industry of that period, the immediate mode of production of life itself? Of course, spiritualistic, *theological* Critical Criticism only knows (at least it imagines it knows) the main political, literary and theological acts of history. Just as it separates thinking from the senses, the soul from the body and itself from the world, it separates history from natural science and industry and sees the origin of history not in vulgar *material* production on the earth but in vaporous clouds in the heavens.

[. . .]

Revelation of the mystery of the emancipation of women, or Louise Morel

On the occasion of the arrest of *Louise Morel*, Rudolph indulges in reflections which he sums up as follows:

> The master often ruins the maid, either by fear, surprise or other use of the opportunities provided by the nature of *the servants' condition*. He reduces her to misery, shame and crime. The *law is not concerned* with this . . . The criminal who has in fact driven a girl to infanticide is not *punished*.

Rudolph's reflections do not go so far as to make the *servants' condition* the object of his most gracious Criticism. Being a *petty* ruler, he is a *great* patroniser of servants' conditions. Still less does he go so far as to understand that the general position of women in modern society is inhuman. Faithful in all respects to his previous theory, he deplores only that there is no *law which punishes* a seducer and links repentance and atonement with terrible chastisement.

Rudolph has only to take a look at the existing legislation in other countries. *English* laws fulfil all his wishes. In their delicacy, which *Blackstone* so highly praises, they go so far as to declare it a *felony* to seduce even a prostitute.

Herr Szeliga exclaims with a *flourish*:

So (!) – *thinks* (!) – *Rudolph* (!) – and now compare *these thoughts* with your *fantasies* about the *emancipation of woman*. The act of this emancipation can be *almost* physically grasped from them, but you are much too practical to start with, and that is why your attempts have failed so often.

In any case we must thank Herr Szeliga for revealing the mystery that an act can be almost physically grasped from thoughts. As for his ridiculous comparison of Rudolph with men who taught the emancipation of woman, compare Rudolph's *thoughts* with the following 'fantasies' of *Fourier*:

Adultery, seduction, are a credit to the seducer, are good tone . . . But, poor girl! Infanticide! What a crime! If she prizes her honour she must efface all traces of dishonour. But if she sacrifices her child to the prejudices of the world her ignominy is all the greater and she is a victim of the prejudices of the law . . . That is the *vicious circle* which every civilised mechanism describes.

Is not the young daughter a ware held up for sale to the first bidder who wishes to obtain exclusive ownership of her? . . . Just as in grammar two negations are the equivalent of an affirmation, we can say that in the *marriage trade two prostitutions are the equivalent of virtue.*

The change in a historical epoch can always be determined by women's progress towards freedom, because here, in the relation of woman to man, of the weak to the strong, the victory of human nature over brutality is most evident. The degree of emancipation of woman is the natural measure of general emancipation.

The humiliation of the female sex is an essential feature of civilisation as well as of barbarism. The only difference is that the civilised system raises every vice that barbarism practises in a simple form to a compound, equivocal, ambiguous, hypocritical mode of existence . . . No one is punished more severely for keeping woman in slavery than man himself. (*Fourier*)

It is superfluous to contrast Rudolph's thoughts with Fourier's masterly characterisation of *marriage*, or with the works of the materialist section of French communism.

[. . .]

From: *Collected Works*, Vol. 4, pp. 34–7, 81–2, 150, 195–6

6

Theses on Feuerbach

It is the Eleventh Thesis – that 'philosophers have only interpreted the world in various ways; the point is to change it' – which everyone remembers. But the other ten theses are a succinct condensation of Marx's complex notion of materialism – and a counter to those who see him in the grips of a simple and mechanistic determinism.

1 The chief defect of all previous materialism (that of Feuerbach included) is that things, reality, sensuousness are conceived only in the form of the *object, or of contemplation*, but not as *sensuous human activity, practice*, not subjectively. Hence, in contradistinction to materialism, the *active* side was set forth abstractly by idealism – which, of course, does not know real, sensuous activity as such. Feuerbach wants sensuous objects, really distinct from conceptual objects, but he does not conceive human activity itself as *objective* activity. In *Das Wesen des Christenthums*, he therefore regards the theoretical attitude as the only genuinely human attitude, while practice is conceived and defined only in its dirty-Jewish form of appearance. Hence he does not grasp the significance of 'revolutionary' of 'practical-critical', activity.

2 The question whether objective truth can be attributed to human thinking is not a question of theory but is a *practical* question. Man must prove the truth, i.e., the reality and power, the this-worldliness of his thinking in practice. The dispute over the reality or non-reality of thinking which is isolated from practice is a purely *scholastic* question.

3 The materialist doctrine concerning the changing of circumstances and upbringing forgets that circumstances are changed by men and that the educator must himself be educated. This doctrine must, therefore, divide society into two parts, one of which is superior to society.

The coincidence of the changing of circumstances and of human activity or self-change can be conceived and rationally understood only as *revolutionary practice*.

4 Feuerbach starts out from the fact of religious self-estrangement, of the duplication of the world into a religious world and a secular one. His work consists in resolving the religious world into its secular basis. But that the secular basis lifts off from itself and establishes itself as an independent realm in the clouds can only be explained by the inner strife and intrinsic contradictoriness of this secular basis. The latter must, therefore, itself be both understood in its contradiction and revolutionised in practice. Thus, for instance, once the earthly family is discovered to be the secret of the holy family, the former must then itself be destroyed in theory and in practice.

5 Feuerbach, not satisfied with *abstract thinking*, wants *sensuous contemplation*; but he does not conceive sensuousness as *practical*, human-sensuous activity.

6 Feuerbach resolves the essence of religion into the essence of *man*. But the essence of man is no abstraction inherent in each single individual. In its reality it is the ensemble of the social relations.

Feuerbach, who does not enter upon a criticism of this real essence, is hence obliged:

(a) To abstract from the historical process and to define the religious sentiment by itself, and to presuppose an abstract – *isolated* – human individual.

(b) Essence, therefore, can be regarded only as 'species', as an inner, mute, general character which unites the many individuals *in a natural way*.

7 Feuerbach, consequently, does not see that the 'religious sentiment' is itself a social product, and that the abstract individual which he analyses belongs to a particular form of society.

8 All social life is essentially *practical*. All mysteries which lead theory to mysticism find their rational solution in human practice and in the comprehension of this practice.

9 The highest point reached by contemplative materialism, that is, materialism which does not comprehend sensuousness as practical activity, is the contemplation of single individuals and of civil society.

10 The standpoint of the old materialism is civil society; the standpoint of the new is human society, or social humanity.

11 The philosophers have only *interpreted* the world in various ways; the point is to *change* it.

From: *Collected Works*, Vol. 5, pp. 3–5

7

The German Ideology

Jointly attributed to Marx and Engels, The German Ideology *is a crucial text. Part One sets out more systematically than ever before Marx's materialist conception of history. It identifies history as a succession of differing stages distinguished, above all, by their material basis. It speaks of the succession from one epoch to another being the product of 'the contradiction between the productive forces and the form of intercourse'. It contains the essentials of the Marxist view of ideology in which 'life is not determined by consciousness, but consciousness by life' and 'the class which is the ruling material force in society . . . is at the same time its ruling intellectual force'. Although* The German Ideology *was unpublished until the 1930s, and despite Marx and Engels' later judgement that they were happy to leave their manuscript to 'the gnawing criticism of the mice', it remains the clearest and fullest statement of the underlying theory of history which was to continue to inform all the writings of Marx's maturity.*

[. . .]

Ideology in general, German ideology in particular

First premises of materialist method

The premises from which we begin are not arbitrary ones, not dogmas, but real premises from which abstraction can only be made in the imagination. They are the real individuals, their activity and the material conditions under which they live, both those which they find already existing and those produced by their activity. These premises can thus be verified in a purely empirical way.

The first premise of all human history is, of course, the existence of living human individuals. Thus the first fact to be established is the physical organisation of these individuals and their consequent relation to the rest of nature. Of course, we cannot here go either into the actual physical nature of man, or into the natural conditions in which man finds himself – geological, orohydrographical, climatic and so on. The writing of history must always set out from these natural bases and their modification in the course of history through the action of men.

Men can be distinguished from animals by consciousness, by religion or anything else you like. They themselves begin to distinguish themselves from animals as soon as they begin to *produce* their means of subsistence, a step which is conditioned by their physical organisation. By producing their means of subsistence men are indirectly producing their actual material life.

The way in which men produce their means of subsistence depends first of all on the nature of the actual means of subsistence they find in existence and have to reproduce. This mode of production must not be considered simply as being the production of the physical existence of the individuals. Rather it is a definite form of activity of these individuals, a definite form of expressing their life, a definite *mode of life* on their part. As individuals express their life, so they are. What they are, therefore, coincides with their production, both with *what* they produce and with *how* they produce. The nature of individuals thus depends on the material conditions determining their production.

This production only makes its appearance with the *increase* of *population*. In its turn this presupposes the *intercourse* of individuals with one another. The form of this intercourse is again determined by production.

The relations of different nations among themselves depend upon the extent to which each has developed its productive forces, the division of labour and internal intercourse. This statement is generally recognised. But not only the relation of one nation to others, but also the whole internal structure of the nation itself depends on the stage of development reached by its production and its internal and external intercourse. How far the productive forces of a nation are developed is shown most manifestly by the degree to which the division of labour has been carried. Each new productive force, insofar as it is not merely a quantitative extension of productive forces already known (for instance the bringing into cultivation of fresh land), causes a further development of the division of labour.

The division of labour inside a nation leads at first to the separation of industrial and commercial from agricultural labour, and hence to the separation of *town* and *country* and to the conflict of their interests. Its further development leads to the separation of commercial from industrial labour. At the same time through the division of labour inside these various branches there develop various divisions among the individuals co-operating in definite kinds of labour. The relative position of these individual groups is determined by the methods employed in agriculture, industry and commerce (patriarchalism, slavery, estates, classes). These same conditions are to be seen (given a more developed intercourse) in the relations of different nations to one another.

The various stages of development in the division of labour are just so many different forms of ownership, i.e. the existing stage in the division of labour determines also the relations of individuals to one another with reference to the material, instrument, and product of labour.

The first form of ownership is tribal ownership. It corresponds to the undeveloped stage of production, at which a people lives by hunting and fishing, by the rearing of beasts or, in the highest stage, agriculture. In the latter case it presupposes a great mass of uncultivated stretches of land. The division of labour is at this stage still very elementary and is confined to a further extension of the natural division of labour existing in the family. The social structure is, therefore, limited to an extension of the family; patriarchal family chieftains, below them the members of the tribe, finally slaves. The slavery latent in the family only develops gradually with the increase of population, the growth of wants, and with the extension of external relations, both of war and of barter.

The second form is the ancient communal and State ownership which proceeds especially from the union of several tribes into a *city* by agreement or by conquest, and which is still accompanied by slavery. Beside communal ownership we already find movable, and later also immovable, private property developing, but as an abnormal form subordinate to communal ownership. The citizens hold power over their labouring slaves only in their community, and on this account alone, therefore, they are bound to the form of communal ownership. It is the communal private property which compels the active citizens to remain in this spontaneously derived form of association over against their slaves. For this reason the whole structure of society based on this communal ownership, and with it the power of the people, decays in the same measure as, in particular, immovable private property evolves. The division of labour is already more developed. We already find the antagonism of town and country; later the antagonism between those states which represent town interests and those which represent country interests, and inside the towns themselves the antagonism between industry and maritime commerce. The class relation between citizens and slaves is now completely developed.

With the development of private property, we find here for the first time the same conditions which we shall find again, only on a more extensive scale, with modern private property. On the one hand, the concentration of private property, which began very early in Rome (as the Licinian agrarian law proves) and proceeded very rapidly from the time of the civil wars and especially under the Emperors; on the other hand, coupled with this, the transformation of the plebeian small peasantry into a proletariat, which, however, owing to its intermediate position between propertied citizens and slaves, never achieved an independent development.

The third form of ownership is feudal or estate property. If antiquity started out from the *town* and its little territory, the Middle Ages started out from the *country*. This different starting-point was determined by the sparseness of the population at that time, which was scattered over a large area and which received no large increase from the conquerors. In contrast to Greece and Rome, feudal development at the outset, therefore, extends over a much wider territory, prepared by the Roman conquests and the spread of agriculture at first associated with it. The last centuries of the declining Roman Empire and its conquest by the barbarians destroyed a number of productive forces; agriculture had declined, industry had decayed for want of a market, trade had died out or been violently suspended, the rural and urban population had decreased. From these conditions and the mode of organisation of the conquest determined by them, feudal property developed under the influence of the Germanic military constitution. Like tribal and communal ownership, it is based again on a community; but the directly producing class standing over against it is not, as in the case of the ancient community, the slaves, but the enserfed small peasantry. As soon as feudalism is fully developed, there also arises antagonism to the towns. The hierarchical structure of landownership, and the armed bodies of retainers associated with it, gave the nobility power over the serfs. This feudal organisation was, just as much as the ancient communal ownership, an association against a subjected producing class; but the form of association and the relation to the direct producers were different because of the different conditions of production.

This feudal system of landownership had its counterpart in the *towns* in the shape of corporative property, the feudal organisation of trades. Here property consisted chiefly in the labour of each individual person. The necessity for association against the organised robber-nobility, the need for communal covered markets in an age when the industrialist was at the same time a merchant, the growing competition of the escaped serfs swarming into the rising towns, the feudal structure of the whole country: these combined to bring about the *guilds*. The gradually accumulated small capital of individual craftsmen and their stable numbers, as against the growing population, evolved the relation of journeyman and apprentice, which brought into being in the towns a hierarchy similar to that in the country.

Thus the chief form of property during the feudal epoch consisted on the one hand of landed property with serf labour chained to it, and on the other of the labour of the individual with small capital commanding the labour of journeymen. The organisation of both was determined by the restricted conditions of production – the small-scale and primitive cultivation of the land, and the craft type of industry. There was little division of labour in the heyday of feudalism. Each country bore in itself the antithesis of town and country; the division into estates was certainly strongly marked; but apart from the differentiation of princes, nobility, clergy and peasants in the country, and masters, journeymen, apprentices and soon also the rabble of casual labourers in the towns, no division of importance took place. In agriculture it was rendered difficult by the strip-system, beside which the cottage industry of the peasants themselves emerged. In industry there was no division of labour at all in the individual trades themselves, and very little between them. The separation of industry and commerce was found already in existence in older towns; in the newer it only developed later, when the towns entered into mutual relations.

The grouping of larger territories into feudal kingdoms was a necessity for the landed nobility as for the towns. The organisation of the ruling class, the nobility, had, therefore, everywhere a monarch at its head.

The fact is, therefore, that definite individuals who are productively active in a definite way enter into these definite social and political relations. Empirical observation must in each separate instance bring out empirically, and without any mystification and speculation, the connection of the social and political structure with production. The social structure and the State are continually evolving out of the life-process of definite individuals, but of individuals, not as they may appear in their own or other people's imagination, but as they *really* are; i.e. as they operate, produce materially, and hence as they work under definite material limits, presuppositions and conditions independent of their will.

The production of ideas, of conceptions, of consciousness, is at first directly interwoven with the material activity and the material intercourse of men, the language of real life. Conceiving, thinking, the mental intercourse of men, appear at this stage as the direct efflux of their material behaviour. The same applies to mental production as expressed in the language of politics, laws, morality, religion, metaphysics, etc. of a people. Men are the producers of their conceptions, ideas, etc. – real, active men, as they are conditioned by a definite development of their productive forces and of the intercourse corresponding to these, up to its furthest forms. Consciousness can never be anything else than conscious existence, and the existence of men is their actual life-process. If in all ideology men and their circumstances appear upside-down as in a *camera obscura*, this phenomenon arises just as much from their historical life-process as the inversion of objects on the retina does from their physical life-process.

In direct contrast to German philosophy which descends from heaven to earth, here we ascend from earth to heaven. That is to say, we do not set out from what men say, imagine, conceive, nor from men as narrated, thought of, imagined, conceived, in order to arrive at men in the flesh. We set out from real, active men, and on the basis of their real life-process we demonstrate the development of the ideological reflexes and echoes of this life-process. The phantoms formed in the human brain are also, necessarily, sublimates of their material life-process, which is empirically verifiable and bound to material premises. Morality, religion, metaphysics, all the rest of ideology and their corresponding forms of consciousness, thus no longer retain the semblance of independence. They have no history, no development; but men, developing their material production and their material intercourse, alter, along with this their real existence, their thinking and the products of their thinking. Life is not determined by consciousness, but consciousness by life. In the first method of approach the starting-point is consciousness taken as the living individual; in the second method, which conforms to real life, it is the real living individuals themselves, and consciousness is considered solely as *their* consciousness.

This method of approach is not devoid of premises. It starts out from the real premises and does not abandon them for a moment. Its premises are men, not in any fantastic isolation and rigidity, but in their actual, empirically perceptible process of development under definite conditions. As soon as this active life-process is described, history ceases to be a collection of dead facts as it is with the empiricists (themselves still abstract), or an imagined activity of imagined subjects, as with the idealists.

Where speculation ends – in real life – there real, positive science begins: the representation of the practical activity, of the practical process of development of men. Empty talk about consciousness ceases, and real knowledge has to take its place. When reality is depicted, philosophy as an independent branch of knowledge loses its medium of existence.

[. . .]

History: fundamental conditions

Since we are dealing with the Germans, who are devoid of premises, we must begin by stating the first premise of all human existence and, therefore, of all history, the premise, namely, that men must be in a position to live in order to be able to 'make history'. But life involves before everything else eating and drinking, a habitation, clothing and many other things. The first historical act is thus the production of the means to satisfy these needs, the production of material life itself. [. . .] Therefore in any interpretation of history one has first of all to observe this fundamental fact in all its significance and all its implications and to accord it its due importance. It is well known that the Germans have never done this, and they have never, therefore, had an *earthly* basis for history and consequently never an historian. The French and the English, even if they have conceived the relation of this fact with so-called history only in an extremely one-sided fashion, particularly as long as they remained in the toils of political ideology, have nevertheless made the first attempts to give the writing of history a materialistic basis by being the first to write histories of civil society, of commerce and industry.

The second point is that the satisfaction of the first need (the action of satisfying, and the instrument of satisfaction which has been acquired) leads to new needs; and this production of new needs is the first historical act. [. . .]

The third circumstance which, from the very outset, enters into historical development, is that men, who daily remake their own life, begin to make other men, to propagate their kind: the relation between man and woman, parents and children, the *family*. The family, which to begin with is the only social relationship, becomes later, when increased needs create new social relations and the increased population new needs, a subordinate one (except in Germany), and must then be treated and analysed according to the existing empirical data, not according to 'the concept of the family', as is the custom in Germany. These three aspects of social activity are not of course to be taken as three different stages, but just as three aspects or, to make it clear to the Germans, three 'moments', which have existed simultaneously since the dawn of history and the first men, and which still assert themselves in history today.

The production of life, both of one's own in labour and of fresh life in procreation, now appears as a double relationship: on the one hand as a natural, on the other as a social relationship. By social we understand the co-operation of several individuals, no matter under what conditions, in what manner and to what end. It follows from this that a certain mode of production, or industrial stage, is always combined with a certain mode of co-operation, or social stage, and this mode of co-operation is itself a 'productive force'. Further, that the multitude of productive forces accessible to men determines the nature of society, hence, that the 'history of humanity' must always be studied and treated in relation to the history of industry and exchange. But it is also clear how in Germany it is impossible to write this sort of history, because the Germans lack not only the necessary power of comprehension and the material but also the 'evidence of their senses', for across the Rhine you cannot have any experience of these things since history has stopped happening. Thus it is quite obvious from the start that there exists a materialistic connection of men with one another, which is determined by their needs and their mode of production, and which is as old as men themselves. This connection is ever taking on new forms, and thus presents a 'history' independently of the existence of any political or religious nonsense which in addition may hold men together.

Only now, after having considered four moments, four aspects of the primary historical relationships, do we find that man also possesses 'consciousness', but, even so, not inherent, not 'pure' consciousness. From the start the 'spirit' is afflicted with the curse of being 'burdened' with matter, which here makes its appearance in the form of agitated layers of air, sounds, in short, of language. Language is as old as consciousness, language *is* practical consciousness that exists also for other men, and for that reason alone it really exists for me personally as well; language, like consciousness, only arises from the need, the necessity, of intercourse with other men. Where there exists a relationship, it exists for me: the animal does not enter into '*relations*' with anything, it does not enter into any relation at all. For the animal, its relation to others does not exist as a relation. Consciousness is, therefore, from the very beginning a social product, and remains so as long as men exist at all. Consciousness is at first, of course, merely consciousness concerning the *immediate* sensuous environment and consciousness of the limited connection with other persons and things outside the individual who is growing self-conscious. At the same time it is consciousness of nature, which first appears to men as a completely alien, all-powerful and unassailable force, with which men's relations are purely animal and by which they are overawed like beasts; it is thus a purely animal consciousness of nature (natural religion) just because nature is as yet hardly modified historically. (We see here immediately: this natural religion or this particular relation of men to nature is determined by the form of society and vice versa. Here, as everywhere, the identity of nature and man appears in such a way that the restricted relation of men to nature determines their restricted relation to one another, and their restricted relation to one another determines men's restricted relation to nature.) On the other hand, man's consciousness of the necessity of associating with the individuals around him is the beginning of the consciousness that he is living in society at all. This beginning is as animal as social life itself at this stage. It is mere herd-consciousness, and at this point man is only distinguished from sheep by the fact that with him consciousness takes the place of instinct or that his instinct is a conscious one. This sheep-like or tribal consciousness receives its further development and extension through increased productivity, the increase of needs, and, what is fundamental to both of these, the increase of population. With these there develops the division of labour, which was originally nothing but the division of labour in the sexual act, then that division of labour which develops spontaneously or 'naturally' by virtue of natural predisposition (e.g. physical strength), needs, accidents, etc. etc. Division of labour only becomes truly such from the moment when a division of material and mental labour appears. (The first form of ideologists, *priests*, is concurrent.) From this moment onwards consciousness *can* really flatter itself that it is something other than consciousness of existing practice, that it *really* represents something without representing something real; from now on consciousness is in a position to emancipate itself from the world and to proceed to the formation of 'pure' theory, theology, philosophy, ethics, etc. But even if this theory, theology, philosophy, ethics, etc. comes into contradiction with the existing relations, this can only occur because existing social relations have come into contradiction with existing forces of production; this, moreover, can also occur in a particular national sphere of relations through the appearance of the contradiction, not within the national orbit, but between this national consciousness and the practice of other nations, i.e. between the national and the general consciousness of a nation (as we see it now in Germany).

Moreover, it is quite immaterial what consciousness starts to do on its own: out of all such muck we get only the one inference that these three moments, the forces of production, the state of society, and consciousness, can and must come into contradiction with one another, because the *division of labour* implies the possibility, nay the fact that intellectual and material activity – enjoyment and labour, production and consumption – devolve on different individuals, and that the only possibility of their not coming into contradiction lies in the negation in its turn of the division of labour. It is self-evident, moreover, that 'spectres', 'bonds', 'the higher being', 'concept', 'scruple', are merely the idealistic, spiritual expression, the conception apparently of the isolated individual, the image of very empirical fetters and limitations, within which the mode of production of life and the form of intercourse coupled with it move.

Private property and communism

With the division of labour, in which all these contradictions are implicit, and which in its turn is based on the natural division of labour in the family and the separation of society into individual families opposed to one another, is given simultaneously the *distribution*, and indeed the *unequal* distribution, both quantitative and qualitative, of labour and its products, hence property: the nucleus, the first form, of which lies in the family, where wife and children are the slaves of the husband. This latent slavery in the family, though still very crude, is the first property, but even at this early stage it corresponds perfectly to the definition of modern economists who call it the power of disposing of the labour-power of others. Division of labour and private property are, moreover, identical expressions: in the one the same thing is affirmed with reference to activity as is affirmed in the other with reference to the product of the activity.

Further, the division of labour implies the contradiction between the interest of the separate individual or the individual family and the communal interest of all individuals who have intercourse with one another. And indeed, this communal interest does not exist merely in the imagination, as the 'general interest', but first of all in reality, as the mutual interdependence of the individuals among whom the labour is divided.

And out of this very contradiction between the interest of the individual and that of the community the latter takes an independent form as the *State*, divorced from the real interest of individual and community, and at the same time as an illusory communal life, always based, however, on the real ties existing in every family and tribal conglomeration – such as flesh and blood, language, division of labour on a larger scale, and other interests – and especially, as we shall enlarge upon later, on the classes, already determined by the division of labour, which in every such mass of men separate out, and of which one dominates all the others. It follows from this that all struggles within the State, the struggle between democracy, aristocracy, and monarchy, the struggle for the franchise, etc., etc., are merely the illusory forms in which the real struggles of the different classes are fought out among one another (of this the German theoreticians have not the faintest inkling, although they have received a sufficient introduction to the subject in the *Deutsch–Französische Jahrbücher* and *Die heilige Familie*). Further, it follows that every class which is struggling for mastery, even when its domination, as is the case with the proletariat, postulates the abolition of the old form of society in its entirety and of domination itself, must first conquer for itself political power in order to represent its interest in turn as the general interest, which in the first moment it is forced to do.

Just because individuals seek *only* their particular interest, which for them does not coincide with their communal interest (in fact the general is the illusory form of communal life), the latter will be imposed on them as an interest 'alien' to them, and 'independent' of them as in its turn a particular, peculiar 'general' interest; or they themselves must remain within this discord, as in democracy. On the other hand, too, the *practical* struggle of these particular interests, which constantly *really* run counter to the communal and illusory communal interests, makes *practical* intervention and control necessary through the illusory 'general' interest in the form of the State.

And finally, the division of labour offers us the first example of how, as long as man remains in natural society, that is, as long as a cleavage exists between the particular and the common interest, as long, therefore, as activity is not voluntarily, but naturally, divided, man's own deed becomes an alien power opposed to him, which enslaves him instead of being controlled by him. For as soon as the distribution of labour comes into being, each man has a particular, exclusive sphere of activity, which is forced upon him and from which he cannot escape. He is a hunter, a fisherman, a herdsman, or a critical critic, and must remain so if he does not want to lose his means of livelihood; while in communist society, where nobody has one exclusive sphere of activity but each can become accomplished in any branch he wishes, society regulates the general production and thus makes it possible for me to do one thing today and another tomorrow, to hunt in the morning, fish in the afternoon, rear cattle in the evening, criticise after dinner, just as I have a mind, without ever becoming hunter, fisherman, herdsman or critic.

This fixation of social activity, this consolidation of what we ourselves produce into an objective power above us, growing out of our control, thwarting our expectations, bringing to naught our calculations, is one of the chief factors in historical development up till now. The social power, i.e., the multiplied productive force, which arises through the co-operation of different individuals as it is determined by the division of labour, appears to these individuals, since their co-operation is not voluntary but has come about naturally, not as their own united power, but as an alien force existing outside them, of the origin and goal of which they are ignorant, which they thus cannot control, which on the contrary passes through a peculiar series of phases and stages independent of the will and the action of man, nay even being the prime governor of these.

How otherwise could for instance property have had a history at all, have taken on different forms, and landed property, for example, according to the different premises given, have proceeded in France from parcellation to centralisation in the hands of a few, in England from centralisation in the hands of a few to parcellation, as is actually the case today? Or how does it happen that trade, which after all is nothing more than the exchange of products of various individuals and countries, rules the whole world through the relation of supply and demand – a relation which, as an English economist says, hovers over the earth like the fate of the ancients, and with invisible hand allots fortune and misfortune to men, sets up empires and overthrows empires, causes nations to rise and to disappear – while with the abolition of the basis of private property, with the communistic regulation of production (and, implicit in this, the destruction of the alien relation between men and what they themselves produce), the power of the relation of supply and demand is dissolved into nothing, and men get exchange, production, the mode of their mutual relation, under their own control again?

In history up to the present it is certainly an empirical fact that separate individuals have, with the broadening of their activity into world-historical activity, become more and more enslaved under a power alien to them (a pressure which they have conceived of as a dirty trick on the part of the so-called universal spirit, etc.), a power which has become more and more enormous and, in the last instance, turns out to be the *world market*. But it is just as empirically established that, by the overthrow of the existing state of society by the communist revolution (of which more below) and the abolition of private property which is identical with it, this power, which so baffles the German theoreticians, will be dissolved; and that then the liberation of each single individual will be accomplished in the measure in which history becomes transformed into world history. From the above it is clear that the real intellectual wealth of the individual depends entirely on the wealth of his real connections. Only then will the separate individuals be liberated from the various national and local barriers, be brought into practical connection with the material and intellectual production of the whole world and be put in a position to acquire the capacity to enjoy this all-sided production of the whole earth (the creations of man). *All-round* dependence, this natural form of the *world-historical* co-operation of individuals, will be transformed by this communist revolution into the control and conscious mastery of these powers, which, born of the action of men on one another, have till now overawed and governed men as powers completely alien to them. Now this view can be expressed again in speculative-idealistic, i.e. fantastic, terms as 'self-generation of the species' ('society as the subject'), and thereby the consecutive series of interrelated individuals connected with each other can be conceived as a single individual, which accomplishes the mystery of generating itself. It is clear here that individuals certainly make *one another*, physically and mentally, but do not make themselves.

This 'alienation' (to use a term which will be comprehensible to the philosophers) can, of course, only be abolished given two practical premises. For it to become an 'intolerable' power, i.e. a power against which men make a revolution, it must necessarily have rendered the great mass of humanity 'propertyless', and produced, at the same time, the contradiction of an existing world of wealth and culture, both of which conditions presuppose a great increase in productive power, a high degree of its development. And, on the other hand, this development of productive forces (which itself implies the actual empirical existence of men in their *world-historical*, instead of local, being) is an absolutely necessary practical premise because without it *want* is merely made general, and with *destitution* the struggle for necessities and all the old filthy business would necessarily be reproduced; and furthermore, because only with this universal development of productive forces is a *universal* intercourse between men established, which produces in all nations simultaneously the phenomenon of the 'propertyless' mass (universal competition), makes each nation dependent on the revolutions of the others, and finally has put *world-historical*, empirically universal individuals in place of local ones. Without this, (1) communism could only exist as a local event; (2) the *forces* of intercourse themselves could not have developed as *universal*, hence intolerable powers: they would have remained home-bred conditions surrounded by superstition; and (3) each extension of intercourse would abolish local communism. Empirically, communism is only possible as the act of the dominant peoples 'all at once' and simultaneously, which presupposes the universal development of productive forces and the world intercourse bound up with communism. Moreover, the mass of *propertyless* workers – the utterly precarious position of labour-power on a mass scale cut off from capital or from even a limited satisfaction and, therefore, no longer merely temporarily deprived of work itself as a secure source of life – presupposes the *world market* through competition. The proletariat can thus only exist *world-historically*, just as communism, its activity, can only have a 'world-historical' existence. World-historical existence of individuals means existence of individuals which is directly linked up with world history.

Communism is for us not a *state of affairs* which is to be established, an *ideal* to which reality [will] have to adjust itself. We call communism the *real* movement which abolishes the present state of things. The conditions of this movement result from the premises now in existence.

The illusion of the epoch

Civil society and the conception of history

The form of intercourse determined by the existing productive forces at all previous historical stages, and in its turn determining these, is *civil society*. The latter, as is clear from what we have said above, has as its premises and basis the simple family and the multiple, the so-called tribe, the more precise determinants of this society are enumerated in our remarks above. Already here we see how this civil society is the true source and theatre of all history, and how absurd is the conception of history held hitherto, which neglects the real relationships and confines itself to high-sounding dramas of princes and states.

Civil society embraces the whole material intercourse of individuals within a definite stage of the development of productive forces. It embraces the whole commercial and industrial life of a given stage and, insofar, transcends the State and the nation, though, on the other hand again, it must assert itself in its foreign relations as nationality, and inwardly must organise itself as State. The word 'civil society' [*bürgerliche Gesellschaft*] emerged in the eighteenth century, when property relationships had already extricated themselves from the ancient and medieval communal society. Civil society as such only develops with the bourgeoisie; the social organisation evolving directly out of production and commerce, which in all ages forms the basis of the State and of the rest of the idealistic superstructure, has, however, always been designated by the same name.

History is nothing but the succession of the separate generations, each of which exploits the materials, the capital funds, the productive forces handed down to it by all preceding generations, and thus, on the one hand, continues the traditional activity in completely changed circumstances and, on the other, modifies the old circumstances with a completely changed activity. This can be speculatively distorted so that later history is made the goal of earlier history, e.g. the goal ascribed to the discovery of America is to further the eruption of the French Revolution. Thereby history receives its own special aims and becomes 'a person ranking with other persons' (to wit: 'Self-Consciousness, Criticism, the Unique', etc.), while what is designated with the words 'destiny', 'goal', 'germ', or 'idea' of earlier history is nothing more than an abstraction formed from later history, from the active influence which earlier history exercises on later history.

The further the separate spheres, which interact on one another, extend in the course of this development, the more the original isolation of the separate nationalities is destroyed by the developed mode of production and intercourse and the division of labour between various nations naturally brought forth by these, the more history becomes world history. Thus, for instance, if in England a machine is invented, which deprives countless workers of bread in India and China, and overturns the whole form of existence of these empires, this invention becomes a world-historical fact. Or again, take the case of sugar and coffee which have proved their world-historical importance in the nineteenth century by the fact that the lack of these products, occasioned by the Napoleonic Continental System, caused the Germans to rise against Napoleon, and thus became the real basis of the glorious Wars of Liberation of 1813. From this it follows that this transformation of history into world history is not indeed a mere abstract act on the part of the 'self-consciousness', the world spirit, or of any other metaphysical spectre, but a quite material, empirically verifiable act, an act the proof of which every individual furnishes as he comes and goes, eats, drinks and clothes himself.

This conception of history depends on our ability to expound the real process of production, starting out from the material production of life itself, and to comprehend the form of intercourse connected with this and created by this mode of production (i.e. civil society in its various stages), as the basis of all history; and to show it in its action as State, to explain all the different theoretical products and forms of consciousness, religion, philosophy, ethics, etc. etc. and trace their origins and growth from that basis; by which means, of course, the whole thing can be depicted in its totality (and therefore, too, the reciprocal action of these various sides on one another). It has not, like the idealistic view of history, in every period to look for a category, but remains constantly on the real *ground* of history; it does not explain practice from the idea but explains the formation of ideas from material practice; and accordingly it comes to the conclusion that all forms and products of consciousness cannot be dissolved by mental criticism, by resolution into 'self-consciousness' or transformation into 'apparitions', 'spectres', 'fancies', etc. but only by the practical overthrow of the actual social relations which gave rise to this idealistic humbug; that not criticism but revolution is the driving force of history, also of religion, of philosophy and all other types of theory. It shows that history does not end by being resolved into 'self-consciousness' as 'spirit of the spirit', but that in it at each stage there is found a material result: a sum of productive forces, an historically created relation of individuals to nature and to one another, which is handed down to each generation from its predecessor; a mass of productive forces, capital funds and conditions, which, on the one hand, is indeed modified by the new generation, but also on the other prescribes for it its conditions of life and gives it a definite development, a special character. It shows that circumstances make men just as much as men make circumstances.

This sum of productive forces, capital funds and social forms of intercourse, which every individual and generation finds in existence as something given, is the real basis of what the philosophers have conceived as 'substance' and 'essence of man', and what they have deified and attacked; a real basis which is not in the least disturbed, in its effect and influence on the development of men, by the fact that these philosophers revolt against it as 'self-consciousness' and the 'Unique'. These conditions of life, which different generations find in existence, decide also whether or not the periodically recurring revolutionary convulsion will be strong enough to overthrow the basis of the entire existing system. And if these material elements of a complete revolution are not present (namely, on the one hand the existing productive forces, on the other the formation of a revolutionary mass, which revolts not only against separate conditions of society up till then, but against the very 'production of life' till then, the 'total activity' on which it was based), then, as far as practical development is concerned, it is absolutely immaterial whether the *idea* of this revolution has been expressed a hundred times already, as the history of communism proves.

In the whole conception of history up to the present this real basis of history has either been totally neglected or else considered as a minor matter quite irrelevant to the course of history. History must, therefore, always be written according to an extraneous standard; the real production of life seems to be primeval history, while the truly historical appears to be separated from ordinary life, something extra-superterrestrial. With this the relation of man to nature is excluded from history and hence the antithesis of nature and history is created. The exponents of this conception of history have consequently only been able to see in history the political actions of princes and States, religious and all sorts of theoretical struggles, and in particular in each historical epoch have had to *share the illusion of that epoch*. For instance, if an epoch imagines itself to be actuated by purely 'political' or 'religious' motives, although 'religion' and 'politics' are only forms of its true motives, the historian accepts this opinion. The 'idea', the 'conception' of the people in question about their real practice, is transformed into the sole determining, active force, which controls and determines their practice. When the crude form in which the division of labour appears with the Indians and Egyptians calls forth the caste-system in their State and religion, the historian believes that the caste-system is the power which has produced this crude social form. While the French and the English at least hold by the political illusion, which is moderately close to reality, the Germans move in the realm of the 'pure spirit', and make religious illusion the driving force of history. The Hegelian philosophy of history is the last consequence, reduced to its 'finest expression', of all this German historiography, for which it is not a question of real, nor even of political, interests, but of pure thoughts, which consequently must appear to Saint Bruno [Bauer] as a series of 'thoughts' that devour one another and are finally swallowed up in 'self-consciousness'.

[. . .]

Ruling class and ruling ideas

The ideas of the ruling class are in every epoch the ruling ideas, i.e. the class which is the ruling *material* force of society, is at the same time its ruling *intellectual* force. The class which has the means of material production at its disposal, has control at the same time over the means of mental production, so that thereby, generally speaking, the ideas of those who lack the means of mental production are subject to it. The ruling ideas are nothing more than the ideal expression of the dominant material relationships, the dominant material relationships grasped as ideas; hence of the relationships which make the one class the ruling one, therefore, the ideas of its dominance. The individuals composing the ruling class possess among other things consciousness, and therefore think. Insofar, therefore, as they rule as a class and determine the extent and compass of an epoch, it is self-evident that they do this in its whole range, hence among other things rule also as thinkers, as producers of ideas, and regulate the production and distribution of the ideas of their age: thus their ideas are the ruling ideas of the epoch. For instance, in an age and in a country where royal power, aristocracy, and bourgeoisie are contending for mastery and where, therefore, mastery is shared, the doctrine of the separation of powers proves to be the dominant idea and is expressed as an 'eternal law'.

The division of labour, which we already saw above (pp. 102–5) as one of the chief forces of history up till now, manifests itself also in the ruling class as the division of mental and material labour, so that inside this class one part appears as the thinkers of the class (its active, conceptive ideologists, who make the perfecting of the illusion of the class about itself their chief source of livelihood), while the others' attitude to these ideas and illusions is more passive and receptive, because they are in reality the active members of this class and have less time to make up illusions and ideas about themselves. Within this class this cleavage can even develop into a certain opposition and hostility between the two parts, which, however, in the case of a practical collision, in which the class itself is endangered, automatically comes to nothing, in which case there also vanishes the semblance that the ruling ideas were not the ideas of the ruling class and had a power distinct from the power of this class. The existence of revolutionary ideas in a particular period presupposes the existence of a revolutionary class; about the premises for the latter sufficient has already been said above (pp. 104–6).

If now in considering the course of history we detach the ideas of the ruling class from the ruling class itself and attribute to them an independent existence, if we confine ourselves to saying that these or those ideas were dominant at a given time, without bothering ourselves about the conditions of production and the producers of these ideas, if we thus ignore the individuals and world conditions which are the source of the ideas, we can say, for instance, that during the time that the aristocracy was dominant, the concepts honour, loyalty, etc. were dominant, during the dominance of the bourgeoisie the concepts freedom, equality, etc. The ruling class itself on the whole imagines this to be so. This conception of history, which is common to all historians, particularly since the eighteenth century, will necessarily come up against the phenomenon that increasingly abstract ideas hold sway, i.e. ideas which increasingly take on the form of universality. For each new class which puts itself in the place of one ruling before it, is compelled, merely in order to carry through its aim, to represent its interest as the common interest of all the members of society, that is, expressed in ideal form: it has to give its ideas the form of universality, and represent them as the only rational, universally valid ones. The class making a revolution appears from the very start, if only because it is opposed to a *class*, not as a class but as the representative of the whole of society; it appears as the whole mass of society confronting the one ruling class. It can do this because, to start with, its interest really is more connected with the common interest of all other non-ruling classes, because under the pressure of hitherto existing conditions its interest has not yet been able to develop as the particular interest of a particular class. Its victory, therefore, benefits also many individuals of the other classes which are not winning a dominant position, but only insofar as it now puts these individuals in a position to raise themselves into the ruling class. When the French bourgeoisie overthrew the power of the aristocracy, it thereby made it possible for many proletarians to raise themselves above the proletariat, but only insofar as they become bourgeois. Every new class, therefore, achieves its hegemony only on a broader basis than that of the class ruling previously, whereas the opposition of the non-ruling class against the new ruling class later develops all the more sharply and profoundly. Both these things determine the fact that the struggle to be waged against this new ruling class, in its turn, aims at a more decided and radical negation of the previous conditions of society than could all previous classes which sought to rule.

This whole semblance, that the rule of a certain class is only the rule of certain ideas, comes to a natural end, of course, as soon as class rule in general ceases to be the form in which society is organised, that is to say, as soon as it is no longer necessary to represent a particular interest as general or the 'general interest' as ruling.

[. . .]

Forms of intercourse

Communism differs from all previous movements in that it overturns the basis of all earlier relations of production and intercourse, and for the first time consciously treats all natural premises as the creatures of hitherto existing men, strips them of their natural character and subjugates them to the power of the united individuals. Its organisation is, therefore, essentially economic, the material production of the conditions of this unity; it turns existing conditions into conditions of unity. The reality, which communism is creating, is precisely the true basis for rendering it impossible that anything should exist independently of individuals, insofar as reality is only a product of the preceding intercourse of individuals themselves. Thus the communists in practice treat the conditions created up to now by production and intercourse as inorganic conditions, without, however, imagining that it was the plan or the destiny of previous generations to give them material, and without believing that these conditions were inorganic for the individuals creating them. The difference between the individual as a person and what is accidental to him, is not a conceptual difference but an historical fact. This distinction has a different significance at different times – e.g. the estate as something accidental to the individual in the eighteenth century, the family more or less too. It is not a distinction that we have to make for each age, but one which each age makes itself from among the different elements which it finds in existence, and indeed not according to any theory, but compelled by material collisions in life. What appears accidental to the later age as opposed to the earlier – and this applies also to the elements handed down by an earlier age – is a form of intercourse which corresponded to a definite stage of development of the productive forces. The relation of the productive forces to the form of intercourse is the relation of the form of intercourse to the occupation or activity of the individuals. (The fundamental form of this activity is, of course, material, on which depend all other forms – mental, political, religious, etc. The various shaping of material life is, of course, in every case dependent on the needs which are already developed, and the production, as well as the satisfaction, of these needs is an historical process, which is not found in the case of a sheep or a dog, although sheep and dogs in their present form certainly, but *malgré eux*, are products of an historical process.) The conditions under which individuals have intercourse with each other, so long as the above-mentioned contradiction is absent, are conditions appertaining to their individuality, in no way external to them; conditions under which these definite individuals, living under definite relationships, can alone produce their material life and what is connected with it, are thus the conditions of their self-activity and are produced by this self-activity. The definite condition under which they produce, thus corresponds, as long as the contradiction has not yet appeared, to the reality of their conditioned nature, their one-sided existence, the one-sidedness of which only becomes evident when the contradiction enters on the scene and thus exists for the later individuals. Then this condition appears as an accidental fetter, and the consciousness that it is a fetter is imputed to the earlier age as well.

These various conditions, which appear first as conditions of self-activity, later as fetters upon it, form in the whole evolution of history a coherent series of forms of intercourse, the coherence of which consists in this: in the place of an earlier form of intercourse, which has become a fetter, a new one is put, corresponding to the more developed productive forces and, hence, to the advanced mode of the self-activity of individuals – a form which in its turn becomes a fetter and is then replaced by another. Since these conditions correspond at every stage to the simultaneous development of the productive forces, their history is at the same time the history of the evolving productive forces taken over by each new generation, and is, therefore, the history of the development of the forces of the individuals themselves.

Since this evolution takes place naturally, i.e. is not subordinated to a general plan of freely combined individuals, it proceeds from various localities, tribes, nations, branches of labour, etc. each of which to start with develops independently of the others and only gradually enters into relation with the others. Furthermore, it takes place only very slowly; the various stages and interests are never completely overcome, but only subordinated to the prevailing interest and trail along beside the latter for centuries afterwards. It follows from this that within a nation itself the individuals, even apart from their pecuniary circumstances, have quite different developments, and that an earlier interest, the peculiar form of intercourse of which has already been ousted by that belonging to a later interest, remains for a long time afterwards in possession of a traditional power in the illusory community (State, law), which has won an existence independent of the individuals; a power which in the last resort can only be broken by a revolution. This explains why, with reference to individual points which allow of a more general summing-up, consciousness can sometimes appear further advanced than the contemporary empirical relationships, so that in the struggles of a later epoch one can refer to earlier theoreticians as authorities.

On the other hand, in countries which, like North America, begin in an already advanced historical epoch, the development proceeds very rapidly. Such countries have no other natural premises than the individuals, who settled there and were led to do so because the forms of intercourse of the old countries did not correspond to their wants. Thus they begin with the most advanced individuals of the old countries, and, therefore, with the correspondingly most advanced form of intercourse, before this form of intercourse has been able to establish itself in the old countries. This is the case with all colonies, insofar as they are not mere military or trading stations. Carthage, the Greek colonies, and Iceland in the eleventh and twelfth centuries, provide examples of this. A similar relationship issues from conquest, when a form of intercourse which has evolved on another soil is brought over complete to the conquered country: whereas in its home it was still encumbered with interests and relationships left over from earlier periods, here it can and must be established completely and without hindrance, if only to assure the conquerors' lasting power. (England and Naples after the Norman conquest, when they received the most perfect form of feudal organisation.)

*   *   *

This contradiction between the productive forces and the form of intercourse, which, as we saw, has occurred several times in past history, without, however, endangering the basis, necessarily on each occasion burst out in a revolution, taking on at the same time various subsidiary forms, such as all-embracing collisions, collisions of various classes, contradiction of consciousness, battle of ideas, etc., political conflict, etc. From a narrow point of view one may isolate one of these subsidiary forms and consider it as the basis of these revolutions; and this is all the more easy as the individuals who started the revolutions had illusions about their own activity according to their degree of culture and the stage of historical development.

Thus all collisions in history have their origin, according to our view, in the contradiction between the productive forces and the form of intercourse. Incidentally, to lead to collisions in a country, this contradiction need not necessarily have reached its extreme limit in this particular country. The competition with industrially more advanced countries, brought about by the expansion of international intercourse, is sufficient to produce a similar contradiction in countries with a backward industry (e.g. the latent proletariat in Germany brought into view by the competition of English industry).

[. . .]

Contradictions of big industry: revolution

Our investigation hitherto started from the instruments of production, and it has already shown that private property was a necessity for certain industrial stages. In *industrie extractive* private property still coincides with labour; in small industry and all agriculture up till now property is the necessary consequence of the existing instruments of production; in big industry the contradiction between the instrument of production and private property appears from the first time and is the product of big industry; moreover, big industry must be highly developed to produce this contradiction. And thus only with big industry does the abolition of private property become possible.

In big industry and competition the whole mass of conditions of existence, limitations, biases of individuals, are fused together into the two simplest forms: private property and labour. With money every form of intercourse, and intercourse itself, is considered fortuitous for the individuals. Thus money implies that all previous intercourse was only intercourse of individuals under particular conditions, not of individuals as individuals. These conditions are reduced to two: accumulated labour or private property, and actual labour. If both or one of these ceases; then intercourse comes to a standstill. The modern economists themselves, e.g. Sismondi, Cherbuliez, etc., oppose 'association of individuals' to 'association of capital'. On the other hand, the individuals themselves are entirely subordinated to the division of labour and hence are brought into the most complete dependence on one another. Private property, insofar as within labour itself it is opposed to labour, evolves out of the necessity of accumulation, and has still, to begin with, rather the form of the communality; but in its further development it approaches more and more the modern form of private property. The division of labour implies from the outset the division of the *conditions* of labour, of tools and materials, and thus the splitting-up of accumulated capital among different owners, and thus, also, the division between capital and labour, and the different forms of property itself. The more the division of labour develops and accumulation grows, the sharper are the forms that this process of differentiation assumes. Labour itself can only exist on the premise of this fragmentation.

Thus two facts are here revealed. First the productive forces appear as a world for themselves, quite independent of and divorced from the individuals, alongside the individuals: the reason for this is that the individuals, whose forces they are, exist split up and in opposition to one another, whilst, on the other hand, these forces are only real forces in the intercourse and association of these individuals. Thus, on the one hand, we have a totality of productive forces, which have, as it were, taken on a material form and are for the individuals no longer the forces of the individuals but of private property, and hence of the individuals only insofar as they are owners of private property themselves. Never, in any earlier period, have the productive forces taken on a form so indifferent to the intercourse of individuals *as* individuals, because their intercourse itself was formerly a restricted one. On the other hand, standing over against these productive forces, we have the majority of the individuals from whom these forces have been wrested away, and who, robbed thus of all real life-content, have become abstract individuals, but who are, however, only by this fact put into a position to enter into relation with one another *as individuals*.

The only connection which still links them with the productive forces and with their own existence – labour – has lost all semblance of self-activity and only sustains their life by stunting it. While in the earlier periods self-activity and the production of material life were separated, in that they devolved on different persons, and while, on account of the narrowness of the individuals themselves, the production of material life was considered as a subordinate mode of self-activity, they now diverge to such an extent that altogether material life appears as the end, and what produces this material life, labour (which is now the only possible but, as we see, negative form of self-activity), as the means.

Thus things have now come to such a pass that the individuals must appropriate the existing totality of productive forces, not only to achieve self-activity, but, also, merely to safeguard their very existence. This appropriation is first determined by the object to be appropriated, the productive forces, which have been developed to a totality and which only exist within a universal intercourse. From this aspect alone, therefore, this appropriation must have a universal character corresponding to the productive forces and the intercourse.

The appropriation of these forces is itself nothing more than the development of the individual capacities corresponding to the material instruments of production. The appropriation of a totality of instruments of production is, for this very reason, the development of a totality of capacities in the individuals themselves.

This appropriation is further determined by the persons appropriating. Only the proletarians of the present day, who are completely shut off from all self-activity, are in a position to achieve a complete and no longer restricted self-activity, which consists in the appropriation of a totality of productive forces and in the thus postulated development of a totality of capacities. All earlier revolutionary appropriations were restricted; individuals, whose self-activity was restricted by a crude instrument of production and a limited intercourse, appropriated this crude instrument of production, and hence merely achieved a new state of limitation. Their instrument of production became their property, but they themselves remained subordinate to the division of labour and their own instrument of production. In all expropriations up to now, a mass of individuals remained subservient to a single instrument of production; in the appropriation by the proletarians, a mass of instruments of production must be made subject to each individual and property to all. Modern universal intercourse can be controlled by individuals, therefore, only when controlled by all.

This appropriation is further determined by the manner in which it must be effected. It can only be effected through a union, which by the character of the proletariat itself can again only be a universal one, and through a revolution, in which, on the one hand, the power of the earlier mode of production and intercourse and social organisation is overthrown, and, on the other hand, there develops the universal character and the energy of the proletariat, without which the revolution cannot be accomplished; and in which, further, the proletariat rids itself of everything that still clings to it from its previous position in society.

Only at this stage does self-activity coincide with material life, which corresponds to the development of individuals into complete individuals and the casting-off of all natural limitations. The transformation of labour into self-activity corresponds to the transformation of the earlier limited intercourse into the intercourse of individuals as such. With the appropriation of the total productive forces through united individuals, private property comes to an end. Whilst previously in history a particular condition always appeared as accidental, now the isolation of individuals and the particular private gain of each man have themselves become accidental.

The individuals, who are no longer subject to the division of labour, have been conceived by the philosophers as an ideal, under the name 'Man'. They have conceived the whole process which we have outlined as the evolutionary process of 'Man', so that at every historical stage 'Man' was substituted for the individuals and shown as the motive force of history. The whole process was thus conceived as a process of the self-estrangement of 'Man', and this was essentially due to the fact that the average individual of the later stage was always foisted on to the earlier stage, and the consciousness of a later age on to the individuals of an earlier. Through this inversion, which from the first is an abstract image of the actual conditions, it was possible to transform the whole of history into an evolutionary process of consciousness.

Finally, from the conception of history we have sketched we obtain these further conclusions: (1) In the development of productive forces there comes a stage when productive forces and means of intercourse are brought into being, which, under the existing relationships, only cause mischief, and are no longer productive but destructive forces (machinery and money); and connected with this a class is called forth, which has to bear all the burdens of society without enjoying its advantages, which, ousted from society, is forced into the most decided antagonism to all other classes; a class which forms the majority of all members of society, and from which emanates the consciousness of the necessity of a fundamental revolution, the communist consciousness, which may, of course, arise among the other classes too through the contemplation of the situation of this class. (2) The conditions under which definite productive forces can be applied are the conditions of the rule of a definite class of society, whose social power, deriving from its property, has its *practical*-idealistic expression in each case in the form of the State; and, therefore, every revolutionary struggle is directed against a class, which till then has been in power. (3) In all revolutions up till now the mode of activity always remained unscathed and it was only a question of a different distribution of this activity, a new distribution of labour to other persons, whilst the communist revolution is directed against the preceding *mode* of activity, does away with *labour*, and abolishes the rule of all classes with the classes themselves, because it is carried through by the class which no longer counts as a class in society, is not recognised as a class, and is in itself the expression of the dissolution of all classes, nationalities, etc. within present society; and (4) both for the production on a mass scale of this communist consciousness, and for the success of the cause itself, the alteration of men on a mass scale is necessary, an alteration which can only take place in a practical movement, a *revolution*; this revolution is necessary, therefore, not only because the *ruling* class cannot be overthrown in any other way, but also because the class *overthrowing* it can only in a revolution succeed in ridding itself of all the muck of ages and become fitted to found society anew.

From: *The German Ideology* (C. J. Arthur ed.), Part 1, pp. 42–3, 46–60, 64–6, 86–7, 91–5

8

Preface to a Contribution to the Critique of Political Economy

Written in 1859, but describing the intellectual position at which Marx had arrived by 1845, this passage offers the very briefest synoptic account of the major principles of historical materialism. Marx describes it as the 'guiding thread' of all his later studies.

[. . .]

In the social production of their life, men enter into definite relations that are indispensable and independent of their will, relations of production which correspond to a definite stage of development of their material productive forces. The sum total of these relations of production constitutes the economic structure of society, the real foundation, on which rises a legal and political superstructure and to which correspond definite forms of social consciousness. The mode of production of material life conditions the social, political and intellectual life process in general. It is not the consciousness of men that determines their being, but, on the contrary, their social being that determines their consciousness. At a certain stage of their development, the material productive forces of society come in conflict with the existing relations of production, or – what is but a legal expression for the same thing – with the property relations within which they have been at work hitherto. From forms of development of the productive forces these relations turn into their fetters. Then begins an epoch of social revolution. With the change of the economic foundation the entire immense superstructure is more or less rapidly transformed. In considering such transformations a distinction should always be made between the material transformation of the economic conditions of production, which can be determined with the precision of natural science, and the legal, political, religious, aesthetic or philosophic – in short, ideological forms in which men become conscious of this conflict and fight it out. Just as our opinion of an individual is not based on what he thinks of himself, so can we not judge of such a period of transformation by its own consciousness; on the contrary, this consciousness must be explained rather from the contradictions of material life, from the existing conflict between the social productive forces and the relations of production. No social order ever perishes before all the productive forces for which there is room in it have developed; and new, higher relations of production never appear before the material conditions of their existence have matured in the womb of the old society itself. Therefore mankind always sets itself only such tasks as it can solve; since, looking at the matter more closely, it will always be found that the task itself arises only when the material conditions for its solution already exist or are at least in the process of formation. In broad outlines Asiatic, ancient, feudal, and modern bourgeois modes of production can be designated as progressive epochs in the economic formation of society. The bourgeois relations of production are the last antagonistic form of the social process of production – antagonistic not in the sense of individual antagonism, but of one arising from the social conditions of life of the individuals; at the same time the productive forces developing in the womb of bourgeois society create the material conditions for the solution of that antagonism. This social formation brings, therefore, the prehistory of human society to a close.

[...]

From: *Collected Works*, Vol. 29, pp. 262–4

9

Letter to Annenkov

Marx spent a good deal of his time and energy criticising other (and, as he saw it, mistaken) trends in nineteenth-century socialist thought. The Letter to Annenkov *(of 1846) contains the essential elements of Marx's critique of the contemporary French socialist-anarchist thinker, Proudhon (a criticism more fully developed in Marx's text* The Poverty of Philosophy*). As well as showing us the contempt in which Marx held many of his theoretical 'rivals', we have here a further clear exposition of the materialist case: 'with the acquisition of new productive faculties man changes his mode of production and with the mode of production he changes all the economic relations which were but the necessary relations of that particular mode of production'.*

[. . .]

What is society, irrespective of its form? The product of man's interaction upon man. Is man free to choose this or that form of society? By no means. If you assume a given state of development of man's productive faculties, you will have a corresponding form of commerce and consumption. If you assume given stages of development in production, commerce or consumption, you will have a corresponding form of social constitution, a corresponding organisation, whether of the family, of the estates or of the classes – in a word, a corresponding civil society. If you assume this or that civil society, you will have this or that political system, which is but the official expression of civil society. This is something Mr Proudhon will never understand, for he imagines he's doing something great when he appeals from the state to civil society, i.e. to official society from the official epitome of society.

Needless to say, man is not free to choose *his productive forces* – upon which his whole history is based – for every productive force is an acquired force, the product of previous activity. Thus the productive forces are the result of man's practical energy, but that energy is in turn circumscribed by the conditions in which man is placed by the productive forces already acquired, by the form of society which exists before him, which he does not create, which is the product of the preceding generation. The simple fact that every succeeding generation finds productive forces acquired by the preceding generation and which serve it as the raw material of further production, engenders a relatedness in the history of man, engenders a history of mankind, which is all the more a history of mankind as man's productive forces, and hence his social relations, have expanded. From this it can only be concluded that the social history of man is never anything else than the history of his individual development, whether he is conscious of this or not. His material relations form the basis of all his relations. These material relations are but the necessary forms in which his material and individual activity is realised.

Mr Proudhon confuses ideas and things. Man never renounces what he has gained, but this does not mean that he never renounces the form of society in which he has acquired certain productive forces. On the contrary. If he is not to be deprived of the results obtained or to forfeit the fruits of civilisation, man is compelled to change all his traditional social forms as soon as the mode of commerce ceases to correspond to the productive forces acquired. Here I use the word *commerce* in its widest sense – as we would say *Verkehr* in German. For instance, privilege, the institution of guilds and corporations, the regulatory system of the Middle Ages, were the only social relations that corresponded to the acquired productive forces and to the pre-existing social conditions from which those institutions had emerged. Protected by the corporative and regulatory system, capital had accumulated, maritime trade had expanded, colonies had been founded – and man would have lost the very fruits of all this had he wished to preserve the forms under whose protection those fruits had ripened. And, indeed, two thunderclaps occurred, the revolutions of 1640 and of 1688. In England, all the earlier economic forms, the social relations corresponding to them, and the political system which was the official expression of the old civil society, were destroyed. Thus, the economic forms in which man produces, consumes and exchanges are *transitory and historical*. With the acquisition of new productive faculties man changes his mode of production and with the mode of production he changes all the economic relations which were but the necessary relations of that particular mode of production.

It is this that Mr Proudhon has failed to understand, let alone demonstrate. Unable to follow the real course of history, Mr Proudhon provides a phantasmagoria which he has the presumption to present as a dialectical phantasmagoria. He no longer feels any need to speak of the seventeenth, eighteenth or nineteenth centuries, for his history takes place in the nebulous realm of the imagination and soars high above time and place. In a word, it is Hegelian trash, it is not history, it is not profane history – history of mankind, but sacred history – history of ideas. As seen by him, man is but the instrument used by the idea or eternal reason in order to unfold itself. The *evolutions* of which Mr Proudhon speaks are presumed to be evolutions such as take place in the mystical bosom of the absolute idea. If the veil of this mystical language be rent, it will be found that what Mr Proudhon gives us is the order in which economic categories are arranged within his mind. It would require no great effort on my part to prove to you that this arrangement is the arrangement of a very disorderly mind.

Mr Proudhon opens his book with a dissertation on *value* which is his hobby-horse. For the time being I shall not embark upon an examination of that dissertation.

The series of eternal reason's economic evolutions begins with the *division of labour*. For Mr Proudhon, the division of labour is something exceedingly simple. But was not the caste system a specific division of labour? And was not the corporative system another division of labour? And is not the division of labour in the manufacturing system, which began in England in the middle of the seventeenth century and ended towards the end of the eighteenth century, likewise entirely distinct from the division of labour in big industry, in modern industry?

Mr Proudhon is so far from the truth that he neglects to do what even profane economists do. In discussing the division of labour, he feels no need to refer to the world *market*. Well! Must not the division of labour in the fourteenth and fifteenth centuries, when there were as yet no colonies, when America was still non-existent for Europe, and when Eastern Asia existed only through the mediation of Constantinople, have been utterly different from the division of labour in the seventeenth century, when colonies were already developed?

And that is not all. Is the whole internal organisation of nations, are their international relations, anything but the expression of a given division of labour? And must they not change as the division of labour changes?

Mr Proudhon has so little understood the question of the division of labour that he does not even mention the separation of town and country which occurred in Germany, for instance, between the ninth and twelfth centuries. Thus, to Mr Proudhon, that separation must be an eternal law because he is unaware either of its origin or of its development. Throughout his book he speaks as though this creation of a given mode of production were to last till the end of time. All that Mr Proudhon says about the division of labour is but a résumé, and a very superficial and very incomplete résumé at that, of what Adam Smith and a thousand others said before him.

The second evolution is *machinery*. With Mr Proudhon, the relation between the division of labour and machinery is a wholly mystical one. Each one of the modes of the division of labour had its specific instruments of production. For instance, between the mid-seventeenth and mid-eighteenth century man did not make everything by hand. He had tools and very intricate ones, such as looms, ships, levers, etc., etc.

Thus nothing could be more absurd than to see machinery as deriving from the division of labour in general.

In passing I should also point out that, not having understood the historical origin of machinery, Mr. Proudhon has still less understood its development. Up till 1825 – when the first general crisis occurred – it might be said that the requirements of consumption as a whole were growing more rapidly than production, and that the development of machinery was the necessary consequence of the needs of the market. Since 1825, the invention and use of machinery resulted solely from the war between masters and workmen. But this is true only of England. As for the European nations, they were compelled to use machinery by the competition they were encountering from the English, in their home markets as much as in the world market. Finally, where North America was concerned, the introduction of machinery was brought about both by competition with other nations and by scarcity of labour, i.e. by the disproportion between the population and the industrial requirements of North America. From this you will be able to see what wisdom Mr Proudhon evinces when he conjures up the spectre of competition as the third evolution, as the antithesis of machinery!

Finally, and generally speaking, it is truly absurd to make *machinery* an economic category alongside the division of labour, competition, credit, etc.

Machinery is no more an economic category than the ox who draws the plough. The present *use* of machinery is one of the relations of our present economic system, but the way in which machinery is exploited is quite distinct from the machinery itself. Powder is still powder, whether you use it to wound a man or to dress his wounds.

Mr Proudhon surpasses himself in causing to grow inside his own brain competition, monopoly, taxes or police, balance of trade, credit and property in the order I have given here. Nearly all the credit institutions had been developed in England by the beginning of the eighteenth century, before the invention of machinery. State credit was simply another method of increasing taxes and meeting the new requirements created by the rise to power of the bourgeois class. Finally, *property* constitutes the last category in Mr Proudhon's system. In the really existing world, on the other hand, the division of labour and all Mr Proudhon's other categories are social relations which together go to make up what is now known as *property*; outside these relations bourgeois property is nothing but a metaphysical or juridical illusion. The property of another epoch, feudal property, developed in a wholly different set of social relations. In establishing property as an independent relation, Mr Proudhon is guilty of more than a methodological error: he clearly proves his failure to grasp the bond linking all forms of *bourgeois* production, or to understand the *historical* and *transitory* nature of the forms of production in any one epoch. Failing to see our social institutions as historical products and to understand either their origin or their development, Mr Proudhon can only subject them to a dogmatic critique.

Hence Mr Proudhon is compelled to resort to a *fiction* in order to explain development. He imagines that the division of labour, credit, machinery, etc., were all invented in the service of his *idée fixe*, the idea of equality. His explanation is sublimely naïve. These things were invented for the sake of equality, but unfortunately they have turned against equality. That is the whole of his argument. In other words, he makes a gratuitous assumption and, because actual development contradicts his fiction at every turn, he concludes that there is a contradiction. He conceals the fact that there is a contradiction only between his *idées fixes* and the real movement.

Thus Mr Proudhon, chiefly because he doesn't know history, fails to see that, in developing his productive faculties, i.e. in living, man develops certain inter-relations, and that the nature of these relations necessarily changes with the modification and the growth of the said productive faculties. He fails to see that *economic categories* are but *abstractions* of those real relations, that they are truths only in so far as those relations continue to exist. Thus he falls into the error of bourgeois economists who regard those economic categories as eternal laws and not as historical laws which are laws only for a given historical development, a specific development of the productive forces. Thus, instead of regarding politico-economic categories as abstractions of actual social relations that are transitory and historical, Mr Proudhon, by a mystical inversion, sees in the real relations only the embodiment of those abstractions.

[. . .]

Mr Proudhon understands perfectly well that men manufacture worsted, linens and silks; and whatever credit is due for understanding such a trifle! What Mr Proudhon does not understand is that, according to their faculties, men also produce the *social relations* in which they produce worsted and linens. Still less does Mr Proudhon understand that those who produce social relations in conformity with their material productivity also produce the *ideas*, *categories*, i.e. the ideal abstract expressions of those same social relations. Indeed, the categories are no more eternal than the relations they express. They are historical and transitory products. To Mr Proudhon, on the contrary, the prime cause consists in abstractions and categories. According to him it is these and not men which make history. *The abstraction, the category regarded as such*, i.e. as distinct from man and his material activity, is, of course, immortal, immutable, impassive. It is nothing but an entity of pure reason, which is only another way of saying that an abstraction, regarded as such, is abstract. An admirable *tautology*!

Hence, to Mr Proudhon, economic relations, seen in the form of categories, are eternal formulas without origin or progress.

To put it another way: Mr Proudhon does not directly assert that to him *bourgeois life* is an *eternal truth*; he says so indirectly, by deifying the categories which express bourgeois relations in the form of thought. He regards the products of bourgeois society as spontaneous entities, endowed with a life of their own, eternal, the moment these present themselves to him in the shape of categories, of thought. Thus he fails to rise above the bourgeois horizon. Because he operates with bourgeois thoughts and assumes them to be eternally true, he looks for the synthesis of those thoughts, their balance, and fails to see that their present manner of maintaining a balance is the only possible one.

In fact he does what all good bourgeois do. They all maintain that competition, monopoly, etc., are, in principle – i.e. regarded as abstract thoughts – the only basis for existence, but leave a great deal to be desired in practice. What they all want is competition without the pernicious consequences of competition. They all want the impossible, i.e. the conditions of bourgeois existence without the necessary consequences of those conditions. They all fail to understand that the bourgeois form of production is an historical and transitory form, just as was the feudal form. This mistake is due to the fact that, to them, bourgeois man is the only possible basis for any society, and that they cannot envisage a state of society in which man will have ceased to be bourgeois.

Hence Mr Proudhon is necessarily *doctrinaire*. The historical movement by which the present world is convulsed resolves itself, so far as he is concerned, into the problem of discovering the right balance, the synthesis of two bourgeois thoughts. Thus, by subtlety, the clever fellow discovers God's secret thought, the unity of two isolated thoughts which are isolated thoughts only because Mr Proudhon has isolated them from practical life, from present-day production, which is the combination of the realities they express. In place of the great historical movement which is born of the conflict between the productive forces already acquired by man, and his social relations which no longer correspond to those productive forces, in the place of the terrible wars now imminent between the various classes of a nation and between the various nations, in place of practical and violent action on the part of the masses, which is alone capable of resolving those conflicts, in place of that movement – vast, prolonged and complex – Mr Proudhon puts the cacky-dauphin movement of his own mind. Thus it is the savants, the men able to filch from God his inmost thoughts, who make history. All the lesser fry have to do is put their revelations into practice.

Now you will understand why Mr Proudhon is the avowed enemy of all political movements. For him, the solution of present-day problems does not consist in public action but in the dialectical rotations of his brain. Because to him the categories are the motive force, it is not necessary to change practical life in order to change the categories; on the contrary, it is necessary to change the categories, whereupon actual society will change as a result.

[. . .]

From: *Collected Works,* Vol. 38, pp. 95–103

10

The Communist Manifesto

It is quite wrong to read the Manifesto as a considered summary of Marx's social and political thought. After all, he was barely thirty when it was written and most of his intellectual life still lay ahead of him. It was produced for immediate consumption in what Marx saw as a near-revolutionary situation across the European continent. Nonetheless, it is a brilliantly lucid account of the materialist conception of history and of the political imperatives Marx derived from it. Part One of the Manifesto remains one of history's more extraordinary and impassioned polemics. It is the fate of many manifestoes to go unfulfilled. Few, however, have been as well written and as widely read as Marx's.

A spectre is haunting Europe – the spectre of Communism. All the Powers of old Europe have entered into a holy alliance to exorcise this spectre: Pope and Czar, Metternich and Guizot, French Radicals and German police-spies.

Where is the party in opposition that has not been decried as Communistic by its opponents in power? Where the Opposition that has not hurled back the branding reproach of Communism, against the more advanced opposition parties, as well as against its reactionary adversaries?

Two things result from this fact:

1 Communism is already acknowledged by all European Powers to be itself a Power.
2 It is high time that Communists should openly, in the face of the whole world, publish their views, their aims, their tendencies, and meet this nursery tale of the Spectre of Communism with a Manifesto of the party itself.

To this end, Communists of various nationalities have assembled in London, and sketched the following Manifesto, to be published in the English, French, German, Italian, Flemish and Danish languages.

I
Bourgeois and proletarians[1]

The history of all hitherto existing society[2] is the history of class struggles.

Freeman and slave, patrician and plebeian, lord and serf, guild-master and journeyman, in a word, oppressor and oppressed, stood in constant opposition to one another, carried on an uninterrupted, now hidden, now open fight, a fight that each time ended, either in a revolutionary re-constitution of society at large, or in the common ruin of the contending classes.

In the earlier epochs of history, we find almost everywhere a complicated arrangement of society into various orders, a manifold gradation of social rank. In ancient Rome we have patricians, knights, plebeians, slaves; in the Middle Ages, feudal lords, vassals, guild-masters, journeymen, apprentices, serfs; in almost all of these classes, again, subordinate gradations.

The modern bourgeois society that has sprouted from the ruins of feudal society has not done away with class antagonisms. It has but established new classes, new conditions of oppression, new forms of struggle in place of the old ones.

Our epoch, the epoch of the bourgeoisie, possesses, however, this distinctive feature: it has simplified the class antagonisms. Society as a whole is more and more splitting up into two great hostile camps, into two great classes directly facing each other: Bourgeoisie and Proletariat.

From the serfs of the Middle Ages sprang the chartered burghers of the earliest towns. From these burgesses the first elements of the bourgeoisie were developed.

The discovery of America, the rounding of the Cape, opened up fresh ground for the rising bourgeoisie. The East-Indian and Chinese markets, the colonisation of America, trade with the colonies, the increase in the means of exchange and in commodities generally, gave to commerce, to navigation, to industry, an impulse never before known, and thereby, to the revolutionary element in the tottering feudal society, a rapid development.

The feudal system of industry, under which industrial production was monopolised by closed guilds, now no longer sufficed for the growing wants of the new markets. The manufacturing system took its place. The guild-masters were pushed on one side by the manufacturing middle class;

division of labour between the different corporate guilds vanished in the face of division of labour in each single workshop.

Meantime the markets kept ever growing, the demand ever rising. Even manufacture no longer sufficed. Thereupon, steam and machinery revolutionised industrial production. The place of manufacture was taken by the giant, Modern Industry, the place of the industrial middle class, by industrial millionaires, the leaders of whole industrial armies, the modern bourgeois.

Modern industry has established the world market, for which the discovery of America paved the way. This market has given an immense development to commerce, to navigation, to communication by land. This development has, in its turn, reacted on the extension of industry; and in proportion as industry, commerce, navigation, railways extended, in the same proportion the bourgeoisie developed, increased its capital, and pushed into the background every class handed down from the Middle Ages.

We see, therefore, how the modern bourgeoisie is itself the product of a long course of development, of a series of revolutions in the modes of production and of exchange.

Each step in the development of the bourgeoisie was accompanied by a corresponding political advance of that class. An oppressed class under the sway of the feudal nobility, an armed and self-governing association in the medieval commune; here independent urban republic (as in Italy and Germany), there taxable 'third estate' of the monarchy (as in France), afterwards, in the period of manufacture proper, serving either the semifeudal or the absolute monarchy as a counterpoise against the nobility, and, in fact, cornerstone of the great monarchies in general, the bourgeoisie has at last, since the establishment of Modern Industry and of the world market, conquered for itself, in the modern representative State, exclusive political sway. The executive of the modern State is but a committee for managing the common affairs of the whole bourgeoisie.

The bourgeoisie, historically, has played a most revolutionary part.

The bourgeoisie, wherever it has got the upper hand, has put an end to all feudal, patriarchal, idyllic relations. It has pitilessly torn asunder the motley feudal ties that bound man to his 'natural superiors', and has left remaining no other nexus between man and man than naked self-interest, than callous 'cash payment'. It has drowned the most heavenly ecstasies of religious fervour, of chivalrous enthusiasm, of philistine sentimentalism, in the icy water of egotistical calculation. It has resolved personal worth into exchange value, and in place of the numberless indefeasible chartered freedoms, has set up that single, unconscionable freedom – Free Trade. In one word, for exploitation, veiled by religious and political illusions, it has substituted naked, shameless, direct, brutal exploitation.

The bourgeoisie has stripped of its halo every occupation hitherto honoured and looked up to with reverent awe. It has converted the physician, the lawyer, the priest, the poet, the man of science, into its paid wage-labourers.

The bourgeoisie has torn away from the family its sentimental veil, and has reduced the family relation to a mere money relation.

The bourgeoisie has disclosed how it came to pass that the brutal display of vigour in the Middle Ages, which Reactionists so much admire, found its fitting complement in the most slothful indolence. It has been the first to show what man's activity can bring about. It has accomplished wonders far surpassing Egyptian pyramids, Roman aqueducts, and Gothic cathedrals; it has conducted expeditions that put in the shade all former Exoduses of nations and crusades.

The bourgeoisie cannot exist without constantly revolutionising the instruments of production, and thereby the relations of production, and with them the whole relations of society. Conservation of the old modes of production in unaltered form, was, on the contrary, the first condition of existence for all earlier industrial classes. Constant revolutionising of production, uninterrupted disturbance of all social conditions, everlasting uncertainty and agitation distinguish the bourgeois epoch from all earlier ones. All fixed, fast-frozen relations, with their train of ancient and venerable prejudices and opinions, are swept away, all new-formed ones become antiquated before they can ossify. All that is solid melts into air, all that is holy is profaned, and man is at last compelled to face with sober senses, his real conditions of life, and his relations with his kind.

The need of a constantly expanding market for its products chases the bourgeoisie over the whole surface of the globe. It must nestle everywhere, settle everywhere, establish connexions everywhere.

The bourgeoisie has through its exploitation of the world market given a cosmopolitan character to production and consumption in every country. To the great chagrin of Reactionists, it has drawn from under the feet of industry the national ground on which it stood. All old-established national industries have been destroyed or are daily being destroyed. They are dislodged by new industries, whose introduction becomes a life and death question for all civilised nations, by industries that no longer work up indigenous raw material, but raw material drawn from the remotest zones; industries whose products are consumed, not only at home, but in every quarter of the globe. In place of the old wants, satisfied by the productions of the country, we find new wants, requiring for their satisfaction the products of distant lands and climes. In place of the old local and national seclusion and self-sufficiency, we have intercourse in every direction, universal inter-dependence of nations. And as in material, so also in intellectual production. The intellectual creations of individual nations become common property. National one-sidedness and narrow-mindedness become more and more impossible, and from the numerous national and local literatures, there arises a world literature.

The bourgeoisie, by the rapid improvement of all instruments of production, by the immensely facilitated means of communication draws all, even the most barbarian, nations into civilisation. The cheap prices of its commodities are the heavy artillery with which it batters down all Chinese walls, with which it forces the barbarians' intensely obstinate hatred of foreigners to capitulate. It compels all nations, on pain of extinction, to adopt the bourgeois mode of production; it compels them to introduce what it calls civilisation into their midst, i.e., to become bourgeois themselves. In one word, it creates a world after its own image.

The bourgeoisie has subjected the country to the rule of the towns. It has created enormous cities, has greatly increased the urban population as compared with the rural, and has thus rescued a considerable part of the population from the idiocy of rural life. Just as it has made the country dependent on the towns, so it has made barbarian and semi-barbarian countries dependent on the civilised ones, nations of peasants on nations of bourgeois, the East on the West.

The bourgeoisie keeps more and more doing away with the scattered state of the population, of the means of production, and of property. It has agglomerated population, centralised means of production, and has concentrated property in a few hands. The necessary consequence of this was political centralisation. Independent, or but loosely connected provinces with separate interests, laws, governments and systems of taxation, became lumped together into one nation, with one government, one code of laws, one national class-interest, one frontier and one customs-tariff.

The bourgeoisie, during its rule of scarce one hundred years, has created more massive and more colossal productive forces than have all preceding generations together. Subjection of Nature's forces to man, machinery, application of chemistry to industry and agriculture, steam-navigation, railways, electric telegraphs, clearing of whole continents for cultivation, canalisation of rivers, whole populations conjured out of the ground – what earlier century had even a presentiment that such productive forces slumbered in the lap of social labour?

We see then: the means of production and of exchange, on whose foundation the bourgeoisie built itself up, were generated in feudal society. At a certain stage in the development of these means of production and of exchange, the conditions under which feudal society produced and exchanged, the feudal organisation of agriculture and manufacturing industry, in one word, the feudal relations of property became no longer compatible with the already developed productive forces; they became so many fetters. They had to be burst asunder; they were burst asunder.

Into their place stepped free competition, accompanied by a social and
political constitution adapted to it, and by the economical and political
sway of the bourgeois class.

A similar movement is going on before our own eyes. Modern bourgeois
society with its relations of production, of exchange and of property, a
society that has conjured up such gigantic means of production and of
exchange, is like the sorcerer, who is no longer able to control the powers
of the nether world whom he has called up by his spells. For many a decade
past the history of industry and commerce is but the history of the revolt
of modern productive forces against modern conditions of production,
against the property relations that are the conditions for the existence of
the bourgeoisie and of its rule. It is enough to mention the commercial
crises that by their periodical return put on its trial, each time more
threateningly, the existence of the entire bourgeois society. In these crises
a great part not only of the existing products, but also of the previously
created productive forces, are periodically destroyed. In these crises there
breaks out an epidemic that, in all earlier epochs, would have seemed an
absurdity – the epidemic of over-production. Society suddenly finds itself
put back into a state of momentary barbarism; it appears as if a famine,
a universal war of devastation had cut off the supply of every means of
subsistence; industry and commerce seem to be destroyed; and why?
Because there is too much civilisation, too much means of subsistence, too
much industry, too much commerce. The productive forces at the disposal
of society no longer tend to further the development of the conditions of
bourgeois property; on the contrary, they have become too powerful for
these conditions, by which they are fettered, and so soon as they overcome
these fetters, they bring disorder into the whole of bourgeois society,
endanger the existence of bourgeois property. The conditions of bourgeois
society are too narrow to comprise the wealth created by them. And how
does the bourgeoisie get over these crises? On the one hand by enforced
destruction of a mass of productive forces; on the other, by the conquest
of new markets, and by the more thorough exploitation of the old ones.
That is to say, by paving the way for more extensive and more destructive
crises, and by diminishing the means whereby crises are prevented.

The weapons with which the bourgeoisie felled feudalism to the ground
are now turned against the bourgeoisie itself.

But not only has the bourgeoisie forged the weapons that bring death
to itself; it has also called into existence the men who are to wield those
weapons – the modern working class – the proletarians.

In proportion as the bourgeoisie, i.e., capital, is developed, in the same
proportion is the proletariat, the modern working class, developed – a class
of labourers, who live only so long as they find work, and who find work
only so long as their labour increases capital. These labourers, who must

sell themselves piecemeal, are a commodity, like every other article of commerce, and are consequently exposed to all the vicissitudes of competition, to all the fluctuations of the market.

Owing to the extensive use of machinery and to division of labour, the work of the proletarians has lost all individual character, and, consequently, all charm for the workman. He becomes an appendage of the machine, and it is only the most simple, most monotonous, and most easily acquired knack, that is required of him. Hence, the cost of production of a workman is restricted, almost entirely, to the means of subsistence that he requires for his maintenance, and for the propagation of his race. But the price of a commodity, and therefore also of labour, is equal to its cost of production. In proportion, therefore, as the repulsiveness of the work increases, the wage decreases. Nay more, in proportion as the use of machinery and division of labour increases, in the same proportion the burden of toil also increases, whether by prolongation of the working hours, by increase of the work exacted in a given time or by increased speed of the machinery, etc.

Modern industry has converted the little workshop of the patriarchal master into the great factory of the industrial capitalist. Masses of labourers, crowded into the factory, are organised like soldiers. As privates of the industrial army they are placed under the command of a perfect hierarchy of officers and sergeants. Not only are they slaves of the bourgeois class, and of the bourgeois State; they are daily and hourly enslaved by the machine, by the overlooker, and, above all, by the individual bourgeois manufacturer himself. The more openly this despotism proclaims gain to be its end and aim, the more petty, the more hateful and the more embittering it is.

The less the skill and exertion of strength implied in manual labour, in other words, the more modern industry becomes developed, the more is the labour of men superseded by that of women. Differences of age and sex have no longer any distinctive social validity for the working class. All are instruments of labour, more or less expensive to use, according to their age and sex.

No sooner is the exploitation of the labourer by the manufacturer, so far, at an end, and he receives his wages in cash, than he is set upon by the other portions of the bourgeoisie, the landlord, the shopkeeper, the pawnbroker, etc.

The lower strata of the middle class – the small tradespeople, shopkeepers, and retired tradesmen generally, the handicraftsmen and peasants – all these sink gradually into the proletariat, partly because their diminutive capital does not suffice for the scale on which Modern Industry is carried on, and is swamped in the competition with the large capitalists, partly because their specialised skill is rendered worthless by new methods of production. Thus the proletariat is recruited from all classes of the population.

The proletariat goes through various stages of development. With its birth begins its struggle with the bourgeoisie. At first the contest is carried on by individual labourers, then by the workpeople of a factory, then by the operatives of one trade, in one locality, against the individual bourgeois who directly exploits them. They direct their attacks not against the bourgeois conditions of production, but against the instruments of production themselves; they destroy imported wares that compete with their labour, they smash to pieces machinery, they set factories ablaze, they seek to restore by force the vanished status of the workman of the Middle Ages.

At this stage the labourers still form an incoherent mass scattered over the whole country, and broken up by their mutual competition. If anywhere they unite to form more compact bodies, this is not yet the consequence of their own active union, but of the union of the bourgeoisie, which class, in order to attain its own political ends, is compelled to set the whole proletariat in motion, and is moreover yet, for a time, able to do so. At this stage, therefore, the proletarians do not fight their enemies, but the enemies of their enemies, the remnants of absolute monarchy, the landowners, the non-industrial bourgeois, the petty bourgeoisie. Thus the whole historical movement is concentrated in the hands of the bourgeoisie; every victory so obtained is a victory for the bourgeoisie.

But with the development of industry the proletariat not only increases in number; it becomes concentrated in greater masses, its strength grows, and it feels that strength more. The various interests and conditions of life within the ranks of the proletariat are more and more equalised, in proportion as machinery obliterates all distinctions of labour, and nearly everywhere reduces wages to the same low level. The growing competition among the bourgeois, and the resulting commercial crises, make the wages of the workers ever more fluctuating. The unceasing improvement of machinery, ever more rapidly developing, makes their livelihood more and more precarious; the collisions between individual workmen and individual bourgeois take more and more the character of collisions between two classes. Thereupon the workers begin to form combinations (Trades' Unions) against the bourgeois; they club together in order to keep up the rate of wages; they found permanent associations in order to make provision beforehand for these occasional revolts. Here and there the contest breaks out into riots.

Now and then the workers are victorious, but only for a time. The real fruit of their battles lies, not in the immediate result, but in the ever-expanding union of the workers. This union is helped on by the improved means of communication that are created by modern industry and that place the workers of different localities in contact with one another. It was just this contact that was needed to centralise the numerous local struggles, all of the same character, into one national struggle between classes. But every class struggle is a political struggle. And that union, to attain which the burghers of the Middle Ages, with their miserable highways, required centuries, the modern proletarians, thanks to railways, achieve in a few years.

This organisation of the proletarians into a class, and consequently into a political party, is continually being upset again by the competition between the workers themselves. But it ever rises up again, stronger, firmer, mightier. It compels legislative recognition of particular interests of the workers, by taking advantage of the divisions among the bourgeoisie itself. Thus the ten-hours' bill in England was carried.

Altogether collisions between the classes of the old society further, in many ways, the course of development of the proletariat. The bourgeoisie finds itself involved in a constant battle. At first with the aristocracy; later on, with those portions of the bourgeoisie itself, whose interests have become antagonistic to the progress of industry; at all times, with the bourgeoisie of foreign countries. In all these battles it sees itself compelled to appeal to the proletariat, to ask for its help, and thus, to drag it into the political arena. The bourgeoisie itself, therefore, supplies the proletariat with its own elements of political and general education, in other words, it furnishes the proletariat with weapons for fighting the bourgeoisie.

Further, as we have already seen, entire sections of the ruling classes are, by the advance of industry, precipitated into the proletariat, or are at least threatened in their conditions of existence. These also supply the proletariat with fresh elements of enlightenment and progress.

Finally, in times when the class struggle nears the decisive hour, the process of dissolution going on within the ruling class, in fact within the whole range of old society, assumes such a violent, glaring character, that a small section of the ruling class cuts itself adrift, and joins the revolutionary class, the class that holds the future in its hands. Just as, therefore, at an earlier period, a section of the nobility went over to the bourgeoisie, so now a portion of the bourgeoisie goes over to the proletariat, and in particular, a portion of the bourgeois ideologists, who have raised themselves to the level of comprehending theoretically the historical movement as a whole.

Of all the classes that stand face to face with the bourgeoisie today, the proletariat alone is a really revolutionary class. The other classes decay and finally disappear in the face of Modern Industry; the proletariat is its special and essential product.

The lower middle class, the small manufacturer, the shopkeeper, the artisan, the peasant, all these fight against the bourgeoisie, to save from extinction their existence as fractions of the middle class. They are therefore not revolutionary, but conservative. Nay more, they are reactionary, for they try to roll back the wheel of history. If by chance they are revolutionary, they are so only in view of their impending transfer into the proletariat, they thus defend not their present, but their future interests, they desert their own standpoint to place themselves at that of the proletariat.

The 'dangerous class', the social scum, that passively rotting mass thrown off by the lowest layers of old society may, here and there, be swept into the movement by a proletarian revolution; its conditions of life, however, prepare it far more for the part of a bribed tool of reactionary intrigue.

In the conditions of the proletariat, those of old society at large are already virtually swamped. The proletarian is without property; his relation to his wife and children has no longer anything in common with the bourgeois family relations; modern industrial labour, modern subjection to capital, the same in England as in France, in America as in Germany, has stripped him of every trace of national character. Law, morality, religion, are to him so many bourgeois prejudices, behind which lurk in ambush just as many bourgeois interests.

All the preceding classes that got the upper hand, sought to fortify their already acquired status by subjecting society at large to their conditions of appropriation. The proletarians cannot become masters of the productive forces of society, except by abolishing their own previous mode of appropriation, and thereby also every other previous mode of appropriation. They have nothing of their own to secure and to fortify; their mission is to destroy all previous securities for, and insurances of, individual property.

All previous historical movements were movements of minorities, or in the interest of minorities. The proletarian movement is the self-conscious, independent movement of the immense majority, in the interest of the immense majority. The proletariat, the lowest stratum of our present society, cannot stir, cannot raise itself up, without the whole superincumbent strata of official society being sprung into the air.

Though not in substance, yet in form, the struggle of the proletariat with the bourgeoisie is at first a national struggle. The proletariat of each country must, of course, first of all settle matters with its own bourgeoisie.

In depicting the most general phases of the development of the proletariat, we traced the more or less veiled civil war, raging within existing society, up to the point where that war breaks out into open revolution, and where the violent overthrow of the bourgeoisie lays the foundation for the sway of the proletariat.

Hitherto, every form of society has been based, as we have already seen, on the antagonism of oppressing and oppressed classes. But in order to oppress a class, certain conditions must be assured to it under which it can, at least, continue its slavish existence. The serf, in the period of serfdom, raised himself to membership in the commune, just as the petty bourgeois, under the yoke of feudal absolutism, managed to develop into a bourgeois. The modern labourer, on the contrary, instead of rising with the progress of industry, sinks deeper and deeper below the conditions of existence of his own class. He becomes a pauper, and pauperism develops more rapidly than population and wealth. And here it becomes evident, that the bourgeoisie is unfit any longer to be the ruling class in society, and to impose its conditions of existence upon society as an over-riding law. It is unfit to rule because it is incompetent to assure an existence to its slave within his slavery, because it cannot help letting him sink into such a state, that it has to feed him, instead of being fed by him. Society can no longer live under this bourgeoisie, in other words, its existence is no longer compatible with society.

The essential condition for the existence, and for the sway of the bourgeois class is the formation and augmentation of capital; the condition for capital is wage-labour. Wage-labour rests exclusively on competition between the labourers. The advance of industry, whose involuntary promoter is the bourgeoisie, replaces the isolation of the labourers, due to competition, by their revolutionary combination, due to association. The development of Modern Industry, therefore, cuts from under its feet the very foundation on which the bourgeoisie produces and appropriates products. What the bourgeoisie, therefore, produces, above all, is its own grave-diggers. Its fall and the victory of the proletariat are equally inevitable.

II

Proletarians and communists

In what relation do the Communists stand to the proletarians as a whole?

The Communists do not form a separate party opposed to other working-class parties.

They have no interests separate and apart from those of the proletariat as a whole.

They do not set up any sectarian principles of their own, by which to shape and mould the proletarian movement.

The Communists are distinguished from the other working-class parties by this only: (1) In the national struggles of the proletarians of the different countries, they point out and bring to the front the common interests of the entire proletariat, independently of all nationality. (2) In the various stages of development which the struggle of the working class against the bourgeoisie has to pass through, they always and everywhere represent the interests of the movement as a whole.

The Communists, therefore, are on the one hand, practically, the most advanced and resolute section of the working-class parties of every country, that section which pushes forward all others; on the other hand, theoretically, they have over the great mass of the proletariat the advantage of clearly understanding the line of march, the conditions, and the ultimate general results of the proletarian movement.

The immediate aim of the Communists is the same as that of all the other proletarian parties: formation of the proletariat into a class, overthrow of the bourgeois supremacy, conquest of political power by the proletariat.

The theoretical conclusions of the Communists are in no way based on ideas or principles that have been invented, or discovered by this or that would-be universal reformer.

They merely express, in general terms, actual relations springing from an existing class struggle, from a historical movement going on under our very eyes. The abolition of existing property relations is not at all a distinctive feature of Communism.

All property relations in the past have continually been subject to historical change consequent upon the change in historical conditions.

The French Revolution, for example, abolished feudal property in favour of bourgeois property.

The distinguishing feature of Communism is not the abolition of property generally, but the abolition of bourgeois property. But modern bourgeois private property is the final and most complete expression of the system of producing and appropriating products, that is based on class antagonisms, on the exploitation of the many by the few.

In this sense, the theory of the Communists may be summed up in the single sentence: Abolition of private property.

We Communists have been reproached with the desire of abolishing the right of personally acquiring property as the fruit of a man's own labour, which property is alleged to be the groundwork of all personal freedom, activity and independence.

Hard-won, self-acquired, self-earned property! Do you mean the property of the petty artisan and of the small peasant, a form of property that preceded the bourgeois form? There is no need to abolish that; the development of industry has to a great extent already destroyed it, and is still destroying it daily.

Or do you mean modern bourgeois private property?

But does wage-labour create any property for the labourer? Not a bit. It creates capital, i.e., that kind of property which exploits wage-labour, and which cannot increase except upon condition of begetting a new supply of wage-labour for fresh exploitation. Property, in its present form, is based on the antagonism of capital and wage-labour. Let us examine both sides of this antagonism.

To be a capitalist is to have not only a purely personal, but a social *status* in production. Capital is a collective product, and only by the united action of many members, nay, in the last resort, only by the united action of all members of society, can it be set in motion.

Capital is, therefore, not a personal, it is a social power.

When, therefore, capital is converted into common property, into the property of all members of society, personal property is not thereby transformed into social property. It is only the social character of the property that is changed. It loses its class character.

Let us now take wage-labour.

The average price of wage-labour is the minimum wage, i.e., that quantum of the means of subsistence, which is absolutely requisite to keep the labourer in bare existence as a labourer. What, therefore, the wage-labourer appropriates by means of his labour, merely suffices to prolong and reproduce a bare existence. We by no means intend to abolish this personal appropriation of the products of labour, an appropriation that is made for the maintenance and reproduction of human life, and that leaves no surplus wherewith to command the labour of others. All that we want to do away with is the miserable character of this appropriation, under which the labourer lives merely to increase capital, and is allowed to live only in so far as the interest of the ruling class requires it.

In bourgeois society, living labour is but a means to increase accumulated labour. In Communist society, accumulated labour is but a means to widen, to enrich, to promote the existence of the labourer.

In bourgeois society, therefore, the past dominates the present; in Communist society, the present dominates the past. In bourgeois society capital is independent and has individuality, while the living person is dependent and has no individuality.

And the abolition of this state of things is called by the bourgeois abolition of individuality and freedom! And rightly so. The abolition of bourgeois individuality, bourgeois independence, and bourgeois freedom is undoubtedly aimed at.

By freedom is meant, under the present bourgeois conditions of production, free trade, free selling and buying.

But if selling and buying disappears, free selling and buying disappears also. This talk about free selling and buying, and all the other 'brave words' of our bourgeoisie about freedom in general, have a meaning, if any, only in contrast with restricted selling and buying, with the fettered traders of the Middle Ages, but have no meaning when opposed to the Communistic abolition of buying and selling, of the bourgeois conditions of production, and of the bourgeoisie itself.

You are horrified at our intending to do away with private property. But in your existing society, private property is already done away with for nine-tenths of the population; its existence for the few is solely due to its non-existence in the hands of those nine-tenths. You reproach us, therefore, with intending to do away with a form of property, the necessary condition for whose existence is the non-existence of any property for the immense majority of society.

In one word, you reproach us with intending to do away with your property. Precisely so; that is just what we intend.

From the moment when labour can no longer be converted into capital, money, or rent, into a social power capable of being monopolised, i.e., from the moment when individual property can no longer be transformed into bourgeois property, into capital, from that moment, you say, individuality vanishes.

You must, therefore, confess that by 'individual' you mean no other person than the bourgeois, than the middle-class owner of property. This person must, indeed, be swept out of the way, and made impossible.

Communism deprives no man of the power to appropriate the products of society; all that it does is to deprive him of the power to subjugate the labour of others by means of such appropriation.

It has been objected that upon the abolition of private property all work will cease, and universal laziness will overtake us.

According to this, bourgeois society ought long ago to have gone to the dogs through sheer idleness; for those of its members who work, acquire nothing, and those who acquire anything, do not work. The whole of this objection is but another expression of the tautology: that there can no longer be any wage-labour when there is no longer any capital.

All objections urged against the Communistic mode of producing and appropriating material products, have, in the same way, been urged against the Communistic modes of producing and appropriating intellectual products. Just as, to the bourgeois, the disappearance of class property is the disappearance of production itself, so the disappearance of class culture is to him identical with the disappearance of all culture.

That culture, the loss of which he laments, is, for the enormous majority, a mere training to act as a machine.

But don't wrangle with us so long as you apply, to our intended abolition of bourgeois property, the standard of your bourgeois notions of freedom, culture, law, etc. Your very ideas are but the outgrowth of the conditions of your bourgeois production and bourgeois property, just as your jurisprudence is but the will of your class made into a law for all, a will, whose essential character and direction are determined by the economical conditions of existence of your class.

The selfish misconception that induces you to transform into eternal laws of nature and of reason, the social forms springing from your present mode of production and form of property – historical relations that rise and disappear in the progress of production – this misconception you share with every ruling class that has preceded you. What you see clearly in the case of ancient property, what you admit in the case of feudal property, you are of course forbidden to admit in the case of your own bourgeois form of property.

Abolition of the family! Even the most radical flare up at this infamous proposal of the Communists.

On what foundation is the present family, the bourgeois family, based? On capital, on private gain. In its completely developed form this family exists only among the bourgeoisie. But this state of things finds its complement in the practical absence of the family among the proletarians, and in public prostitution.

The bourgeois family will vanish as a matter of course when its complement vanishes, and both will vanish with the vanishing of capital.

Do you charge us with wanting to stop the exploitation of children by their parents? To this crime we plead guilty.

But, you will say, we destroy the most hallowed of relations, when we replace home education by social.

And your education! Is not that also social, and determined by the social conditions under which you educate, by the intervention, direct or indirect, of society, by means of schools, etc.? The Communists have not invented the intervention of society in education; they do but seek to alter the character of that intervention, and to rescue education from the influence of the ruling class.

The bourgeois clap-trap about the family and education, about the hallowed co-relation of parent and child, becomes all the more disgusting, the more, by the action of Modern Industry, all family ties among the proletarians are torn asunder, and their children transformed into simple articles of commerce and instruments of labour.

But you Communists would introduce community of women, screams the whole bourgeoisie in chorus.

The bourgeois sees in his wife a mere instrument of production. He hears that the instruments of production are to be exploited in common, and, naturally, can come to no other conclusion than that the lot of being common to all will likewise fall to the women.

He has not even a suspicion that the real point aimed at is to do away with the status of women as mere instruments of production.

For the rest, nothing is more ridiculous than the virtuous indignation of our bourgeois at the community of women which, they pretend, is to be openly and officially established by the Communists. The Communists have no need to introduce community of women; it has existed almost from time immemorial.

Our bourgeois, not content with having the wives and daughters of their proletarians at their disposal, not to speak of common prostitutes, take the greatest pleasure in seducing each other's wives.

Bourgeois marriage is in reality a system of wives in common and thus, at the most, what the Communists might possibly be reproached with, is that they desire to introduce, in substitution for a hypocritically concealed, an openly legalised community of women. For the rest, it is self-evident that the abolition of the present system of production must bring with it the abolition of the community of women springing from that system, i.e., of prostitution both public and private.

The Communists are further reproached with desiring to abolish countries and nationality.

The working men have no country. We cannot take from them what they have not got. Since the proletariat must first of all acquire political supremacy, must rise to be the leading class of the nation, must constitute itself *the* nation, it is so far, itself national, though not in the bourgeois sense of the word.

National differences and antagonisms between peoples are daily more and more vanishing, owing to the development of the bourgeoisie, to freedom of commerce, to the world market, to uniformity in the mode of production and in the conditions of life corresponding thereto.

The supremacy of the proletariat will cause them to vanish still faster. United action, of the leading civilised countries at least, is one of the first conditions for the emancipation of the proletariat.

In proportion as the exploitation of one individual by another is put an end to, the exploitation of one nation by another will also be put an end to. In proportion as the antagonism between classes within the nation vanishes, the hostility of one nation to another will come to an end.

The charges against Communism made from a religious, a philosophical, and, generally, from an ideological standpoint, are not deserving of serious examination.

Does it require deep intuition to comprehend that man's ideas, views and conceptions, in one word, man's consciousness, changes with every change in the conditions of his material existence, in his social relations and in his social life?

What else does the history of ideas prove, than that intellectual production changes its character in proportion as material production is changed? The ruling ideas of each age have ever been the ideas of its ruling class.

When people speak of ideas that revolutionise society, they do but express the fact, that within the old society, the elements of a new one have been created, and that the dissolution of the old ideas keeps even pace with the dissolution of the old conditions of existence.

When the ancient world was in its last throes, the ancient relitions were overcome by Christianity. When Christian ideas succumbed in the 18th century to rationalist ideas, feudal society fought its death battle with the then revolutionary bourgeoisie. The ideas of religious liberty and freedom of conscience merely gave expression to the sway of free competition within the domain of knowledge.

'Undoubtedly,' it will be said, 'religious, moral, philosophical and juridical ideas have been modified in the course of historical development. But religion, morality, philosophy, political science, and law, constantly survived this change.

'There are, besides, eternal truths, such as Freedom, Justice, etc., that are common to all states of society. But Communism abolishes eternal truths, it abolishes all religion and all morality, instead of constituting them on a new basis; it therefore acts in contradiction to all past historical experience.'

What does this accusation reduce itself to? The history of all past society has consisted in the development of class antagonisms, antagonisms that assumed different forms at different epochs.

But whatever form they may have taken, one fact is common to all past ages, viz., the exploitation of one part of society by the other. No wonder, then, that the social consciousness of past ages, despite all the multiplicity and variety it displays, moves within certain common forms, or general ideas, which cannot completely vanish except with the total disappearance of class antagonisms.

The Communist revolution is the most radical rupture with traditional property relations; no wonder that its development involves the most radical rupture with traditional ideas.

But let us have done with the bourgeois objections to Communism.

We have seen above, that the first step in the revolution by the working class is to raise the proletariat to the position of ruling class, to win the battle of democracy.

The proletariat will use its political supremacy to wrest, by degrees, all capital from the bourgeoisie, to centralise all instruments of production in the hands of the State, i.e., of the proletariat organised as the ruling class; and to increase the total of productive forces as rapidly as possible.

Of course, in the beginning, this cannot be effected except by means of despotic inroads on the rights of property, and on the conditions of bourgeois production; by means of measures, therefore, which appear economically insufficient and untenable, but which, in the course of the movement, outstrip themselves, necessitate further inroads upon the old social order, and are unavoidable as a means of entirely revolutionising the mode of production.

These measures will of course be different in different countries.

Nevertheless in the most advanced countries, the following will be pretty generally applicable:

1 Abolition of property in land and application of all rents of land to public purposes.
2 A heavy progressive or graduated income tax.
3 Abolition of all right of inheritance.
4 Confiscation of the property of all emigrants and rebels.
5 Centralisation of credit in the hands of the State, by means of a national bank with State capital and an exclusive monopoly.
6 Centralisation of the means of communication and transport in the hands of the State.
7 Extension of factories and instruments of production owned by the State; the bringing into cultivation of waste-lands, and the improvement of the soil generally in accordance with a common plan.
8 Equal liability of all to labour. Establishment of industrial armies, especially for agriculture.
9 Combination of agriculture with manufacturing industries; gradual abolition of the distinction between town and country, by a more equable distribution of the population over the country.
10 Free education for all children in public schools. Abolition of children's factory labour in its present form. Combination of education with industrial production, etc., etc.

When, in the course of development, class distinctions have disappeared, and all production has been concentrated in the hands of a vast association of the whole nation, the public power will lose its political character. Political power, properly so called, is merely the organised power of one class for oppressing another. If the proletariat during its contest with the bourgeoisie is compelled, by the force of circumstances, to organise itself as a class, if, by means of a revolution, it makes itself the ruling class, and, as such, sweeps away by force the old conditions of production, then it will, along with these conditions, have swept away the conditions for the existence of class antagonisms and of classes generally, and will thereby have abolished its own supremacy as a class.

In place of the old bourgeois society, with its classes and class antagonisms, we shall have an association, in which the free development of each is the condition for the free development of all.

[. . .]

The Communists disdain to conceal their views and aims. They openly declare that their ends can be attained only by the forcible overthrow of all existing social conditions. Let the ruling classes tremble at a Communistic revolution. The proletarians have nothing to lose but their chains. They have a world to win.

WORKING MEN OF ALL COUNTRIES, UNITE!

From: *Collected Works,* Vol. 6, pp. 481-2, 485–505, 519

Notes

1 By bourgeoisie is meant the class of modern Capitalists, owners of the means of social production and employers of wage-labour. By proletariat, the class of modern wage-labourers who, having no means of production of their own, are reduced to selling their labour-power in order to live. (*Note by Engels to the English edition of 1888*)
2 That is, all *written* history. In 1847, the pre-history of society, the social organisation existing previous to recorded history, was all but unknown. Since then, Haxthausen discovered common ownership of land in Russia, Maurer proved it to be the social foundation from which all Teutonic races started in history, and by and by village communities were found to be, or to have been the primitive form of society everywhere from India to Ireland. The inner organisation of this primitive Communistic society was laid bare, in its typical form, by Morgan's crowning discovery of the true nature of the *gens* and its relation to the *tribe*. With the dissolution of these primeval communities society begins to be differentiated into separate and finally antagonistic classes. I have attempted to retrace this process of dissolution in *Der Ursprung der Familie, des Privateigenthums und des Staats*, 2nd edition, Stuttgart, 1886. (*Note by Engels to the English edition of 1888*)

11

Address of the Central Committee to the Communist League

In the wake of the defeat of the revolutionary uprisings of 1848, Marx and Engels drew a number of tactical conclusions which they felt would apply to the next (and coming) wave of revolutionary activity. In essence, the workers could no longer trust even the 'progressive' section of the middle class consistently to support the overthrow of the old order. In any future uprising, the workers must retain an independent military force and seek to outflank bourgeois-democratic 'reformers' by pressing for the immediate introduction of socialist measures. The battle cry of the workers' party must be 'The Revolution in Permanence'. Although the 'new wave' of uprisings in Germany never came, the 1850 Address has been seen as the authoritative source for the much later advocacy of a strategy of 'Permanent Revolution' in Russia, first by Trotsky and subsequently by Lenin.

[...]

Brothers! We told you as early as 1848 that the German liberal bourgeois would soon come to power and would immediately turn their newly acquired power against the workers. You have seen how this has been fulfilled. In fact, it was the bourgeois who, immediately after the March movement of 1848, took possession of the state power and used this power in order at once to force the workers, their allies in the struggle, back into their former oppressed position. Though the bourgeoisie was not able to accomplish this without uniting with the feudal party, which had been ousted in March, without finally even relinquishing power once again to this feudal absolutist party, still it has secured conditions for itself which, in the long run, owing to the financial embarrassment of the government, would place power in its hands and would safeguard all its interests, if it were possible that the revolutionary movement would already now assume a so-called peaceful development. To safeguard its rule the bourgeoisie would not even need to make itself obnoxious by violent measures against the people, since all these violent steps have already been taken by the feudal counter-revolution. Developments, however, will not take this peaceful course. On the contrary, the revolution, which will accelerate these developments, is near at hand, whether it will be called forth by an independent uprising of the French proletariat or by an invasion of the Holy Alliance against the revolutionary Babylon.

And the role which the German liberal bourgeois played in 1848 against the people, this so treacherous role will be taken over in the impending revolution by the democratic petty bourgeois, who at present take the same attitude in the opposition as the liberal bourgeois before 1848. This party, the democratic party, which is far more dangerous to the workers than the previous liberal party, consists of three elements:

1 The most advanced sections of the big bourgeoisie, which pursue the aim of the immediate and complete overthrow of feudalism and absolutism. This faction is represented by the one-time Berlin agreers, the tax resisters.
2 The democratic-constitutional petty bourgeois, whose main aim during the previous movement was the establishment of a more or less democratic federal state as striven for by their representatives, the Lefts in the Frankfurt Assembly, and later by the Stuttgart parliament, and by themselves in the campaign for the Imperial Constitution.
3 The republican petty bourgeois, whose ideal is a German federative republic after the manner of Switzerland, and who now call themselves red and social-democratic because they cherish the pious wish of abolishing the pressure of big capital on small capital, of the big bourgeois on the petty bourgeois. The representatives of this faction were the members of the democratic congresses and committees, the leaders of the democratic associations, the editors of the democratic newspapers.

Now, after their defeat, all these factions call themselves republicans or reds, just as the republican petty bourgeois in France now call themselves socialists. Where, as in Württemberg, Bavaria, etc., they still find opportunity to pursue their aims constitutionally, they seize the occasion to retain their old phrases and to prove by deeds that they have not changed in the least. It is evident, incidentally, that the altered name of this party does not make the slightest difference to its attitude to the workers, but merely proves that it is now obliged to turn against the bourgeoisie, which is united with absolutism, and to seek the support of the proletariat.

The petty-bourgeois democratic party in Germany is very powerful; it comprises not only the great majority of the burgher inhabitants of the towns, the small people in industry and trade and the master craftsmen; it numbers among its followers also the peasants and the rural proletariat, insofar as the latter has not yet found a support in the independent urban proletariat.

The relation of the revolutionary workers' party to the petty-bourgeois democrats is this: it marches together with them against the faction which it aims at overthrowing, it opposes them in everything by which they seek to consolidate their position in their own interests.

Far from desiring to transform the whole of society for the revolutionary proletarians, the democratic petty bourgeois strive for a change in social conditions by means of which the existing society will be made as tolerable and comfortable as possible for them. Hence they demand above all a diminution of state expenditure by curtailing the bureaucracy and shifting the bulk of the taxes on to the big landowners and bourgeois. Further, they demand the abolition of the pressure of big capital on small, through public credit institutions and laws against usury, by which means it will be possible for them and the peasants to obtain advances on favourable conditions from the state instead of from the capitalists; they also demand the establishment of bourgeois property relations in the countryside by the complete abolition of feudalism. To accomplish all this they need a democratic state structure, either constitutional or republican, that will give them and their allies, the peasants, a majority; also a democratic communal structure that will give them direct control over communal property, and a number of functions now performed by the bureaucrats.

The domination and speedy increase of capital is further to be counteracted partly by restricting the right of inheritance and partly by transferring as many jobs of work as possible to the state. As far as the workers are concerned, it is certain above all that they are to remain wage-workers as before; the democratic petty bourgeois only desire better wages and a more secure existence for the workers and hope to achieve this through partial employment by the state and through charity measures; in short, they hope to bribe the workers by more or less concealed alms and to sap their revolutionary vigour by making their position tolerable for the moment. The demands of the petty-bourgeois democrats here summarised are not put forward by all of their factions and only very few of their members consider these demands in their aggregate as a definite aim. The further individual people or factions among them go, the more of these demands will they make their own, and those few who see their own programme in what has been outlined above would believe that thereby they have put forward the utmost that can be demanded from the revolution. But these demands can in no wise suffice for the party of the proletariat. While the democratic petty bourgeois wish to bring the revolution to a conclusion as quickly as possible, and with the achievement, at most, of the above demands, it is our interest and our task to make the revolution permanent, until all more or less possessing classes have been forced out of their position of dominance, the proletariat has conquered state power, and the association of proletarians, not only in one country but in all the dominant countries of the world, has advanced so far that competition among the proletarians in these countries has ceased and that at least the decisive productive forces are concentrated in the hands of the proletarians. For us the issue cannot be the alteration of private property but only its annihilation, not the smoothing over of class antagonisms but the abolition of classes, not the improvement of the existing society but the foundation of a new one. That, during the further development of the revolution, petty-bourgeois democracy will for a moment obtain predominating influence in Germany is not open to doubt. The question, therefore, is what the attitude of the proletariat and in particular of the League will be in relation to it:

1 during the continuance of the present relations, under which the petty-bourgeois democrats are likewise oppressed;
2 in the next revolutionary struggle, which will give them the upper hand;
3 after this struggle, during the period of preponderance over the overthrown classes and the proletariat.

1 At the present moment, when the democratic petty bourgeois are everywhere oppressed, they preach in general unity and reconciliation to the proletariat, they offer it their hand and strive for the establishment of a large opposition party which will embrace all shades of opinion in the democratic party, that is, they strive to entangle the workers in a party organisation in which general social-democratic phrases predominate, and serve to conceal their special interests, and in which the definite demands of the proletariat must not be brought forward for the sake of beloved peace. Such a union would turn out solely to their advantage and altogether to the disadvantage of the proletariat. The proletariat would lose its whole independent, laboriously achieved position and once more be reduced to an appendage of official bourgeois democracy. This union must, therefore, be most decisively rejected. Instead of once again stooping to serve as the applauding chorus of the bourgeois democrats, the workers, and above all the League, must exert themselves to establish an independent secret and public organisation of the workers' party alongside the official democrats and make each community the central point and nucleus of workers'

associations in which the attitude and interests of the proletariat will be discussed independently of bourgeois influences. How far the bourgeois democrats are from seriously considering an alliance in which the proletarians would stand side by side with them with equal power and equal rights is shown, for example, by the Breslau democrats who, in their organ, the *Neue Oder-Zeitung*, most furiously attack the independently organised workers, whom they style socialists. In the case of a struggle against a common adversary no special union is required. As soon as such an adversary has to be fought directly, the interests of both parties, for the moment, coincide, and, as previously so also in the future, this alliance, calculated to last only for the moment, will come about of itself. It is self-evident that in the impending bloody conflicts, as in all earlier ones, it is the workers who, in the main, will have to win the victory by their courage, determination and self-sacrifice. As previously so also in this struggle, the mass of the petty bourgeois will as long as possible remain hesitant, undecided and inactive, and then, as soon as the issue has been decided, will seize the victory for themselves, will call upon the workers to maintain tranquillity and return to their work, will guard against so-called excesses and bar the proletariat from the fruits of victory. It is not in the power of the workers to prevent the petty-bourgeois democrats from doing this, but it is in their power to make it difficult for them to gain the upper hand as against the armed proletariat, and to dictate such conditions to them that the rule of the bourgeois democrats will from the outset bear within it the seeds of its downfall, and that its subsequent extrusion by the rule of the proletariat will be considerably facilitated. Above all things, the workers must counteract, as much as is at all possible, during the conflict and immediately after the struggle, the bourgeois endeavours to allay the storm, and must compel the democrats to carry out their present terrorist phrases. They must work to prevent the direct revolutionary excitement from being suppressed again immediately after the victory. On the contrary, they must keep it alive as long as possible. Far from opposing so-called excesses, instances of popular revenge against hated individuals or public buildings that are associated only with hateful recollections, such instances must not only be tolerated but the lead in them must be taken. During the struggle and after the struggle, the workers must, at every opportunity, put forward their own demands alongside the demands of the bourgeois democrats. They must demand guarantees for the workers as soon as the democratic bourgeois set about taking the government into their hands. If necessary they must wring these guarantees by force and in general they must see to it that the new rulers pledge themselves to all possible concessions and promises – the surest way to compromise them. In general, they must in every way restrain as far as possible the intoxication of victory and the enthusiasm for the new state of things which follows every victorious street battle by a calm and dispassionate assessment of the situation and by unconcealed mistrust in the new government. Alongside the new official governments they must immediately establish their own revolutionary workers' governments, whether in the form of municipal committees and municipal councils or in the form of workers' clubs or workers' committees, so that the bourgeois-democratic governments not only immediately lose the support of the workers but from the outset see themselves supervised and threatened by authorities backed by the whole mass of the workers. In a word, from the first moment of victory, mistrust must be directed no longer against the defeated reactionary party, but against the workers' previous allies, against the party that wishes to exploit the common victory for itself alone.

2 But in order to be able energetically and threateningly to oppose this party, whose treachery to the workers will begin from the first hour of victory, the workers must be armed and organised. The arming of the whole proletariat with rifles, muskets, cannon and ammunition must be carried out at once, the revival of the old civic militia directed against the workers must be resisted. However, where the latter is not feasible the workers must try to organise themselves independently as a proletarian guard with commanders elected by themselves and with a general staff of their own choosing, and to put themselves under the command not of the state authority but of the revolutionary municipal councils set up by the workers. Where workers are employed at the expense of the state they must see that they are armed and organised in a separate corps with commanders of their own choosing or as part of the proletarian guard. Arms and ammunition must not be surrendered on any pretext; any attempt at disarming must be frustrated, if necessary, by force. Destruction of the influence of the bourgeois democrats upon the workers, immediate independent and armed organisation of the workers and the enforcement of conditions as difficult and compromising as possible for the inevitable momentary rule of bourgeois democracy – these are the main points which the proletariat and hence the League must keep in view during and after the impending insurrection.

3 As soon as the new governments have consolidated their positions to some extent, their struggle against the workers will begin. Here in order to be able to offer energetic opposition to the democratic petty bourgeois, it is above all necessary for the workers to be independently organised and centralised in clubs. After the overthrow of the existing governments, the Central Authority will, as soon as at all possible, betake itself to Germany, immediately convene a congress and put before it the necessary proposals for the centralisation of the workers' clubs under a leadership established in the chief seat of the movement. The speedy organisation of at least a provincial association of the workers' clubs is one of the most important

points for strengthening and developing the workers' party; the immediate consequence of the overthrow of the existing governments will be the election of a national representative assembly. Here the proletariat must see to it:

1 that no groups of workers are barred on any pretext by any kind of trickery on the part of local authorities or government commissaries;
2 that everywhere workers' candidates are put up alongside the bourgeois-democratic candidates, that they are as far as possible, members of the League, and that their election is promoted by all possible means. Even where there is no prospect whatever of their being elected, the workers must put up their own candidates in order to preserve their independence, to count their forces and to lay before the public their revolutionary attitude and party standpoint. In this connection they must not allow themselves to be bribed by such arguments of the democrats as, for example, that by so doing they are splitting the democratic party and giving the reactionaries the possibility of victory. The ultimate purpose of all such phrases is to dupe the proletariat. The advance which the proletarian party is bound to make by such independent action is infinitely more important than the disadvantage that might be incurred by the presence of a few reactionaries in the representative body. If from the outset the democrats come out resolutely and terroristically against the reactionaries, the influence of the latter in the elections will be destroyed in advance.

The first point on which the bourgeois democrats will come into conflict with the workers will be the abolition of feudalism. As in the first French Revolution, the petty bourgeois will give the feudal lands to the peasants as free property, that is to say, try to leave the rural proletariat in existence and form a petty-bourgeois peasant class, which will go through the same cycle of impoverishment and indebtedness which the French peasant is now still caught in.

The workers must oppose this plan in the interest of the rural proletariat and in their own interest. They must demand that the confiscated feudal property remain state property and be converted into workers' colonies cultivated by the associated rural proletariat with all the advantages of large-scale agriculture, through which the principle of common property immediately obtains a firm basis in the midst of the tottering bourgeois property relations. Just as the democrats combine with the peasants so must the workers combine with the rural proletariat. Further, the democrats will work either directly for a federative republic or, if they cannot avoid a single and indivisible republic, they will at least attempt to cripple the central government by the utmost possible autonomy and independence for the communities and provinces. The workers, in opposition to this plan, must not only strive for a single and indivisible German republic, but also within this republic for the most determined centralisation of power in the hands of the state authority. They must not allow themselves to be misguided by the democratic talk of freedom for the communities, of self-government, etc. In a country like Germany, where there are still so many remnants of the Middle Ages to be abolished, where there is so much local and provincial obstinacy to be broken, it must under no circumstances be permitted that every village, every town and every province should put a new obstacle in the path of revolutionary activity, which can proceed with full force only from the centre. – It is not to be tolerated that the present state of affairs should be renewed, that Germans must fight separately in every town and in every province for one and the same advance. Least of all is it to be tolerated that a form of property which still lags behind modern private property and everywhere is necessarily disintegrating into it – that communal property with the quarrels between poor and rich communities resulting from it, as well as communal civil law, with its trickery against the workers, which exists alongside state civil law, should be perpetuated by a so-called free communal constitution. As in France in 1793 so today in Germany, it is the task of the really revolutionary party to carry through the strictest centralisation.

We have seen how the democrats will come to power with the next movement, how they will be compelled to propose more or less socialist measures. It will be asked what measures the workers ought to propose in reply. At the beginning of the movement, of course, the workers cannot yet propose any directly communist measures. But they can:

1 Compel the democrats to interfere in as many spheres as possible of the hitherto existing social order, to disturb its regular course and to compromise themselves as well as to concentrate the utmost possible productive forces, means of transport, factories, railways, etc., in the hands of the state.
2 They must carry to the extreme the proposals of the democrats, who in any case will not act in a revolutionary but in a merely reformist manner, and transform them into direct attacks upon private property; thus, for example, if the petty bourgeois propose purchase of the railways and factories, the workers must demand that these railways and factories should be simply confiscated by the state without compensation as being the property of reactionaries. If the democrats propose proportional taxation, the workers must demand progressive taxation; if the democrats themselves put forward a moderately progressive taxation, the workers must insist on a taxation with rates that rise so steeply that big capital will be ruined by it; if the democrats demand the regulation of

state debts, the workers must demand state bankruptcy. Thus, the demands of the workers must everywhere be governed by the concessions and measures of the democrats.

If the German workers are not able to attain power and achieve their own class interests without completely going through a lengthy revolutionary development, they at least know for a certainty this time that the first act of this approaching revolutionary drama will coincide with the direct victory of their own class in France and will be very much accelerated by it.

But they themselves must do the utmost for their final victory by making it clear to themselves what their class interests are, by taking up their position as an independent party as soon as possible and by not allowing themselves to be misled for a single moment by the hypocritical phrases of the democratic petty bourgeois into refraining from the independent organisation of the party of the proletariat. Their battle cry must be: The Revolution in Permanence.

From: *Collected Works,* Vol. 10, pp. 277–87

12

The Eighteenth Brumaire of Louis Bonaparte

The articles collected as The Class Struggles in France *and* The Eighteenth Brumaire of Louis Bonaparte *constitute Marx's contemporary (and materialist) history of events in France in the immediate aftermath of the failed uprising of 1848, including the coup d'état of Louis Bonaparte in 1851. Here we include the most important sections from the* Eighteenth Brumaire. *It is notable, above all, for Marx's nuanced reading of the politics of class and class fractions, his characterization of the relationship between state and society, and his insistence upon 'smashing' rather than adapting the apparatus of the existing state. Few commentators on the vexed relationship between social structures and human agency have bettered Marx's pithy formulation: 'Men make their own history [but] they do not make it under circumstances chosen by themselves'.*

Hegel remarks somewhere that all facts and personages of great importance in world history occur, as it were, twice. He forgot to add: the first time as tragedy, the second as farce. Caussidière for Danton, Louis Blanc for Robespierre, the Montagne of 1848 to 1851 for the Montagne of 1793 to 1795, the Nephew for the Uncle. And the same caricature occurs in the circumstances attending the second edition of the eighteenth Brumaire!

Men make their own history, but they do not make it just as they please; they do not make it under circumstances chosen by themselves, but under circumstances directly encountered, given and transmitted from the past. The tradition of all the dead generations weighs like a nightmare on the brain of the living. And just when they seem engaged in revolutionising themselves and things, in creating something that has never yet existed, precisely in such periods of revolutionary crisis they anxiously conjure up the spirits of the past to their service and borrow from them names, battle-cries and costumes in order to present the new scene of world history in this time-honoured disguise and this borrowed language. Thus Luther donned the mask of the Apostle Paul, the revolution of 1789 to 1814 draped itself alternately as the Roman Republic and the Roman Empire, and the revolution of 1848 knew nothing better to do than to parody, now 1789, now the revolutionary tradition of 1793 to 1795. In like manner a beginner who has learnt a new language always translates it back into his mother tongue, but he has assimilated the spirit of the new language and can freely express himself in it only when he finds his way in it without recalling the old and forgets his native tongue in the use of the new.

Consideration of this world-historical necromancy reveals at once a salient difference. Camille Desmoulins, Danton, Robespierre, Saint-Just, Napoleon, the heroes as well as the parties and the masses of the old French Revolution, performed the task of their time in Roman costume and with Roman phrases, the task of unchaining and setting up modern *bourgeois* society. The first ones knocked the feudal basis to pieces and mowed off the feudal heads which had grown on it. The other created inside France the conditions under which free competition could first be developed, parcelled landed property exploited and the unchained industrial productive forces of the nation employed; and beyond the French borders he everywhere swept the feudal institutions away, so far as was necessary to furnish bourgeois society in France with a suitable up-to-date environment on the European Continent. The new social formation once established, the antediluvian Colossi disappeared and with them resurrected Romanity – the Brutuses, Gracchi, Publicolas, the tribunes, the senators, and Caesar himself. Bourgeois society in its sober reality had begotten its true interpreters and mouthpieces in the Says, Cousins, Royer-Collards, Benjamin Constants and Guizots; its real commanders sat behind the counter, and the hogheaded Louis XVIII was its political chief. Wholly absorbed in the production of wealth and in peaceful competitive struggle, it no longer comprehended that ghosts from the days of Rome had watched over its cradle. But unheroic as bourgeois society is, it nevertheless took heroism, sacrifice, terror, civil war and battles of peoples to bring it into being. And in the classically austere traditions of the Roman Republic its gladiators found the ideals and the art forms, the self-deceptions that they needed in order to conceal from themselves the bourgeois limitations of the content of their struggles and to maintain their passion on the high plane of great historical tragedy. Similarly, at another stage of development, a century earlier, Cromwell and the English people had borrowed speech, passions and illusions from the Old Testament for their bourgeois revolution. When the real aim had been achieved, when the bourgeois transformation of English society had been accomplished, Locke supplanted Habakkuk.

Thus the resurrection of the dead in those revolutions served the purpose of glorifying the new struggles, not of parodying the old; of magnifying the given task in imagination, not of fleeing from its solution in reality; of finding once more the spirit of revolution, not of making its ghost walk about again.

From 1848 to 1851 only the ghost of the old revolution walked about, from Marrast, the *republican in yellow gloves,* who disguised himself as the old Bailly, down to the adventurer who hides his commonplace repulsive features under the iron death mask of Napoleon. An entire people, which had imagined that by means of a revolution it had imparted to itself an accelerated power of motion, suddenly finds itself set back into a defunct epoch and, in order that no doubt as to the relapse may be possible, the old dates arise again, the old chronology, the old names, the old edicts, which had long become a subject of antiquarian erudition, and the old myrmidons of the law, who had seemed long decayed. The nation feels like that mad Englishman in Bedlam who fancies that he lives in the times of the ancient Pharaohs and daily bemoans the hard labour that he must perform in the Ethiopian mines as a gold digger, immured in this subterranean prison, a dimly burning lamp fastened to his head, the overseer of the slaves behind him with a long whip, and at the exits a confused welter of barbarian mercenaries, who understand neither the forced labourers in the mines nor one another, since they speak no common language. 'And all this is expected of me,' sighs the mad Englishman, 'of me, a freeborn Briton, in order to make gold for the old Pharaohs.' 'In order to pay the debts of the Bonaparte family,' sighs the French nation. The Englishman, so long as he was in his right mind, could not get rid of the fixed idea of making gold. The French, so long as they were engaged in revolution, could not get rid of the memory of Napoleon, as the election of December 10 proved. They hankered to return from the perils of revolution to the fleshpots of Egypt, and December 2, 1851 was the answer. They have not only a caricature of the old Napoleon, they have the old Napoleon himself, caricatured as he must appear in the middle of the nineteenth century.

The social revolution of the nineteenth century cannot draw its poetry from the past, but only from the future. It cannot begin with itself before it has stripped off all superstition about the past. Earlier revolutions required recollections of past world history in order to dull themselves to their own content. In order to arrive at its own content, the revolution of the nineteenth century must let the dead bury their dead. There the words went beyond the content; here the content goes beyond the words.

The February revolution was a surprise attack, a *taking* of the old society *unawares,* and the people proclaimed this unexpected *coup de main* as a deed of historic importance, ushering in the new epoch. On December 2 the February revolution is conjured away by a cardsharper's trick, and what seems overthrown is no longer the monarchy but the liberal concessions that were wrung from it by centuries of struggle. Instead of *society* having conquered a new content for itself, it seems that the *state* only returned to its oldest form, to the shamelessly simple domination of the sabre and the cowl. This is the answer to the *coup de main* of February 1848, given by the *coup de tête*[1] of December 1851. Easy come, easy go. Meanwhile the intervening time has not passed by unused. During the years 1848 to 1851 French society made up, and that by an abbreviated because revolutionary method, for the studies and experiences which, in a regular, so to speak, textbook course of development, would have had to precede the February revolution, if it was to be more than a ruffling of the surface. Society now seems to have fallen back behind its point of departure; it has in truth first to create for itself the revolutionary point of departure, the situation, the relations, the conditions under which alone modern revolution becomes serious.

Bourgeois revolutions, like those of the eighteenth century, storm swiftly from success to success, their dramatic effects outdo each other, men and things seem set in sparkling brilliants, ecstasy is the everyday spirit, but they are short-lived, soon they have attained their zenith, and a long crapulent depression seizes society before it learns soberly to assimilate the results of its storm-and-stress period. On the other hand, proletarian revolutions, like those of the nineteenth century, criticise themselves constantly, interrupt themselves continually in their own course, come back to the apparently accomplished in order to begin it afresh, deride with unmerciful thoroughness the inadequacies, weaknesses and paltrinesses of their first attempts, seem to throw down their adversary only in order that he may draw new strength from the earth and rise again, more gigantic, before them, and recoil again and again from the indefinite prodigiousness of their own aims, until a situation has been created which makes all turning back impossible, and the conditions themselves cry out:

Hic Rhodus, hic salta!
Here is the rose, here dance!

For the rest, every fairly competent observer, even if he had not followed the course of French development step by step, must have had a presentiment that an unheard-of fiasco was in store for the revolution. It was enough to hear the self-complacent howl of victory with which Messieurs the Democrats congratulated each other on the beneficial consequences of the second Sunday in May 1852. In their minds the second Sunday in May 1852 had become a fixed idea, a dogma, like the day on which Christ should reappear and the millennium begin, in the minds of the Chiliasts. As ever, weakness had taken refuge in a belief in miracles, fancied the enemy overcome when it had only conjured him away in imagination, and lost all understanding of the present in a passive glorification of the future in store for it and of the deeds it had in reserve but which it merely did not want as yet to make public. Those heroes who seek to disprove their proven incapacity by offering each other their sympathy and getting together in a crowd had tied up their bundles, collected their laurel wreaths in advance and were just then engaged in discounting on the exchange market the republics *in partibus* for which they had already providently organised the government personnel with all the calm of their unassuming disposition. December 2 struck them like a thunderbolt from a clear sky, and the peoples that in periods of pusillanimous depression gladly let their inward apprehension be drowned out by the loudest bawlers will have perhaps convinced themselves that the times are past when the cackle of geese could save the Capitol.

The Constitution, the National Assembly, the dynastic parties, the blue and the red republicans, the heroes of Africa, the thunder from the platform, the sheet lightning of the daily press, the entire literature, the political names and the intellectual reputations, the civil law and the penal code, the *liberté, égalité, fraternité* and the second Sunday in May 1852 – all has vanished like a phantasmagoria before the spell of a man whom even his enemies do not make out to be a magician. Universal suffrage seems to have survived only for a moment, in order that with its own hand it may make its last will and testament before the eyes of all the world and declare in the name of the people itself: 'All that comes to birth is fit for overthrow, as nothing worth.'

It is not enough to say, as the French do, that their nation was taken unawares. A nation and a woman are not forgiven the unguarded hour in which the first adventurer that came along could violate them. The riddle is not solved by such turns of speech, but merely formulated differently. It remains to be explained how a nation of thirty-six million can be surprised and delivered unresisting into captivity by three swindlers.

Let us recapitulate in general outline the phases that the French Revolution went through from 24 February 1848 to December 1851.

Three main periods are unmistakable: *the February period*; 4 May 1848 to 28 May 1849: *the period of the constitution of the republic* or *of the Constituent National Assembly*; 28 May 1849 to 2 December 1851: *the period of the constitutional republic* or *of the Legislative National Assembly*.

The *first period*, from February 24, or the overthrow of Louis Philippe, to 4 May 1848, the meeting of the Constituent Assembly, the *February period* proper, may be described as the *prologue* to the revolution. Its character was officially expressed in the fact that the government improvised by it, declared itself that it was *provisional* and, like the government, everything that was mooted, attempted or enunciated during this period proclaimed itself to be only *provisional.* Nothing and nobody ventured to lay claim to the right of existence and of real action. All the elements that had prepared or determined the revolution, the dynastic opposition, the republican bourgeoisie, the democratic-republican petty bourgeoisie and the Social-Democratic workers, provisionally found their place in the February *government.*

It could not be otherwise. The February days originally aimed at an electoral reform, by which the circle of the politically privileged among the possessing class itself was to be widened and the exclusive domination of the finance aristocracy overthrown. When it came to the actual conflict, however, when the people mounted the barricades, the National Guard maintained a passive attitude, the army offered no serious resistance and the monarchy ran away, the republic appeared to be a matter of course. Every party construed it in its own way. Having secured it arms in hand, the proletariat impressed its stamp upon it and proclaimed it to be a *social republic.* There was thus indicated the general content of the modern revolution, a content which was in most singular contradiction to everything that, with the material available, with the degree of education attained by the masses, under the given circumstances and relations, could be immediately realised in practice. On the other hand, the claims of all the remaining elements that had collaborated in the February revolution were recognised by the lion's share that they obtained in the government. In no period do we, therefore, find a more confused mixture of high-flown phrases and actual uncertainty and clumsiness, of more enthusiastic striving for innovation and more thorough domination of the old routine, of more apparent harmony of the whole of society and more profound estrangement of its elements. While the Paris proletariat still revelled in the vision of the wide prospects that had opened before it and indulged in earnest discussions on social problems, the old forces of society had grouped themselves, rallied, reflected and found unexpected support in the mass of the nation, the peasants and petty bourgeois, who all at once stormed on to the political stage, after the barriers of the July monarchy had fallen.

The *second period,* from 4 May 1848 to the end of May 1849, is the period of the *constitution,* the *foundation, of the bourgeois republic.* Directly after the February days not only had the dynastic opposition been surprised by the republicans and the republicans by the Socialists, but all France by Paris. The National Assembly, which met on 4 May 1848, had emerged from the national elections and represented the nation. It was a living protest against the aspirations of the February days and was to reduce the results of the revolution to the bourgeois scale. In vain the Paris proletariat, which immediately grasped the character of this National Assembly, attempted on May 15, a few days after it met, forcibly to negate its existence, to dissolve it, to disintegrate again into its constituent parts the organic form in which the proletariat was threatened by the reacting spirit of the nation. As is known, May 15 had no other result save that of removing Blanqui and his comrades, that is, the real leaders of the proletarian party, from the public stage for the entire duration of the cycle we are considering.

The *bourgeois monarchy* of Louis Philippe can be followed only by a *bourgeois republic*, that is to say, whereas a limited section of the bourgeoisie ruled in the name of the king, the whole of the bourgeoisie will now rule on behalf of the people. The demands of the Paris proletariat are utopian nonsense, to which an end must be put. To this declaration of the Constituent National Assembly the Paris proletariat replied with the *June insurrection*, the most colossal event in the history of European civil wars. The bourgeois republic triumphed. On its side stood the finance aristocracy, the industrial bourgeoisie, the middle class, the petty bourgeois, the army, the lumpenproletariat organised as the Mobile Guard, the intellectuals, the clergy and the rural population. On the side of the Paris proletariat stood none but itself. More than 3,000 insurgents were butchered after the victory, and 15,000 were deported without trial. With this defeat the proletariat recedes into the *background* of the revolutionary stage. It attempts to press forward again on every occasion, as soon as the movement appears to make a fresh start, but with ever decreased expenditure of strength and always slighter results. As soon as one of the social strata situated above it gets into revolutionary ferment, the proletariat enters into an alliance with it and so shares all the defeats that the different parties suffer, one after another. But these subsequent blows become the weaker, the greater the surface of society over which they are distributed. The more important leaders of the proletariat in the Assembly and in the press successively fall victim to the courts, and ever more equivocal figures come to head it. In part it throws itself into *doctrinaire experiments, exchange banks and workers' associations, hence into a movement in which it renounces the revolutionising of the old world by means of the latter's own great, combined resources, and seeks, rather, to achieve its salvation behind society's back, in private fashion, within its limited conditions of existence, and hence necessarily suffers shipwreck.* It seems to be unable either to rediscover revolutionary greatness in itself or to win new energy from the connections newly entered into, until *all classes* with which it contended in June themselves lie prostrate beside it. But at least it succumbs with the honours of the great, world-historic struggle; not only France, but all Europe trembles at the June earthquake, while the ensuing defeats of the upper classes are so cheaply bought that they require barefaced exaggeration by the victorious party to be able to pass for events at all, and become the more ignominious the further the defeated party is from the proletarian party.

The defeat of the June insurgents, to be sure, had indeed prepared and levelled the ground on which the bourgeois republic could be founded and built up, but it had shown at the same time that in Europe the questions at issue are other than that of 'republic or monarchy'. It had revealed that here *bourgeois republic* signifies the unlimited despotism of one class over other classes. It had proved that in countries with an old civilisation, with a developed formation of classes, with modern conditions of production and with an intellectual consciousness in which all traditional ideas have been dissolved by the work of centuries, *the republic* signifies *in general only the political form of the revolutionising of bourgeois society* and not its *conservative form of life*, as, for example, in the United States of North America, where, though classes already exist, they have not yet become fixed, but continually change and interchange their component elements in constant flux, where the modern means of production, instead of coinciding with a stagnant surplus population, rather compensate for the relative deficiency of heads and hands, and where, finally, the feverish, youthful movement of material production, which has to make a new world its own, has left neither time nor opportunity for abolishing the old spirit world.

During the June days all classes and parties had united in the *Party of Order* against the proletarian class as the *Party of Anarchy*, of socialism, of communism. They had 'saved' society from '*the enemies of society*'. They had given out the watch-words of the old society, '*property, family, religion, order*', to their army as passwords and had proclaimed to the counter-revolutionary crusaders: 'By this sign thou shalt conquer!' From this moment, as soon as one of the numerous parties which had gathered under this sign against the June insurgents seeks to hold the revolutionary battlefield in its own class interest, it goes down before the cry: 'Property, family, religion, order.' Society is saved just as often as the circle of its rulers contracts, as a more exclusive interest is maintained against a wider one. Every demand of the simplest bourgeois financial reform, of the most ordinary liberalism, of the most formal republicanism, of the most shallow democracy, is simultaneously castigated as an 'attempt on society' and stigmatised as 'socialism'. And, finally, the high priests of 'religion and order' themselves are driven with kicks from their Pythian tripods, hauled out of their beds in the darkness of night, put in prison-vans, thrown into dungeons or sent into exile; their temple is razed to the ground, their mouths are sealed, their pens broken, their law torn to pieces in the name of religion, of property, of the family, of order. Bourgeois fanatics for order are shot down on their balconies by mobs of drunken soldiers, their domestic sanctuaries profaned, their houses bombarded for amusement –

in the name of property, of the family, of religion and of order. Finally, the scum of bourgeois society forms the *holy phalanx of order* and the hero Krapülinski installs himself in the Tuileries as the *'saviour of society'*.

[. . .]

On the threshold of the February revolution, the *social republic* appeared as a phrase, as a prophecy. In the June days of 1848, it was drowned in the blood of the *Paris proletariat*, but it haunts the subsequent acts of the drama like a ghost. The *democratic republic* announces its arrival. On June 13, 1849 it is dissipated together with its *petty bourgeois*, who have taken to their heels, but in its flight it blows its own trumpet with redoubled boastfulness. The *parliamentary republic*, together with the bourgeoisie, takes possession of the entire stage; it enjoys its existence to the full, but December 2, 1851 buries it to the accompaniment of the anguished cry of the coalitioned royalists: 'Long live the Republic!'

The French bourgeoisie balked at the power of the working proletariat; it has brought the lumpenproletariat to power, with the chief of the Society of December 10 at the head. The bourgeoisie kept France in breathless fear of the future terrors of red anarchy; Bonaparte discounted this future for it when, on December 4, he had the eminent bourgeois of the Boulevard Montmartre and the Boulevard des Italiens shot down at their windows by the liquor-inspired army of order. The bourgeoisie apotheosised the sword; the sword rules it. It destroyed the revolutionary press; its own press has been destroyed. It placed popular meetings under police supervision; its salons are under the supervision of the police. It disbanded the democratic National Guards; its own National Guard is disbanded. It imposed a state of siege; a state of siege is imposed upon it. It supplanted the juries by military commissions; its juries are supplanted by military commissions. It subjected public education to the sway of the priests; the priests subject it to their own education. It transported people without trial; it is being transported without trial. It repressed every stirring in society by means of the state power; every stirring in its society is suppressed by the state power. Out of enthusiasm for its purse, it rebelled against its own politicians and men of letters; its politicians and men of letters are swept aside, but its purse is being plundered now that its mouth has been gagged and its pen broken. The bourgeoisie never wearied of crying out to the revolution what Saint Arsenius cried out to the Christians: *'Fuge, tace, quiesce!* Flee, be silent, keep still!' Bonaparte cries to the bourgeoisie: *'Fuge, tace, quiesce!* Flee, be silent, keep still!'

The French bourgeoisie had long ago found the solution to Napoleon's dilemma: 'In fifty years Europe will be republican or Cossack.' It had found the solution to it in the 'Cossack republic'. No Circe, by means of black magic, has distorted that work of art, the bourgeois republic, into a monstrous shape. That republic has lost nothing but the semblance of respectability. Present-day France was contained in a finished state within the parliamentary republic. It only required a bayonet thrust for the abcess to burst and the monster to spring forth before our eyes.

The immediate aim of the February revolution was to overthrow the Orleans dynasty and that part of the bourgeoisie which ruled under it. It was not until December 2, 1851 that this aim was achieved. Then the immense possessions of the house of Orleans, the real basis of its influence, were confiscated, and what had been expected after the February revolution came to pass after December: the imprisonment, flight, deposition, banishment, disarming and humiliation of the men who from 1830 on had wearied France with their appeals. But only part of the commercial bourgeoisie ruled under Louis Philippe. Its other factions formed a dynastic and a republican opposition or stood entirely outside the so-called legal country. Only the parliamentary republic included all factions of the commercial bourgeoisie in its political sphere. Moreover, under Louis Philippe the commercial bourgeoisie excluded the landowning bourgeoisie. Only the parliamentary republic placed them side by side as possessing equal rights, wedded the July monarchy to the Legitimist monarchy and amalgamated two epochs of the rule of property into one. Under Louis Philippe the privileged part of the bourgeoisie concealed its rule beneath the crown; in the parliamentary republic the rule of the bourgeoisie – after it had united all its elements and made its empire the empire of its class – revealed itself. So the revolution had first created the form in which the rule of the bourgeois class received its broadest, most general and ultimate expression and could therefore also be overthrown, without being able to rise again.

Only now was the sentence executed which was passed in February upon the Orleanist bourgeoisie, i.e. the most viable faction of the French bourgeoisie. Now a crushing blow was struck at its parliament, its legal courts, its commercial courts, its provincial representations, its notary's office, its university, its tribune and its tribunals, its press and its literature, its administrative income and its court fees, its army salaries and its state pensions, in its spirit and in its body. *Blanqui* had made the disbanding of the bourgeois guards the first demand on the revolution, and the bourgeois guards, who in February extended their hand to the revolution in order to hinder its progress, disappeared from the scene in December. The Pantheon itself is again turned into an ordinary church. With the last form of the bourgeois regime, the spell too has been broken which transfigured its eighteenth-century founders into saints. Therefore when on December 2 Guizot learned about the success of the coup d'état, he exclaimed: *C'est le triomphe complet et définitif du socialisme! This is the complete and final triumph of socialism!* That means: this is the final and complete collapse of the rule of the bourgeoisie.[2]

Why did the Paris proletariat not rise in revolt after December 2?

The overthrow of the bourgeoisie had as yet been only decreed: the decree had not been carried out. Any serious insurrection of the proletariat would at once have put fresh life into the bourgeoisie, would have reconciled it with the army and ensured a second June defeat for the workers.

On December 4 the proletariat was incited by bourgeois and *épicier*[3] to fight. On the evening of that day several legions of the National Guard promised to appear, armed and uniformed, on the scene of battle. For the bourgeois and *épicier* had got wind of the fact that in one of his decrees of December 2 Bonaparte abolished the secret ballot and enjoined them to record their 'yes' or 'no' in the official registers after their names. The resistance of December 4 intimidated Bonaparte. During the night he caused placards to be posted on all the street corners of Paris, announcing the restoration of the secret ballot. The bourgeois and *épicier* believed that they had gained their end. Those who failed to appear next morning were the bourgeois and *épicier*.

By a *coup de main* during the night of December 1 to 2, Bonaparte had robbed the Paris proletariat of its leaders, the barricade commanders. An army without officers, averse to fighting under the banner of the Montagnards because of the memories of June 1848 and 1849 and May 1850, it left to its vanguard, the secret societies, the task of saving the insurrectionary honour of Paris, which the bourgeoisie had so unresistingly surrendered to the soldiery that, later on, Bonaparte could sneeringly give as his motive for disarming the National Guard – his fear that its arms would be turned against itself by the anarchists!

'It is the complete and definitive triumph of socialism'. Thus Guizot characterized December 2. But if the overthrow of the parliamentary republic contains within itself the germ of the triumph of the proletarian revolution, its immediate and palpable result was *the victory of Bonaparte over parliament, of the executive power over the legislative power, of force without words over the force of words*. In parliament the nation made its general will the law, that is, it made the law of the ruling class its general will. Before the executive power it renounces all will of its own and submits to the superior command of an alien will, to authority. The executive power, in contrast to the legislative power, expresses the heteronomy of a nation, in contrast to its autonomy. France, therefore, seems to have escaped the despotism of a class only to fall back beneath the despotism of an individual, and, what is more, beneath the authority of an individual without authority. The struggle seems to be settled in such a way that all classes, equally impotent and equally mute, fall on their knees before the rifle butt.

But the revolution is thorough. It is still journeying through purgatory. It does its work methodically. By December 2, 1851 it had completed one half of its preparatory work; it is now completing the other half. First it perfected the parliamentary power, in order to be able to overthrow it. Now that it has attained this, it perfects the *executive power*, reduces it to its purest expression, isolates it, sets it up against itself as the sole target, in order to concentrate all its forces of destruction against it. And when it has done this second half of its preliminary work, Europe will leap from its seat and exultantly exclaim: Well burrowed, old mole!

This executive power with its enormous bureaucratic and military organisation, with its extensive and artificial state machinery, with a host of officials numbering half a million, besides an army of another half million, this appalling parasitic body, which enmeshes the body of French society like a net and chokes all its pores, sprang up in the days of the absolute monarchy, with the decay of the feudal system, which it helped to hasten. The seignorial privileges of the landowners and towns became transformed into so many attributes of the state power, the feudal dignitaries into paid officials and the motley pattern of conflicting medieval plenary powers into the regulated plan of a state authority whose work is divided and centralised as in a factory. The first French Revolution, with its task of breaking all separate local, territorial, urban and provincial powers in order to create the civil unity of the nation, was bound to develop what the absolute monarchy had begun: the centralisation, but at the same time the extent, the attributes and the agents of governmental power. Napoleon perfected this state machinery. The Legitimist monarchy and the July monarchy added nothing but a greater division of labour, growing in the same measure as the division of labour within bourgeois society created new groups of interests, and, therefore, new material for state administration. Every *common* interest was straightway severed from society, counterposed to it as a higher, *general* interest, snatched from the activity of society's members themselves and made an object of government activity, whether it was a bridge, a schoolhouse and the communal property of a village community, or the railways, the national wealth and the national university of France. Finally, in its struggle against the revolution, the parliamentary republic found itself compelled to strengthen, along with the repressive measures, the resources and centralisation of governmental power. All revolutions perfected this machine instead of breaking it. The parties that contended in turn for domination regarded the possession of this huge state edifice as the principal spoils of the victor.

But under the absolute monarchy, during the first revolution, under Napoleon, bureaucracy was only the means of preparing the class rule of the bourgeoisie. Under the Restoration, under Louis Philippe, under the parliamentary republic, it was the instrument of the ruling class, however much it strove for power of its own.

Only under the second Bonaparte does the state seem to have made itself completely independent. As against civil society, the state machine has consolidated its position so thoroughly that the chief of the Society of December 10 suffices for its head, a casual adventurer from abroad, raised up as leader by a drunken soldiery, which he has bought with liquor and sausages, and which he must continually ply with more sausage. Hence the downcast despair, the feeling of most dreadful humiliation and degradation that oppresses the breast of France and makes her catch her breath. She feels dishonoured.

And yet the state power is not suspended in mid air. Bonaparte represents a class, and the most numerous class of French society at that, the *small-holding peasantry*.

Just as the Bourbons were the dynasty of big landed property and just as the Orleans were the dynasty of money, so the Bonapartes are the dynasty of the peasants, that is, the mass of the French people. Not the Bonaparte who submitted to the bourgeois parliament, but the Bonaparte who dispersed the bourgeois parliament is the chosen man of the peasantry. For three years the towns had succeeded in falsifying the meaning of the election of December 10 and in cheating the peasants out of the restoration of the empire. The election of December 10, 1848 has been consummated only by the coup d'état of December 2, 1851.

The small-holding peasants form a vast mass, the members of which live in similar conditions but without entering into manifold relations with one another. Their mode of production isolates them from one another instead of bringing them into mutual intercourse. The isolation is increased by France's bad means of communication and by the poverty of the peasants. Their field of production, the smallholding, admits of no division of labour in its cultivation, no application of science and, therefore, no diversity of development, no variety of talent, no wealth of social relationships. Each individual peasant family is almost self-sufficient; it itself directly produces the major part of its consumption and thus acquires its means of life more through exchange with nature than in intercourse with society. A smallholding, a peasant and his family; alongside them another smallholding, another peasant and another family. A few score of these make up a village, and a few score of villages make up a department. In this way, the great mass of the French nation is formed by simple addition of homologous magnitudes, much as potatoes in a sack form a sack of potatoes. Insofar as millions of families live under economic conditions of existence that separate their mode of life, their interests and their culture from those of the other classes, and put them in hostile opposition to the latter; they form a class. Insofar as there is merely a local interconnection among these small-holding peasants, and the identity of their interests begets no community, no national bond and no political organisation among them; they do not form a class. They are consequently incapable of enforcing their class interests in their own name, whether through a parliament or through a convention. They cannot represent themselves, they must be represented. Their representative must at the same time appear as their master, as an authority over them, as an unlimited governmental power that protects them against the other classes and sends them rain and sunshine from above. The political influence of the small-holding peasants, therefore, finds its final expression in the executive power subordinating society to itself.

Historical tradition gave rise to the belief of the French peasants in the miracle that a man named Napoleon would bring all the glory back to them. And an individual turned up who gives himself out as the man because he bears the name of Napoleon, as a result of the *Code Napoléon*, which lays down that Inquiry into paternity is forbidden. After a vagabondage of twenty years and after a series of grotesque adventures, the legend finds fulfilment and the man becomes Emperor of the French. The fixed idea of the Nephew was realised, because it coincided with the fixed idea of the most numerous class of the French people.

But, it may be objected, what about the peasant risings in half of France, the raids on the peasants by the army, the mass incarceration and transportation of peasants?

Since Louis XIV, France has experienced no similar persecution of the peasants 'for demagogic practices'.

But let there be no misunderstanding. The Bonaparte dynasty represents not the revolutionary, but the conservative peasant; not the peasant that strikes out beyond the condition of his social existence, the smallholding, but rather the peasant who wants to consolidate this holding; not the country folk who, linked up with the towns, want to overthrow the old order through their own energies, but on the contrary those who, in stupefied seclusion within this old order, want to see themselves and their smallholdings saved and favoured by the ghost of the empire. It represents not the enlightenment, but the superstition of the peasant; not his judgement, but his prejudice; not his future, but his past; not his modern Cévennes, but his modern Vendée.

The three years' rigorous rule of the parliamentary republic had freed a part of the French peasants from the Napoleonic illusion and had revolutionised them, even if only superficially; but the bourgeoisie violently repressed them whenever they set themselves in motion. Under the parliamentary republic the modern and the traditional consciousness of the French peasant contended for mastery. This progress took the form of an incessant struggle between the schoolmasters and the priests. The bourgeoisie struck down the schoolmasters. For the first time the peasants made efforts to behave independently in the face of the activity of the government. This was shown in the continual conflict between the *maires* and the prefects. The bourgeoisie deposed the *maires*. Finally, during the period of the parliamentary republic, the peasants of different localities rose against their own offspring, the army. The bourgeoisie punished them with states of siege and punitive expeditions. And this same bourgeoisie now cries out about the stupidity of the masses, the *vile multitude*, that has betrayed it to Bonaparte. It has itself forcibly strengthened the imperial sentiments of the peasant class, it conserved the conditions that form the birthplace of this peasant religion. The bourgeoisie, to be sure, is bound to fear the stupidity of the masses as long as they remain conservative, and the insight of the masses as soon as they become revolutionary.

In the risings after the coup d'état, a part of the French peasants protested, arms in hand, against their own vote of December 10, 1848. The school they had gone through since 1848 had sharpened their wits. But they had made themselves over to the underworld of history; history held them to their word, and the majority was still so prejudiced that in precisely the reddest departments the peasant population voted openly for Bonaparte. In its view, the National Assembly had hindered his progress. He had now merely broken the fetters that the towns had imposed on the will of the countryside. In some parts the peasants even entertained the grotesque notion of a convention side by side with Napoleon.

After the first revolution had transformed the peasants from semi-villeins into freeholders, Napoleon confirmed and regulated the conditions on which they could exploit undisturbed the soil of France which had only just fallen to their lot and slake their youthful passion for property. But what is now causing the ruin of the French peasant is his smallholding itself, the division of the land, the form of property which Napoleon consolidated in France. It is precisely the material conditions which made the French feudal peasant a small-holding peasant and Napoleon an emperor. Two generations have sufficed to produce the inevitable result: progressive deterioration of agriculture, progressive indebtedness of the agriculturist. The 'Napoleonic' form of property, which at the beginning of the nineteenth century was the condition for the liberation and enrichment of the French country folk, has developed in the course of this century into the law of their enslavement and pauperisation. And precisely this law is the first of the '*idées napoléoniennes*' which the second Bonaparte has to uphold. If he still shares with the peasants the illusion that the cause of their ruin is to be sought, not in this small-holding property itself, but outside it, in the influence of secondary circumstances, his experiments will burst like soap bubbles when they come in contact with the relations of production.

The economic development of small-holding property has radically changed the relation of the peasants to the other classes of society. Under Napoleon, the fragmentation of the land in the countryside supplemented free competition and the beginning of big industry in the towns. The peasant class was the ubiquitous protest against the landed aristocracy which had just been overthrown. The roots that small-holding property struck in French soil deprived feudalism of all nutriment. Its landmarks formed the natural fortifications of the bourgeoisie against any *coup de main* on the part of its old overlords. But in the course of the nineteenth century the feudal lords were replaced by urban usurers; the feudal obligation that went with the land was replaced by the mortgage; aristocratic landed property was replaced by bourgeois capital. The smallholding of the peasant is now only the pretext that allows the capitalist to draw profits, interest and rent from the soil, while leaving it to the tiller of the soil himself to see how he can extract his wages. The mortgage debt burdening the soil of France imposes on the French peasantry payment of an amount of interest equal to the annual interest on the entire British national debt. Small-holding property, in this enslavement by capital to which its development inevitably pushes forward, has transformed the mass of the French nation into troglodytes. Sixteen million peasants (including women and children) dwell in hovels, a large number of which have but one opening, others only two and the most favoured only three. And windows are to a house what the five senses are to the head. The bourgeois order, which at the beginning of the century set the state to stand guard over the newly arisen smallholding and manured it with laurels, has become a vampire that sucks out its blood and brains and throws them into the alchemist's cauldron of capital. The *Code Napoléon* is now nothing but a *codex* of distraints, forced sales and compulsory auctions. To the four million (including children, etc.) officially recognised paupers, vagabonds, criminals and prostitutes in France must be added five million who hover on the margin of existence and either have their haunts in the countryside itself or, with their rags and their children, continually desert the countryside for the towns and the towns for the countryside. The interests of the peasants, therefore, are no longer, as under Napoleon, in accord with, but in opposition to the interests of the bourgeoisie, to capital. Hence the peasants find their natural ally and leader in the *urban proletariat*, whose task is the overthrow of the bourgeois order. But *strong and unlimited government* – and this is the second '*idée napoléonienne*', which the second Napoleon has to carry out – is called upon to defend this 'material' order by force. This '*ordre matériel*' also serves as the catchword in all of Bonaparte's proclamations against the rebellious peasants.

Besides the mortgage which capital imposes on it, the small-holding is burdened by *taxes*. Taxes are the source of life for the bureaucracy, the army, the priests and the court, in short, for the whole apparatus of the executive power. Strong government and heavy taxes are identical. By its very nature, small-holding property forms a suitable basis for an all-powerful and innumerable bureaucracy. It creates a uniform level of relationships and persons over the whole surface of the land. Hence it also permits of uniform action from a supreme centre on all points of this uniform mass. It annihilates the aristocratic intermediate grades between the mass of the people and the state power. On all sides, therefore, it calls forth the direct interference of this state power and the interposition of its immediate organs. Finally, it produces an unemployed surplus population for which there is no place either on the land or in the towns, and which accordingly reaches out for state offices as a sort of respectable alms, and provokes the creation of state posts. By the new markets which he opened at the point of the bayonet, by the plundering of the Continent, Napoleon repaid the compulsory taxes with interest. These taxes were a spur to the industry of the peasant, whereas now they rob his industry of its last resources and complete his inability to resist pauperism. And an enormous bureaucracy, well-braided and well-fed, is the '*idée napoléonienne*' which is most congenial of all to the second Bonaparte. How could it be otherwise, seeing that alongside the actual classes of society he is forced to create an artificial caste, for which the maintenance of his regime becomes a bread-and-butter question? Accordingly, one of his first financial operations was the raising of officials' salaries to their old level and the creation of new sinecures.

Another '*idée napoléonienne*' is the domination of the *priests* as an instrument of government. But while in its accord with society, in its dependence on natural forces and its submission to the authority which protected it from above, the smallholding that had newly come into being was naturally religious, the smallholding that is ruined by debts, at odds with society and authority, and driven beyond its own limitations naturally becomes irreligious. Heaven was quite a pleasing accession to the narrow strip of land just won, especially as it makes the weather; it becomes an insult as soon as it is thrust forward as substitute for the smallholding. The priest then appears as only the anointed bloodhound of the earthly police – another '*idée napoléonienne*'. On the next occasion, the expedition against Rome will take place in France itself, but in a sense opposite to that of M. de Montalembert.

Lastly, the culminating point of the '*idées napoléoniennes*' is the preponderance of the *army*. The army was the *point d'honneur* of the smallholding peasants, it was they themselves transformed into heroes, defending their new possessions against the outer world, glorifying their recently won nationhood, plundering and revolutionising the world. The uniform was their own state dress; war was their poetry; the smallholding, extended and rounded off in imagination, was their fatherland, and patriotism the ideal form of their sense of property. But the enemies against whom the French peasant has now to defend his property are not the Cossacks; they are the bailiffs and the tax collectors. The smallholding lies no longer in the so-called fatherland, but in the register of mortgages. The army itself is no longer the flower of the peasant youth; it is the swamp-flower of the peasant lumpenproletariat. It consists in large measure of *remplaçants*, of substitutes, just as the second Bonaparte is himself only a *remplaçant*, the substitute for Napoleon. It now performs its deeds of valour by hunting down the peasants like chamois, and in organised drives, by doing *gendarme* duty, and if the internal contradictions of his system chase the chief of the Society of December 10 over the French border, his army, after some acts of brigandage, will reap, not laurels, but thrashings.

One sees: *all 'idées napoléoniennes' are ideas of the undeveloped small-holding in the freshness of its youth*; for the smallholding that has outlived its day they are an absurdity. They are only the hallucinations of its death struggle, words that are transformed into phrases, spirits transformed into ghosts. But the parody of the empire was necessary to free the mass of the French nation from the weight of tradition and to work out in pure form the opposition between the state power and society. With the progressive undermining of small-holding property, the state structure erected upon it collapses. The centralisation of the state that modern society requires arises only on the ruins of the military-bureaucratic government machinery which was forged in opposition to feudalism.

The condition of the French peasants provides us with the answer to the riddle of the *general elections of December 20 and 21*, which bore the second Bonaparte up Mount Sinai, not to receive laws, but to give them.

Manifestly, the bourgeoisie had now no choice but to elect Bonaparte. When the puritans at the Council of Constance complained of the dissolute lives of the popes and wailed about the necessity of moral reform, Cardinal Pierre d'Ailly thundered at them: 'Only the devil in person can still save the Catholic Church, and you ask for angels.' In like manner, after the coup d'état, the French bourgeoisie cried: Only the chief of the Society of December 10 can still save bourgeois society! Only theft can still save property; only perjury, religion; bastardy, the family; disorder, order!

As the executive authority which has made itself an independent power, Bonaparte feels it to be his mission to safeguard 'bourgeois order'. But the strength of this bourgeois order lies in the middle class. He looks on himself, therefore, as the representative of the middle class and issues decrees in this sense. Nevertheless, he is somebody solely due to the fact that he has broken the political power of this middle class and daily breaks it anew. Consequently, he looks on himself as the adversary of the political and literary power of the middle class. But by protecting its material power, he generates its political power anew. The cause must accordingly be kept alive; but the effect, where it manifests itself, must be done away with. But this cannot pass off without slight confusions of cause and effect, since in their interaction both lose their distinguishing features. New decrees that obliterate the border line. As against the bourgeoisie, Bonaparte looks on himself, at the same time, as the representative of the peasants and of the people in general, who wants to make the lower classes of the people happy within the framework of bourgeois society. New decrees that cheat the 'true Socialists' of their statecraft in advance. But, above all, Bonaparte looks on himself as the chief of the Society of December 10, as the representative of the lumpenproletariat, to which he himself, his entourage, his government and his army belong, and whose prime consideration is to benefit itself and draw California lottery prizes from the state treasury. And he vindicates his position as chief of the Society of December 10 with decrees, without decrees and despite decrees.

This contradictory task of the man explains the contradictions of his government, the confused, blind to-ing and fro-ing which seeks now to win, now to humiliate first one class and then another and arrays all of them uniformly against him, whose practical uncertainty forms a highly comical contrast to the imperious, categorical style of the government decrees, a style which is faithfully copied from the uncle.

Industry and trade, hence the business affairs of the middle class, are to prosper in hothouse fashion under the strong government. The grant of innumerable railway concessions. But the Bonapartist lumpenproletariat is to enrich itself. The initiated engage in jiggery-pokery on the *bourse* with the railway concessions. But no capital is forthcoming for the railways. Obligation of the Bank to make advances on railway shares. But, at the same time, the Bank is to be exploited for personal ends and therefore must be cajoled. Release of the Bank from the obligation to publish its report weekly. Leonine agreement of the Bank with the government. The people are to be given employment. Initiation of public works. But the public works increase the obligations of the people in respect of taxes. Hence reduction of the taxes by an onslaught on the *rentiers*, by conversion of the five percent bonds to four-and-a-half per cent. But, once more, the middle class must receive a sweetener. Therefore doubling of the wine tax for the people, who buy it retail and halving of the wine tax for the middle class, who drink it wholesale. Dissolution of the actual workers' associations, but promises of miracles of association in the future. The peasants are to be helped. Mortgage banks that expedite their getting into debt and accelerate the concentration of property. But these banks are to be used to make money out of the confiscated estates of the House of Orleans. No capitalist wants to agree to this condition, which is not in the decree, and the mortgage bank remains a mere decree, etc., etc.

Bonaparte would like to appear as the patriarchal benefactor of all classes. But he cannot give to one class without taking from another. Just as at the time of the Fronde it was said of the Duke of Guise that he was the most *obligeant* man in France because he had turned all his estates into his partisans' obligations to him, so Bonaparte would fain be the most *obligeant* man in France and turn all the property, all the labour of France into a personal obligation to himself. He would like to steal the whole of France in order to be able to make a present of her to France or, rather, in order to be able to buy France anew with French money, for as the chief of the Society of December 10 he must needs buy what ought to belong to him. And all the state institutions, the Senate, the Council of State, the legislative body, the Legion of Honour, the soldiers' medals, the wash-houses, the public works, the railways, the General Staff of the National Guard excluding privates, and the confiscated estates of the House of Orleans – all become parts of the institution of purchase. Every place in the army and in the government machine becomes a means of purchase. But the most important feature of this process, whereby France is taken in order to be given back, is the percentages that find their way into the pockets of the head and the members of the Society of December 10 during the transaction. The witticism with which Countess Lehon, the mistress of M. de Morny, characterised the confiscation of the Orleans estates: 'It is the first flight [theft] of the eagle', is applicable to every flight of this *eagle*, which is more like a *raven*. He himself and his adherents call out to one another daily like that Italian Carthusian admonishing the miser who, with boastful display, counted up the goods on which he could yet live for years to come: 'Thou countest thy goods, thou shouldst first count thy years.' Lest they make a mistake in the years, they count the minutes. A gang of shady characters push their way forward to the court, into the ministries, to the head of the administration and the army, a crowd of the best of whom it must be said that no one knows whence he comes, a noisy, disreputable, rapacious bohème that crawls into braided coats with the same grotesque dignity as the high dignitaries of Soulouque. One can visualise clearly this upper stratum of the Society of December 10, if one reflects that *Véron-Crevel* is its preacher of morals and *Granier de Cassagnac* its thinker. When Guizot, at the time of his ministry, utilised this Granier on a hole-and-corner newspaper against the dynastic opposition, he used to boast of him with the quip: '*C'est le roi des drôles,*' 'he is the king of buffoons.' One would do wrong to recall the Regency or Louis XV in connection with Louis Bonaparte's court and clique. For 'often already, France has experienced a government of mistresses; but never before a government of kept men'.

Driven by the contradictory demands of his situation and being at the same time, like a conjurer, under the necessity of keeping the public gaze fixed on himself, as Napoleon's substitute, by springing constant surprises, that is to say, under the necessity of executing a coup d'état *en miniature* every day, Bonaparte throws the entire bourgeois economy into confusion, violates everything that seemed inviolable to the revolution of 1848, makes some tolerant of revolution, others desirous of revolution, and produces actual anarchy in the name of order, while at the same time stripping its halo from the entire state machine, profanes it and makes it at once loathsome and ridiculous. The cult of the Holy Coat of Trier he duplicates in Paris with the cult of the Napoleonic imperial mantle. But when the imperial mantle finally falls on the shoulders of Louis Bonaparte, the bronze statue of Napoleon will crash from the top of the Vendôme Column.

From: *Collected Works*, vol. 11, pp. 103–112, 181–97

Notes

1 Rash act.
2 In the original text, these two paragraphs appear as footnotes.
3 Pejorative term for shopkeeper.

13

Letter to Weydemeyer

This brief fragment is famous for Marx's own evaluation of what was original in his contribution to socialist thought: the identity of classes with given periods in the development of society's productive forces and the necessity of a 'dictatorship of the proletariat' in the transition to a classless society.

[. . .]

Now as for myself, I do not claim to have discovered either the existence of classes in modern society or the struggle between them. Long before me, bourgeois historians had described the historical development of this struggle between the classes, as had bourgeois economists their economic anatomy. My own contribution was (1) to show that the *existence of classes* is merely bound up with *certain historical phases in the development of production*; (2) that the class struggle necessarily leads to the *dictatorship of the proletariat*; (3) that this dictatorship itself constitutes no more than a transition to the *abolition of all classes* and to a *classless society*. Ignorant louts such as Heinzen, who deny not only the struggle but the very existence of classes, only demonstrate that, for all their bloodthirsty, mock-humanist yelping, they regard the social conditions in which the bourgeoisie is dominant as the final product, the *non plus ultra* of history, and that they themselves are simply the servants of the bourgeoisie, a servitude which is the more revolting, the less capable are the louts of grasping the very greatness and transient necessity of the bourgeois regime itself.

[. . .]

Your

K. Marx

From: *Collected Works*, vol. 39, pp. 62, 65

14

Two Articles on India

It has often been argued that Marx's thinking was profoundly Eurocentric. Whilst an unrestrained critic of capitalism, he was an ardent admirer of the productive possibilities to which it had given rise and, so it is suggested, rather dismissive of the rights and claims of 'less developed' peoples. In some ways, his treatment of the rule of the British in India is characteristic. On the one hand, he denounces 'the profound hypocrisy and inherent barbarism of bourgeois civilization'. At the same time, he insists that 'the bourgeois period of history has to create the material basis of the new world'. In his view, the subjugation of peoples in the less developed parts of the globe may be a regrettable but unavoidable part of the wider transition towards a classless but highly industrialized world order.

[. . .]

England has broken down the entire framework of Indian society, without any symptoms of reconstitution yet appearing. This loss of his old world, with no gain of a new one, imparts a particular kind of melancholy to the present misery of the Hindoo, and separates Hindostan, ruled by Britain, from all its ancient traditions, and from the whole of its past history.

There have been in Asia, generally, from immemorial times, but three departments of Government; that of Finance, or the plunder of the interior; that of War, or the plunder of the exterior; and, finally, the department of Public Works. Climate and territorial conditions, especially the vast tracts of desert, extending from the Sahara, through Arabia, Persia, India, and Tartary, to the most elevated Asiatic highlands, constituted artificial irrigation by canals and water-works the basis of Oriental agriculture. As in Egypt and India, inundations are used for fertilizing the soil in Mesopotamia, Persia, etc.; advantage is taken of a high level for feeding irrigative canals. This prime necessity of an economical and common use of water, which, in the Occident, drove private enterprise to voluntary association, as in Flanders and Italy, necessitated, in the Orient where civilization was too low and the territorial extent too vast to call into life voluntary association, the interference of the centralizing power of Government. Hence an economical function devolved upon all Asiatic Governments, the function of providing public works. This artificial fertilization of the soil, dependent on a Central Government, and immediately decaying with the neglect of irrigation and drainage, explains the otherwise strange fact that we now find whole territories barren and desert that were once brilliantly cultivated, as Palmyra, Petra, the ruins in Yemen, and large provinces of Egypt, Persia, and Hindostan; it also explains how a single war of devastation has been able to depopulate a country for centuries, and to strip it of all its civilization.

Now, the British in East India accepted from their predecessors the department of finance and of war, but they have neglected entirely that of public works. Hence the deterioration of an agriculture which is not capable of being conducted on the British principle of free competition, of *laissez-faire* and *laissez-aller*. But in Asiatic empires we are quite accustomed to see agriculture deteriorating under one government and reviving again under some other government. There the harvests correspond to good or bad government, as they change in Europe with good or bad seasons. Thus the oppression and neglect of agriculture, bad as it is, could not be looked upon as the final blow dealt to Indian society by the British intruder, had it not been attended by a circumstance of quite different importance, a novelty in the annals of the whole Asiatic world. However changing the political aspect of India's past must appear, its social condition has remained unaltered since its remotest antiquity, until the first decennium of the 19th century.

[. . .]

Modern industry, resulting from the railway system, will dissolve the hereditary divisions of labor, upon which rest the Indian castes, those decisive impediments to Indian progress and Indian power.

All the English bourgeoisie may be forced to do will neither emancipate nor materially mend the social condition of the mass of the people, depending not only on the development of the productive powers, but on their appropriation by the people. But what they will not fail to do is to lay down the material premises for both. Has the bourgeoisie ever done more? Has it ever effected a progress without dragging individuals and people through blood and dirt, through misery and degradation?

The Indians will not reap the fruits of the new elements of society scattered among them by the British bourgeoisie, till in Great Britain itself the now ruling classes shall have been supplanted by the industrial proletariat, or till the Hindoos themselves shall have grown strong enough to throw off the English yoke altogether. At all events, we may safely expect to see, at a more or less remote period, the regeneration of that great and interesting country, whose gentle natives are, to use the expression of Prince Soltykov, even in the most inferior classes, 'more subtle and adroit than the Italians,' whose submission even is counterbalanced by a certain calm nobility, who, notwithstanding their natural langor, have astonished the British officers by their bravery, whose country has been the source of our languages, our religions, and who represent the type of the ancient German in the Jat, and the type of the ancient Greek in the Brahmin.

I cannot part with the subject of India without some concluding remarks.

The profound hypocrisy and inherent barbarism of bourgeois civilization lies unveiled before our eyes, turning from its home, where it assumes respectable forms, to the colonies, where it goes naked. They are the defenders of property, but did any revolutionary party ever originate agrarian revolutions like those in Bengal, in Madras, and in Bombay? Did they not, in India, to borrow an expression of that great robber, Lord Clive himself, resort to atrocious extortion, when simple corruption could not keep pace with their rapacity? While they prated in Europe about the inviolable sanctity of the national debt, did they not confiscate in India the dividends of the rajahs, who had invested their private savings in the Company's own funds? While they combatted the French revolution under the pretext of defending 'our holy religion,' did they not forbid, at the same time, Christianity to be propagated in India, and did they not, in order to make money out of the pilgrims streaming to the temples of Orissa and Bengal, take up the trade in the murder and prostitution perpetrated in the temple of Juggernaut? These are the men of 'Property, Order, Family, and Religion.'

The devastating effects of English industry, when contemplated with regard to India, a country as vast as Europe, and containing 150 millions of acres, are palpable and confounding. But we must not forget that they are only the organic results of the whole system of production as it is now constituted. That production rests on the supreme rule of capital. The centralization of capital is essential to the existence of capital as an independent power. The destructive influence of that centralization upon the markets of the world does but reveal, in the most gigantic dimensions, the inherent organic laws of political economy now at work in every civilized town. The bourgeois period of history has to create the material basis of the new world – on the one hand universal intercourse founded upon the mutual dependency of mankind, and the means of that intercourse; on the other hand the development of the productive powers of man and the transformation of material production into a scientific domination of natural agencies. Bourgeois industry and commerce create these material conditions of a new world in the same way as geological revolutions have created the surface of the earth. When a great social revolution shall have mastered the results of the bourgeois epoch, the market of the world and the modern powers of production, and subjected them to the common control of the most advanced peoples, then only will human progress cease to resemble that hideous, pagan idol, who would not drink the nectar but from the skulls of the slain.

From: *Collected Works,* Vol. 12, pp. 126–8, 221–2

15

Grundrisse

It was clear by 1850, that there was to be no early return to the revolutionary ferment of 1848. This was the period in which, however reluctantly, Marx 'withdrew to his study'. Much of the next twenty years was devoted to his detailed studies of the nature of capitalism, culminating in the first volume of Das Kapital *in 1867. The* Grundrisse *contains several hundred pages of preliminary notes on this topic. Written in 1857–8, they remained unpublished until the time of the Second World War and became available in an English translation only in the 1970s. Many of its ideas anticipate the arguments that were to appear in* Capital, *but others have disappeared in this later work. The introduction to the* Grundrisse *also makes it clear that what appears in the three volumes of* Capital *was only a fraction of a much more ambitious research project which Marx never lived to complete. Included here are sections on the methodology of political economy, on the character of labour in a postcapitalist society, on the nature of individual freedom and on the consequences of automation.*

The subject of our discussion is first of all *material* production. Individuals producing in society, thus the socially determined production of individuals, naturally constitutes the starting point. The individual and isolated hunter or fisher who forms the starting point with Smith and Ricardo belongs to the insipid illusions of the eighteenth century. They are adventure stories which do not by any means represent, as students of the history of civilisation imagine, a reaction against over-refinement and a return to a misunderstood natural life. They are no more based on such a naturalism than is Rousseau's *contrat social*, which makes naturally independent individuals come in contact and have mutual intercourse by contract. They are the fiction and only the aesthetic fiction of the small and great adventure stories. They are, rather, the anticipation of 'civil society', which had been in course of development since the sixteenth century and made gigantic strides towards maturity in the eighteenth. In this society of free competition the individual appears free from the bonds of nature, etc., which in former epochs of history made him part of a definite, limited human conglomeration. To the prophets of the eighteenth century, on whose shoulders Smith and Ricardo are still standing, this eighteenth-century individual, constituting the joint product of the dissolution of the feudal form of society and of the new forces of production which had developed since the sixteenth century, appears as an ideal whose existence belongs to the past; not as a result of history, but as its starting point. Since that individual appeared to be in conformity with nature and corresponded to their conception of human nature, he was regarded as a product not of history but of nature. This illusion has been characteristic of every new epoch in the past. Steuart, who, as an aristocrat, stood more firmly on historical ground and was in many respects opposed to the spirit of the eighteenth century, escaped this simplicity of view.

The further back we go into history, the more the individual and, therefore, the producing individual seems to depend on and belong to a larger whole: at first it is, quite naturally, the family and the clan, which is but an enlarged family; later on, it is the community growing up in its different forms out of the clash and the amalgamation of clans. It is only in the eighteenth century, in 'civil society', that the different forms of social union confront the individual as a mere means to his private ends, as an external necessity. But the period in which this view of the isolated individual becomes prevalent is the very one in which the interrelations of society (general from this point of view) have reached the highest state of development. Man is in the most literal sense of the word a *zoon politikon*, not only a social animal, but an animal which can develop into an individual only in society. Production by isolated individuals outside society – something which might happen as an exception to a civilised man who by accident got into the wilderness and already potentially possessed within himself the forces of society – is as great an absurdity as the idea of the development of language without individuals living together and talking to one another. We need not dwell on this any longer. It would not be necessary to touch upon this point at all, had not this nonsense – which however was justified and made sense in the eighteenth century – been transplanted, in all seriousness, into the field of political economy by Bastiat, Carey, Proudhon and others. Proudhon and others naturally find it very pleasant, when they do not know the historical origin of a certain economic phenomenon, to give it a quasi-historico-philosophical explanation by going into mythology. Adam or Prometheus hit upon the scheme cut and dried, whereupon it was adopted, etc. Nothing is more tediously dry than the dreaming platitude.

Whenever we speak, therefore, of production, we always have in mind production at a certain stage of social development, or production by social individuals. Hence, it might seem that in order to speak of production at all, we must either trace the historical process of development through its various phases, or declare at the outset that we are dealing with a certain historical period, as, for example, with modern capitalist production, which, as a matter of fact, constitutes the proper subject of this work. But all stages of production have certain landmarks in common, common purposes. 'Production in general' is an abstraction, but it is a rational abstraction, in so far as it singles out and fixes the common features, thereby saving us repetition. Yet these general or common features discovered by comparison constitute something very complex, whose constituent elements have different destinations. Some of these elements belong to all epochs, others are common to a few. Some of them are common to the most modern as well as to the most ancient epochs. No production is conceivable without them; but while even the most completely developed languages have laws and conditions in common with the least developed ones, what is characteristic of their development are the points of departure from the general and common. The conditions which generally govern production must be differentiated in order that the essential points of difference should not be lost sight of in view of the general uniformity which is due to the fact that the subject, mankind, and the object, nature, remain the same. The failure to remember this one fact is the source of all the wisdom of modern economists who are trying to prove the eternal nature and harmony of existing social conditions.

[. . .]

When we consider a given country from a politico-economic standpoint, we begin with its population, its subdivision into classes, location in city, country or by the sea, occupation in different branches of production; then we study its exports and imports, annual production and consumption, prices of commodities, etc. It seems to be the correct procedure to commence with the real and the concrete, the actual prerequisites; in the case of political economy, to commence with population, which is the basis and the author of the entire productive activity of society. Yet on closer consideration it proves to be wrong. Population is an abstraction, if we leave out for example the classes of which it consists. These classes, again, are but an empty word unless we know what are the elements on which they are based, such as wage-labour, capital, etc. These imply, in their turn, exchange, division of labour, prices, etc. Capital, for example, does not mean anything without wage-labour, value, money, price, etc. If we start out, therefore, with population, we do so with a chaotic conception of the whole, and by closer analysis we will gradually arrive at simpler ideas; thus we shall proceed from the imaginary concrete to less and less complex abstractions, until we arrive at the simplest determinations. This once attained, we might start on our return journey until we finally came back to population, but this time not as a chaotic notion of an integral whole, but as a rich aggregate of many determinations and relations. The former method is the one which political economy had adopted in the past as its inception. The economists of the seventeenth century, for example, always started out with the living aggregate: population, nation, state, several states, etc., but in the end they invariably arrived by means of analysis at certain leading abstract general principles such as division of labour, money, value, etc. As soon as these separate elements had been more or less established by abstract reasoning, there arose the systems of political economy which start from simple conceptions such as labour, division of labour, demand, exchange value, and conclude with state, international exchange and world market. The latter is manifestly the scientifically correct method. The concrete is concrete because it is a combination of many determinations, i.e. a unity of diverse elements. In our thought it therefore appears as a process of synthesis, as a result, and not as a starting point, although it is the real starting point and, therefore, also the starting point of observation and conception. By the former method the complete conception passes into an abstract definition; by the latter the abstract definitions lead to the reproduction of the concrete subject in the course of reasoning. Hegel fell into the error, therefore, of considering the real as the result of self-co-ordinating, self-absorbed and spontaneously operating thought, while the method of advancing from the abstract to the concrete is but the way of thinking by which the concrete is grasped and is reproduced in our mind as concrete. It is by no means, however, the process which itself generates the concrete. The simplest economic category, say, exchange value, implies the existence of population, population that is engaged in production under certain conditions; it also implies the existence of certain types of family, clan or state, etc. It can have no other existence except as an abstract one-sided relation of an already given concrete and living aggregate.

As a category, however, exchange value leads an antediluvian existence. Thus the consciousness for which comprehending thought is what is most real in man, for which the world is only real when comprehended (and philosophical consciousness is of this nature), mistakes the movement of categories for the real act of production (which unfortunately receives only its impetus from outside), whose result is the world; that is true – here we have, however, again a tautology – in so far as the concrete aggregate, as a thought aggregate, the concrete subject of our thought, is in fact a product of thought, of comprehension; not, however, in the sense of a product of a self-emanating conception which works outside of and stands above observation and imagination, but of a conceptual working-over of observation and imagination. The whole, as it appears in our heads as a thought-aggregate, is the product of a thinking mind which grasps the world in the only way open to it, a way which differs from the one employed by the artistic, religious or practical mind. The concrete subject continues to lead an independent existence after it has been grasped, as it did before, outside the head, so long as the head contemplates it only speculatively, theoretically. So that in the employment of the theoretical method in political economy, the subject, society, must constantly be kept in mind as the premise from which we start.

But have these simple categories no independent historical or natural existence antedating the more concrete ones? That depends. For instance in his *Philosophy of Right* Hegel rightly starts out with possession, as the simplest legal relation of individuals. But there is no such thing as possession before the family or the relations of lord and serf, which relations are a great deal more concrete, have come into existence. On the other hand, one would be right in saying that there are families and clans which only *possess*, but do not *own* things. The simpler category thus appears as a relation of simple family and clan communities with respect to property. In society the category appears as a simple relation of a developed organisation, but the concrete substratum from which the relation of possession springs is always implied. One can imagine an isolated savage in possession of things. But in that case possession is no legal relation. It is not true that the family came as the result of the historical evolution of possession. On the contrary, the latter always implies the existence of this 'more concrete category of law'. Yet this much may be said, that the simple categories are the expression of relations in which the less developed concrete entity may have been realised without entering into the manifold relations and bearings which are mentally expressed in the concrete category; but when the concrete entity attains fuller development it will retain the same category as a subordinate relation.

Money may exist and actually had existed in history before capital or banks or wage-labour came into existence. With that in mind, it may be said that the more simple category can serve as an expression of the predominant relations of an undeveloped whole or of the subordinate relations of a more developed whole, relations which had historically existed before the whole developed in the direction expressed in the more concrete category. To this extent, the course of abstract reasoning, which ascends from the most simple to the complex, corresponds to the actual process of history.

On the other hand, it may be said that there are highly developed but historically less mature forms of society in which the highest economic forms are to be found, such as co-operation, advanced division of labour, etc., and yet there is no money in existence, e.g. Peru. In Slav communities also, money, as well as exchange to which it owes its existence, does not appear at all or very little within the separate communities, but it appears on their boundaries in their intercommunal traffic; in general, it is erroneous to consider exchange as a constituent element originating within the community. It appears at first more in the mutual relations between different communities than in those between the members of the same community. Furthermore, although money begins to play its part everywhere at an early stage, it plays in antiquity the part of a predominant element only in unidirectionally developed nations, viz. trading nations, and even in the most cultured antiquity, in Greece and Rome, it attains its full development, which constitutes the prerequisite of modern bourgeois society, only in the period of their decay. Thus this quite simple category attained its culmination in the past only at the most advanced stages of society. Even then it did not pervade all economic relations; in Rome for example at the time of its highest development, taxes and payments in kind remained the basis. As a matter of fact, the money system was fully developed there only so far as the army was concerned; it never came to dominate the entire system of labour. Thus, although the simple category may have existed historically before the more concrete one, it can attain its complete internal and external development only in complex forms of society, while the more concrete category has reached its full development in a less advanced form of society.

Labour is quite a simple category. The idea of labour in that sense, as labour in general, is also very old. Yet 'labour' thus simply defined by political economy is as much a modern category as the conditions which have given rise to this simple abstraction. The monetary system, for example, defines wealth quite objectively, as a thing external to itself in money. Compared with this point of view, it was a great step forward when the industrial or commercial system came to see the source of wealth not in the object but in the activity of persons, viz. in commercial and industrial labour. But even the latter was thus considered only in the limited sense of a money-producing activity. The physiocratic system marks still further progress in that it considers a certain form of labour, viz. agriculture, as the source of wealth, and wealth itself not in the disguise of money, but as a product in general, as the general result of labour. But corresponding to the limitations of the activity, this product is still only a natural product. Agriculture is productive, land is the source of production *par excellence*. It was a tremendous advance on the part of Adam Smith to throw aside all the limitations which mark wealth-producing activity and to define it as labour in general, neither industrial nor commercial nor agricultural, or one as much as the other. Along with the universal character of wealth-creating activity we now have the universal character of the object defined as wealth, viz. product in general, or labour in general, but as past, objectified labour. How difficult and how great was the transition is evident from the way Adam Smith himself falls back from time to time into the physiocratic system. Now it might seem as though this amounted simply to finding an abstract expression for the simplest relation into which men have been mutually entering as producers from times of yore, no matter under what form of society. In one sense this is true. In another it is not.

The indifference as to the particular kind of labour implies the existence of a highly developed aggregate of different species of concrete labour, none of which is any longer the predominant one. So the most general abstractions commonly arise only where there is the highest concrete development, where one feature appears to be jointly possessed by many and to be common to all. Then it cannot be thought of any longer in one particular form. On the other hand, this abstraction of labour is only the result of a concrete aggregate of different kinds of labour. The indifference to the particular kind of labour corresponds to a form of society in which individuals pass with ease from one kind of work to another, which makes it immaterial to them what particular kind of work may fall to their share. Labour has become here, not only categorially but really, a means of creating wealth in general and has no longer coalesced with the individual in one particular manner. This state of affairs has found its highest development in the most modern of bourgeois societies, the United States. It is only here that the abstraction of the category 'labour', 'labour in general', labour *sans phrase*, the starting point of modern political economy, becomes realised in practice. Thus the simplest abstraction which modern political economy sets up as its starting point, and which expresses a relation dating back to antiquity and prevalent under all forms of society, appears truly realised in this abstraction only as a category of the most modern society. It might be said that what appears in the United States as a historical product – viz. the indifference as to the particular kind of labour – appears among the Russians, for example, as a spontaneously natural disposition. But it makes all the difference in the world whether barbarians have a natural predisposition which makes them applicable alike to everything, or whether civilised people apply themselves to everything. And, besides, this indifference of the Russians as to the kind of work they do corresponds to their traditional practice of remaining in the rut of a quite definite occupation until they are thrown out of it by external influences.

This example of labour strikingly shows how even the most abstract categories, in spite of their applicability to all epochs – just because of their abstract character – are by the very definiteness of the abstraction a product of historical conditions as well, and are fully applicable only to and under those conditions.

Bourgeois society is the most highly developed and most highly differentiated historical organisation of production. The categories which serve as the expression of its conditions and the comprehension of its own organisation enable it at the same time to gain an insight into the organisation and the relationships of production which have prevailed under all the past forms of society, on the ruins and constituent elements of which it has arisen, and of which it still drags along some unsurmounted remains, while what had formerly been mere intimation has now developed to complete significance. The anatomy of the human being is the key to the anatomy of the ape. But the intimations of a higher animal in lower ones can be understood only if the animal of the higher order is already known. The bourgeois economy furnishes a key to ancient economy, etc. This is, however, by no means true of the method of those economists who blot out all historical differences and see the bourgeois form in all forms of society. One can understand the nature of tribute, tithes, etc., after one has learned the nature of rent. But they must not be considered identical.

Since, furthermore, bourgeois society is only a form resulting from the development of antagonistic elements, some relations belonging to earlier forms of society are frequently to be found in it, though in a crippled state or as a travesty of their former self, as for example communal property. While it may be said, therefore, that the categories of bourgeois economy contain what is true of all other forms of society, the statement is to be taken with a pinch of salt. They may contain these in a developed or crippled or caricatured form, but always essentially different. The so-called historical development amounts in the last analysis to this, that the last form considers its predecessors as stages leading up to itself and always perceives them from a single point of view, since it is very seldom and only under certain conditions that it is capable of self-criticism; of course, we do not speak here of such historical periods as appear to their own contemporaries to be periods of decay. The Christian religion became capable of assisting us to an objective view of past mythologies as soon as it was ready for self-criticism to a certain extent, potentially, so to speak. In the same way bourgeois political economy first came to understand the feudal, the ancient and the oriental societies as soon as the self-criticism of bourgeois society had commenced. In as far as bourgeois political economy has not gone into the mythology of identifying the bourgeois system purely with the past, its criticism of the feudal system against which it still had to wage war resembled Christian criticism of the heathen religions or Protestant criticism of Catholicism.

In the study of economic categories, as in the case of every historical and social science, it must be borne in mind that, as in reality so in our mind, the subject, in this case modern bourgeois society, is given, and that the categories are therefore only forms of being, manifestations of existence, and frequently only one-sided aspects of this subject, this definite society; and that, expressly for that reason, the origin of political economy *as a science* does not by any means date from the time to which it is referred to *as such*. This is to be firmly kept in mind because it has an immediate and important bearing on the matter of the subdivisions of the science.

For instance, nothing seems more natural than to start with rent, with landed property, since it is bound up with land, the source of all production and all existence, and with the first form of production in all more or less settled communities, viz. agriculture. But nothing would be more erroneous. Under all forms of society there is a certain industry which predominates over all the rest and whose condition therefore determines the rank and influence of all the rest.

It is the universal light with which all the other colours are tinged and by whose peculiarity they are modified. It is a special ether which determines the specific gravity of everything that appears in it.

Let us take for example pastoral nations (mere hunting and fishing tribes are not as yet at the point from which real development commences). They engage in a certain form of agriculture, sporadically. The nature of land-ownership is determined thereby. It is held in common and retains this form more or less according to the extent to which these nations hold on to traditions; such, for example, is land ownership among the Slavs. Among nations whose agriculture is carried on by a settled population – the settled state constituting a great advance – where agriculture is the predominant industry, such as in ancient and feudal societies, even the manufacturing industry and its organisations, as well as the forms of property which pertain to it, have more or less the characteristic features of the prevailing system of land ownership; society is then either entirely dependent upon agriculture, as in the case of ancient Rome, or, as in the Middle Ages, it imitates in its civic relations the forms of organisation prevailing in the country. Even capital, with the exception of pure money capital, has, in the form of the traditional working tool, the characteristics of land ownership in the Middle Ages.

The reverse is true of bourgeois society. Agriculture comes to be more and more merely a branch of industry and is completely dominated by capital. The same is true of rent. In all the forms of society in which land ownership is the prevalent form, the influence of the natural element is the predominant one. In those where capital predominates, the prevailing element is the one historically created by society. Rent cannot be understood without capital, whereas capital can be understood without rent. Capital is the all-dominating economic power of bourgeois society. It must form the starting point as well as the end and be developed before land ownership. After each has been considered separately, their mutual relation must be analysed.

It would thus be impractical and wrong to arrange the economic categories in the order in which they were the determining factors in the course of history. Their order of sequence is rather determined by the relation which they bear to one another in modern bourgeois society, and which is the exact opposite of what seems to be their natural order or the order of their historical development. What we are interested in is not the place which economic relations occupy in the historical succession of different forms of society. Still less are we interested in the order of their succession 'in the idea' (*Proudhon*), which is but a hazy conception of the course of history. We are interested in their organic connection within modern bourgeois society.

The sharp line of demarcation (abstract precision) which so clearly distinguished the trading nations of antiquity, such as the Phoenicians and the Carthaginians, was due to that very pre-dominance of agriculture. Capital as trading or money capital appears in that abstraction where capital does not constitute as yet the predominating element of society. The Lombards and the Jews occupied the same position among the agricultural societies of the Middle Ages.

As a further illustration of the fact that the same category plays different parts at different stages of society, we may mention the following: one of the latest forms of bourgeois society, viz. joint stock companies, appear also at its beginning in the form of the great chartered monopolistic trading companies.

The concept of national wealth which is imperceptibly formed in the minds of the economists of the seventeenth century, and which in part continues to be entertained by those of the eighteenth century, is that wealth is produced solely for the state, but that the power of the latter is proportional to that wealth. It was as yet an unconsciously hypocritical way in which wealth announced itself and its own production as the aim of modern states, considering the latter merely as a means to the production of wealth.

The order of treatment must manifestly be as follows: first, the general abstract definitions which are more or less applicable to all forms of society, but in the sense indicated above. Second, the categories which go to make up the inner organisation of bourgeois society and constitute the foundations of the principal classes: capital, wage-labour, landed property; their mutual relations; city and country; the three great social classes, the exchange between them; circulation, credit (private). Third, the organisation of bourgeois society in the form of the state, considered in relation to itself; the 'unproductive' classes; taxes; public debts; public credit; population; colonies; emigration. Fourth, the international organisation of production; international division of labour; international exchange; import and export; rate of exchange. Fifth, the world market and crises.

[. . .]

Exchange and the division of labour mutually condition one another. Given that everyone works for himself but that his product is not created for himself, he must of course exchange it, not only in order to obtain a share in general productive capacity, but in order to transform his own production into means of subsistence for himself. Exchange, negotiated through exchange value and money, implies a universal interdependence between the producers, but at the same time the complete isolation of their private interests and a division of social labour, whose unity and mutual fulfilment exists as an external, natural relationship, independent of the individuals. The tension between universal supply and demand constitutes the social network that binds the indifferent individuals together.

The very necessity of first transforming the product or the activity of the individuals into the form of *exchange value* or *money*, that they acquire and demonstrate their social power only in this material form, shows both that: (1) the individuals are now producing only in and for society; and (2) that their production is not directly social, not the offspring of an association that divides the labour among its members. The individuals are subordinated to social production, which exists externally to them, as a sort of fate; but social production is not subordinated to the individuals who manipulate it as their communal capacity.

Nothing, therefore, could be more incorrect and absurd than to presume, on the basis of exchange value and money, the control of associated individuals over their general production. . . .

The *private exchange* of all the products of labour, capacities and activities is opposed to the distribution founded on the spontaneous or political hierarchy of individuals within patriarchal, ancient or feudal societies (where exchange only plays a secondary role and hardly affects the entire life of communities, since it only occurs between them and does not dominate all the relationships of production and commerce). But private exchange is opposed just as much to the free exchange of associated individuals on the basis of collective appropriation and control of the means of production. (This last association is not arbitrary: it presupposes the development of material and intellectual conditions which cannot be discussed here.)

The division of labour results in concentration, co-ordination, co-operation, the antagonism of private interests and class interests, competition, the centralisation of capital, monopolies and joint stock companies – so many contradictory forms of unity which in turn engenders all these contradictions. In the same way private exchange creates world trade, private independence gives rise to complete dependence on the so-called world market, and the fragmented acts of exchange make a system of banks and credit necessary, whose accounts at least settle the balances of private exchange. National trade acquires a semblance of existence in the foreign exchange market – although the private interests within each nation divide them into as many nations as they possess full-grown individuals, and the interests of exporters and importers of the same nation are here opposed. No one would imagine that it was therefore possible to transform the foundations of internal and external trade by means of stock exchange reform. But within bourgeois society, which is founded on exchange value, relationships of commerce and production develop which are so many mines about to explode beneath them.

[. . .]

Considered in the act of production itself, the labour of the individual is used by him as money to buy the product directly, that is, the object of his own activity; but it is particular money, used to buy this particular product. In order to be money in general, it must originate from general and not special labour; that is, it must originally be established as an element of general production. But on this presupposition it is not basically exchange that gives it its general character, but its presupposed social character will determine its participation in the products. The social character of production would make the product from the start a collective and general product. The exchange originally found in production – which is an exchange not of exchange values but of activities determined by communal needs and communal aims – would from the start imply the participation of individuals in the collective world of products.

On the basis of exchange values, it is exchange that first makes of labour something general. In the other system labour is established as such before the exchange; that is, the exchange of products is not at all the medium by which participation of the individual in general production is brought about. There must of course be mediation. In the first case, we start with the autonomous production of private individuals (however much it is determined and modified subsequently by complex relationships) and mediation is carried out by the exchange of goods, exchange value and money, which are all expressions of one and the same relationship. In the second case, the presupposition itself is mediated, i.e. the precondition is collective production; the community is the foundation of production. The labour of the individual is established from the start as collective labour. But whatever the particular form of the product which he creates or helps to create, what he has bought with his labour is not this or that product, but a definite participation in collective production. Therefore he has no special product to exchange. His product is not an exchange value. The product does not have to change into any special form in order to have a general character for the individual. Instead of a division of labour necessarily engendered by the exchange of values, there is an organisation of labour, which has as its consequence the participation of the individual in collective consumption.

In the first case, the social character of production is established subsequently by the elevation of products to exchange values, and the exchange of these values. In the second case, the social character of production is a precondition, and participation in the world of production and in consumption is not brought about by the exchange of labour or the products of labour which are independent of it. It is brought about by the social conditions of production, within which the individual acts.

Thus the desire to turn individual labour directly into money (which also includes the product of labour), i.e. into a realised exchange value, means that the worker's labour must be designated as general labour. In other words, this means that those conditions are denied in which he must necessarily become money and exchange value, and is dependent on private exchange. This requirement can be satisfied only in conditions in which it is no longer set. On the basis of exchange values, neither the labour of the individual nor his product are directly general; to obtain this character, an objective mediation is required, money distinct from the product.

If we suppose communal production, the determination of time remains, of course, essential. The less time society requires in order to produce wheat, cattle, etc., the more time it gains for other forms of production, material or intellectual. As with a single individual, the universality of its development, its enjoyment and its activity depends on saving time. In the final analysis, all forms of economics can be reduced to an economics of time. Likewise, society must divide up its time purposefully in order to achieve a production suited to its general needs; just as the individual has to divide his time in order to acquire, in suitable proportions, the knowledge he needs or to fulfil the various requirements of his activity.

On the basis of community production, the first economic law thus remains the economy of time, and the methodical distribution of working time between the various branches of production; and this law becomes indeed of much greater importance. But all this differs basically from the measurement of exchange values (labour and the products of labour) by labour time. The work of individuals participating in the same branch of activity, and the different kinds of labour are not only quantitatively but also qualitatively different. What is the precondition of a merely quantitative difference between things? The fact that their quality is the same.

Thus units of labour can be measured quantitatively only if they are of equal and identical quality.

[. . .]

Thus on the one hand production which is founded on capital creates universal industry – i.e. surplus labour, value-producing labour; on the other hand it creates a system of general exploitation of natural human attributes, a system of general profitability, whose vehicles seem to be just as much science, as all the physical and intellectual characteristics. There is nothing which can escape, by its own elevated nature or self-justifying characteristics, from this cycle of social production and exchange. Thus capital first creates bourgeois society and the universal appropriation of nature and of social relationships themselves by the members of society. Hence the great civilising influence of capital, its production of a stage of society compared with which all earlier stages appear to be merely *local progress* and idolatry of nature. Nature becomes for the first time simply an object for mankind, purely a matter of utility; it ceases to be recognised as a power in its own right; and the theoretical knowledge of its independent laws appears only as a stratagem designed to subdue it to human requirements, whether as the object of consumption or as the means of production. Pursuing this tendency, capital has pushed beyond national boundaries and prejudices, beyond the deification of nature and the inherited, self-sufficient satisfaction of existing needs confined within well-defined bounds, and the reproduction of the traditional way of life. It is destructive of all this, and permanently revolutionary, tearing down all obstacles that impede the development of productive forces, the expansion of needs, the diversity of production and the exploitation and exchange of natural and intellectual forces.

But because capital sets up any such boundary as a limitation, and is thus *ideally* over and beyond it, it does not in any way follow that it has *really* surmounted it, and since any such limitation contradicts its vocation, capitalist production moves in contradictions which are constantly overcome, only to be, again, constantly re-established. Still more so. The universality towards which it is perpetually driving finds limitations in its own nature, which at a certain stage of its development will make it appear as itself the greatest barrier to this tendency, leading thus to its own self-destruction.

[. . .]

Although free competition has abolished the obstacles created by the relationships and means of pre-capitalist production, it should first be remembered that what were restrictions for capital were inherent frontiers for earlier means of production, within which they developed and moved naturally. These frontiers became obstacles only after productive forces and commercial relationships had sufficiently developed for capital to be the ruling principle of production. The frontiers that it tore down were obstacles to its own movement, development and realisation. It did not abolish all frontiers by any means, or all obstacles; only those that did not correspond to its needs, those that were obstacles for it. Within its own limitations – however much these may seem, from a higher point of view, to be obstacles in production, and have been fixed as such by the historical development of capital – it feels itself free and unhampered, that is, bounded only by itself, but its own conditions of existence.

In the same way the industry of the guilds in its heyday found that the guild organisation gave it the freedom it needed, i.e. the production relationships corresponding to it. Guild industry gave rise to these relationships, developing them as its own inherent conditions, and thus not at all as external, restricting obstacles. The historical aspect of the negation of guild industry, etc., by capital, by means of free competition, means nothing more than that capital, sufficiently strengthened by a means of circulation adequate for its nature, tore down the historical barriers which interfered with and restricted its movement. But competition is far removed from possessing merely this historical significance, or from playing merely this negative role. *Free competition* is the relation of capital to itself as another capital, i.e. it is the real behaviour of capital as such. It is only then that the internal laws of capital – which appear only as tendencies in the early historical stages of its evolution – can be established; production founded on capital only establishes itself in so far as free competition develops, since free competition is the free development of the conditions and means of production founded on capital and of the process which constantly reproduces these conditions. It is not individuals but capital that establishes itself freely in free competition. So long as production founded on capital is the necessary and therefore the most suitable form in which social productive forces can develop, the movement of individuals within the pure conditions of capital will seem to be free. This liberty is then assured dogmatically by constant reference to the barriers that have been torn down by free competition. Free competition expresses the real development of capital. Because of it, individual capital finds imposed upon itself an external necessity that corresponds to the nature of capital, to the means of production founded on it, to the concept of capital. The mutual constraint that different portions of capital impose on each other, on labour, etc. (the competition of workers between themselves is only another form of the competition of capital), is the *free* and at the same time the *real* development of wealth as capital. So much so, that the profoundest economic theorists, Ricardo for example, begin by *presuming* the absolute domination of free competition, in order to study and formulate the laws that are suitable to capital, laws which at the same time appear as the vital tendencies that dominate it. Free competition, however, is the form suitable to the productive process of capital. The more it develops, the more clearly the shape of its movement is seen. What Ricardo, for example, has thus recognised (despite himself) is the historical nature of capital, and the limited character of free competition, which is still only the free movement of portions of capital, i.e. their movement within conditions that have nothing in common with those of any dissolved preliminary stages, but are their own conditions. The domination of capital is the prerequisite of free competition, just as the despotism of the Roman emperors was the prerequisite of the free Roman civil law. So long as capital is weak, it will rely on crutches taken from past means of production or from means of production that are disappearing as it comes onto the scene. As soon as it feels strong, it throws the crutches away and moves according to its own laws. As soon as it begins to feel and to be aware that it is itself an obstacle to development, it takes refuge in forms that, although they appear to complete the mastery of capital, are at the same time, by curbing free competition, the heralds of its dissolution, and of the dissolution of the means of production which are based on it. What lies in the nature of capital is only expressed in reality as an external necessity through competition, which means no more than that the various portions of capital impose the inherent conditions of capital on one another and on themselves. No category of the bourgeois economy – not even the first one, the determination of value – can become real by means of free competition, i.e. through the real process of capital, which appears as the interaction of portions of capital on one another and of all the other relationships of production and circulation that are determined by capital.

Hence the absurdity of considering free competition as being the final development of human liberty, and the negation of free competition as being the negation of individual liberty and of social production founded on individual liberty. It is only free development on a limited foundation – that of the dominion of capital. This kind of individual liberty is thus at the same time the most complete suppression of all individual liberty and total subjugation of individuality to social conditions which take the form of material forces – and even of all-powerful objects that are independent of the individuals relating to them. The only rational answer to the deification of free competition by the middle-class prophets, or its diabolisation by the socialists, lies in its own development. If it is said that, within the limits of free competition, individuals by following their pure self-interest realise their social, or rather their general, interest, this means merely that they exert pressure upon one another under the conditions of capitalist production and that this clash between them can only give rise to the conditions under which their interaction took place. Moreover, once the illusion that competition is the supposedly absolute form of free individuality disappears, this proves that the conditions of competition, i.e. of production founded on capital, are already felt and thought of as a barrier, that they indeed already are such and will increasingly become so. The assertion that free competition is the final form of the development of productive forces, and thus of human freedom, means only that the domination of the middle class is the end of the world's history – of course quite a pleasant thought for yesterday's parvenus!

[. . .]

So long as the means of labour remains a means of labour, in the proper sense of the word, as it has been directly and historically assimilated by capital into its valorisation process, it only undergoes a formal change, in that it appears to be the means of labour not only from its material aspect, but at the same time as a special mode of existence of capital determined by the general process of capital – it has become *fixed capital*. But once absorbed into the production process of capital, the means of labour undergoes various metamorphoses, of which the last is the *machine*, or rather, an *automatic system of machinery* ('automatic' meaning that this is only the most perfected and most fitting form of the machine, and is what transforms the machinery into a system).

This is set in motion by an automaton, a motive force that moves of its own accord. The automaton consists of a number of mechanical and intellectual organs, so that the workers themselves can be no more than the conscious limbs of the automaton. In the machine and still more in machinery as an automatic system, the means of labour is transformed as regards its use value, i.e. as regards its material existence, into an existence suitable for fixed capital and capital in general; and the form in which it was assimilated as a direct means of labour into the production process of capital is transformed into one imposed by capital itself and in accordance with it. In no respect is the machine the means of labour of the individual worker. Its distinctive character is not at all, as with the means of labour, that of transmitting the activity of the worker to its object; rather this activity is so arranged that it now only transmits and supervises and protects from damage the work of the machine and its action on the raw material.

With the tool it was quite the contrary. The worker animated it with his own skill and activity; his manipulation of it depended on his dexterity. The machine, which possesses skill and force in the worker's place, is itself the virtuoso, with a spirit of its own in the mechanical laws that take effect in it; and, just as the worker consumes food, so the machine consumes coal, oil, etc. (instrumental material), for its own constant self-propulsion. The worker's activity, limited to a mere abstraction, is determined and regulated on all sides by the movement of the machinery, not the other way round. The knowledge that obliges the inanimate parts of the machine, through their construction, to work appropriately as an automaton, does not exist in the consciousness of the worker, but acts upon him through the machine as an alien force, as the power of the machine itself. The appropriation of living labour by objectified labour – of valorising strength or activity by self-sufficient value – which is inherent in the concept of capital, is established as the character of the production process itself – when production is based on machinery – as a function of its material elements and material movement. The production process has ceased to be a labour process in the sense that labour is no longer the unity dominating and transcending it. Rather labour appears merely to be a conscious organ, composed of individual living workers at a number of points in the mechanical system; dispersed, subjected to the general process of the machinery itself, it is itself only a limb of the system, whose unity exists not in the living workers but in the living (active) machinery, which seems to be a powerful organism when compared to their individual, insignificant activities. With the stage of machinery, objectified labour appears in the labour process itself as the dominating force opposed to living labour, a force represented by capital in so far as it appropriates living labour.

That the labour process is no more than a simple element in the valorisation process is confirmed by the transformation on the material plane of the working tool into machinery, and of the living worker into a mere living accessory of the machine; they become no more than the means whereby its action can take place.

As we have seen, capital necessarily tends towards an increase in the productivity of labour and as great a diminution as possible in necessary labour. This tendency is realised by means of the transformation of the instrument of labour into the machine. In machinery, objectified labour is materially opposed to living labour as its own dominating force; it subordinates living labour to itself not only by appropriating it, but in the real process of production itself. The character of capital as value that appropriates value-creating activity is established by fixed capital, existing as machinery, in its relationship as the use value of labour power. Further, the value objectified in machinery appears as a prerequisite, opposed to which the valorising power of the individual worker disappears, since it has become infinitely small.

In the large-scale production created by machines, any relationship of the product to the direct requirements of the producer disappears, as does any immediate use value. The form of production, and the circumstances in which production takes place are so arranged that it is only produced as a vehicle for value, its use value being only a condition for this.

In machinery, objectified labour appears not only in the form of a product, or of a product utilised as a means of labour, but also in the force of production itself. The development of the means of labour into machinery is not fortuitous for capital; it is the historical transformation of the traditional means of labour into means adequate for capitalism. The accumulation of knowledge and skill, of the general productive power of society's intelligence, is thus absorbed into capital in opposition to labour and appears as the property of capital, or more exactly of fixed capital, to the extent that it enters into the production process as an actual means of production. Thus machinery appears as the *most adequate form of fixed capital*; and the latter, in so far as capital can be considered as being related to itself, is the most adequate form of capital in general. On the other hand, in so far as fixed capital is firmly tied to its existence as a particular use value, it no longer corresponds to the concept of capital which, as a value, can take up or throw off any particular form of use value, and incarnate itself in any of them indifferently. Seen from this aspect of the external relationships of capital, *circulating capital* seems to be the most adequate form of capital as opposed to fixed capital.

In so far as machinery develops with the accumulation of social knowledge and productive power generally, it is not in labour but in capital that general social labour is represented. Society's productivity is measured in fixed capital, exists within it in an objectified form; and conversely, the productivity of capital evolves in step with this general progress that capital appropriates gratis. We shall not go into the development of machinery in detail here. We are considering it only from the general aspect, to the extent that the means of labour, in its material aspect, loses its immediate form and opposes the worker materially as capital. Science thus appears, in the machine, as something alien and exterior to the worker; and living labour is subsumed under objectified labour, which acts independently. The worker appears to be superfluous in so far as his action is not determined by the needs of capital.

[. . .]

It is a fact that as the productive forces of labour develop, the objective conditions of labour (objectified labour) must grow in proportion to living labour. This is actually a tautology, for the growth of the productive forces of labour means merely that less direct labour is required in order to make a larger product, so that social wealth expresses itself more and more in the labour conditions that have been created by labour itself. From the point of view of capital, it does not appear that one of the elements of social activity (objectified labour) has become the ever more powerful body of the other element (subjective, living labour); rather it appears (and this is important for wage-labour) that the objective conditions of labour become more and more colossally independent of living labour – which is shown by their very extent – and social wealth becomes, in ever greater and greater proportions, an alien and dominating force opposing the worker. Stress is placed not on the state of objectification but on the state of alienation, estrangement and abandonment, on the fact that the enormous objectified power which social labour has opposed to itself as one of its elements belongs not to the worker but to the conditions of production that are personified in capital. So long as the creation of this material form of activity, objectified in contrast to immediate labour power, occurs on the basis of capital and wage-labour, and so long as this process of objectification in fact seems to be a process of alienation as far as the worker is concerned, or to be the appropriation of alien labour from the capitalist's point of view, so long will this distortion and this inversion really exist and not merely occur in the imagination of both workers and capitalists. But this process of inversion is obviously merely a historical necessity, a necessity for the development of productive forces from a definite historical starting point, or basis, but in no way an *absolute* necessity of production; it is, rather, ephemeral. The result and the immanent aim of the process is to destroy and transform this basis itself, as well as this form of the process. Bourgeois economists are so bogged down in their traditional ideas of the historical development of society in a single stage that the necessity of the *objectification* of the social forces of labour seems to them inseparable from the necessity of its *alienation* in relation to living labour.

But as living labour loses its *immediate*, individual character, whether subjective or entirely external, as individual activity becomes directly general or *social*, the objective elements of production lose this form of alienation. They are then produced as property, as the organic social body in which individuals are reproduced as individuals, but as social individuals. The conditions for their being such in the reproduction of their life, in their productive life process, can only be established by the historical economic process; these conditions are both objective and subjective conditions, which are the only two different forms of the same conditions.

The fact that the workers possess no property and the fact that objectified labour has property in living labour (in other words, that capital appropriates the labour of others) constitute the two opposite poles of the same relationship, and are the fundamental conditions of the bourgeois means of production and are in no sense a matter of indifference or chance. These means of distribution are the relations of production themselves, but *sub specie distributionis* ('from the point of view of distribution'). Thus it is quite absurd to say, as J. S. Mill does for example (*Principles of Political*

Economy), that: 'The laws and conditions of the production of wealth partake of the character of physical truths. ... It is not so with the distribution of wealth. This is a matter of human institutions solely.' The 'laws and conditions' of the production of wealth and the laws of 'distribution of wealth' are the same laws in a different form; they both change and undergo the same historical process; they are, in general, never more than elements in a historical process.

No special sagacity is required in order to understand that, beginning with free labour or wage-labour for example, which arose after the abolition of slavery, machines can only develop in opposition to living labour, as a hostile power and alien property, i.e. they must, as capital, oppose the worker. But it is equally easy to see that machines do not cease to be agents of social production, once they become, for example, the property of associated workers. But in the first case, their means of distribution (the fact that they do not belong to the workers) is itself a condition of the means of production that is founded on wage-labour. In the second case, an altered means of distribution will derive from a new, altered basis of production emerging from the historical process.

From: *Grundrisse* (D. McLellan ed.) pp. 16–19, 33–43,
67–9, 74–6, 94–5, 128–35, 150–2

16

Capital

Capital is rightly regarded as the most complete statement of the mature Marx's analysis of the political economy of capitalism. Beginning with the commodity form, Marx's ambition is to show that (once properly understood) categories that are commonplace in traditional political economy – the labour theory of value and the tendency for the rate of profit to fall – reveal capitalism as an economic system premised upon class exploitation and one which contains within it the seeds of its own destruction. The extensive selections from Volume One of Capital *make it possible to follow Marx's argument in some detail. Also included are some briefer passages from Volume Three which deal with the tendential fall in profit rates and the emergence of joint-stock companies. This section finishes with the famously incomplete note on 'the three big classes of modern society'.*

Preface to the first German edition

[. . .]

Every beginning is difficult, holds in all sciences. To understand the first chapter, especially the section that contains the analysis of commodities, will, therefore, present the greatest difficulty. That which concerns more especially the analysis of the substance of value and the magnitude of value, I have, as much as it was possible, popularised. The value-form, whose fully developed shape is the money-form, is very elementary and simple. Nevertheless, the human mind has for more than 2,000 years sought in vain to get to the bottom of it, whilst on the other hand, to the successful analysis of much more composite and complex forms, there has been at least an approximation. Why? Because the body, as an organic whole, is more easy of study than are the cells of that body. In the analysis of economic forms, moreover, neither microscopes nor chemical reagents are of use. The force of abstraction must replace both. But in bourgeois society the commodity-form of the product of labour – or the value-form of the commodity – is the economic cell-form. To the superficial observer, the analysis of these forms seems to turn upon minutiae. It does in fact deal with minutiae, but they are of the same order as those dealt with in microscopic anatomy.

[. . .]

The physicist either observes physical phenomena where they occur in their most typical form and most free from disturbing influence, or, wherever possible, he makes experiments under conditions that assure the occurrence of the phenomenon in its normality. In this work I have to examine the capitalist mode of production, and the conditions of production and exchange corresponding to that mode. Up to the present time, their classic ground is England. That is the reason why England is used as the chief illustration in the development of my theoretical ideas. If, however, the German reader shrugs his shoulders at the condition of the English industrial and agricultural labourers, or in optimist fashion comforts himself with the thought that in Germany things are not nearly so bad; I must plainly tell him, *De te tabula narratur!* ('This story is about you!').

Intrinsically, it is not a question of the higher or lower degree of development of the social antagonisms that result from the natural laws of capitalist production. It is a question of these laws themselves, of these tendencies working with iron necessity towards inevitable results. The country that is more developed industrially only shows, to the less developed, the image of its own future.

But apart from this. Where capitalist production is fully naturalised among the Germans (for instance, in the factories proper) the condition of things is much worse than in England, because the counterpoise of the Factory Acts is wanting. In all other spheres, we, like all the rest of Continental Western Europe, suffer not only from the development of capitalist production, but also from the incompleteness of that develop-ment. Alongside of modern evils, a whole series of inherited evils oppress us, arising from the passive survival of antiquated modes of production, with their inevitable train of social and political anachronisms. We suffer not only from the living, but from the dead. *Le mort saisit le vif!* (The dead seize the living!)

[. . .]

Let us not deceive ourselves on this. As in the 18th century, the American war of independence sounded the tocsin for the European middle-class, so in the 19th century, the American Civil War sounded it for the European working-class. In England the progress of social disintegration is palpable. When it has reached a certain point, it must re-act on the Continent. There it will take a form more brutal or more humane, according to the degree of development of the working-class itself. Apart from higher motives, therefore, their own most important interests dictate to the classes that are for the nonce the ruling ones, the removal of all legally removable hindrances to the free development of the working-class. For this reason, as well as others, I have given so large a space in this volume to the history, the details, and the results of English factory legislation. One nation can and should learn from others. And even when a society has got upon the right track for the discovery of the natural laws of its movement – and it is the ultimate aim of this work, to lay bare the economic law of motion of modern society – it can neither clear by bold leaps, nor remove by legal enactments, the obstacles offered by the successive phases of its normal development. But it can shorten and lessen the birth-pangs.

To prevent possible misunderstanding, a word. I paint the capitalist and the landlord in no sense *couleur de rose*. But here individuals are dealt with only in so far as they are the personifications of economic categories, embodiments of particular class-relations and class-interests. My stand-point, from which the evolution of the economic formation of society is viewed as a process of natural history, can less than any other make the individual responsible for relations whose creature he socially remains, however much he may subjectively raise himself above them.

[. . .]

Part I

Commodities and money

Commodities

The wealth of those societies in which the capitalist mode of production prevails, presents itself as 'an immense accumulation of commodities,' its unit being a single commodity. Our investigation must therefore begin with the analysis of a commodity.

A commodity is, in the first place, an object outside us, a thing that by its properties satisfies human wants of some sort or another. The nature of such wants, whether, for instance, they spring from the stomach or from fancy, makes no difference. Neither are we here concerned to know how the object satisfies these wants, whether directly as means of subsistence, or indirectly as means of production.

Every useful thing, as iron, paper, etc., may be looked at from the two points of view of quality and quantity. It is an assemblage of many properties, and may therefore be of use in various ways. To discover the various uses of things is the work of history. So also is the establishment of socially-recognised standards of measure for the quantities of these useful objects. The diversity of these measures has its origin partly in the diverse nature of the objects to be measured, partly in convention.

The utility of a thing makes it a use-value. But this utility is not a thing of air. Being limited by the physical properties of the commodity, it has no existence apart from that commodity. A commodity, such as iron, corn, or a diamond, is therefore, so far as it is a material thing, a use-value, something useful. This property of a commodity is independent of the amount of labour required to appropriate its useful qualities. When treating of use-value, we always assume to be dealing with definite quantities, such as dozens of watches, yards of linen, or tons of iron. The use-values of commodities furnish the material for a special study, that of the commercial knowledge of commodities. Use-values become a reality only by use or consumption: they also constitute the substance of all wealth, whatever may be the social form of that wealth. In the form of society we are about to consider, they are, in addition, the material depositories of exchange-value.

Exchange-value, at first sight, presents itself as a quantitative relation, as the proportion in which values in use of one sort are exchanged for those of another sort, a relation constantly changing with time and place. Hence exchange-value appears to be something accidental and purely relative, and consequently an intrinsic value, i.e., an exchange-value that is inseparably connected with, inherent in commodities, seems a contradiction in terms. Let us consider the matter a little more closely.

A given commodity, e.g., a quarter of wheat is exchanged for x blacking, y silk, or z gold, etc. – in short, for other commodities in the most different proportions. Instead of one exchange-value, the wheat has, therefore, a great many. But since x blacking, y silk, or z gold, etc., each represents the exchange-value of one quarter of wheat, x blacking, y silk, z gold, etc., must, as exchange-values, be replaceable by each other, or equal to each other. Therefore, first: the valid exchange-values of a given commodity express something equal; secondly, exchange-value, generally, is only the mode of expression, the phenomenal form, of something contained in it, yet distinguishable from it.

Let us take two commodities, e.g., corn and iron. The proportions in which they are exchangeable, whatever those proportions may be, can always be represented by an equation in which a given quantity of corn is equated to some quantity of iron: e.g., 1 quarter corn = x cwt. iron. What does this equation tell us? It tells us that in two different things – in 1 quarter of corn and x cwt. of iron, there exists in equal quantities something common to both. The two things must therefore be equal to a third, which in itself is neither the one nor the other. Each of them, so far as it is exchange-value, must therefore be reducible to this third.

A simple geometrical illustration will make this clear. In order to calculate and compare the areas of rectilinear figures, we decompose them into triangles. But the area of the triangle itself is expressed by something totally different from its visible figure, namely, by half the product of the base into the altitude. In the same way the exchange-values of commodities must be capable of being expressed in terms of something common to them all, of which thing they represent a greater or less quantity.

This common 'something' cannot be either a geometrical, a chemical, or any other natural property of commodities. Such properties claim our attention only in so far as they affect the utility of those commodities, make them use-values. But the exchange of commodities is evidently an act characterised by a total abstraction from use-value. Then one use-value is just as good as another, provided only it be present in sufficient quantity. Or, as old Barbon says, 'one sort of wares are as good as another, if the values be equal. There is no difference or distinction in things of equal value. . . . An hundred pounds' worth of lead or iron, is of as great value as one hundred pounds' worth of silver or gold.' As use-values, commodities are, above all, of different qualities, but as exchange-values they are merely different quantities, and consequently do not contain an atom of use-value.

If then we leave out of consideration the use-value of commodities, they have only one common property left, that of being products of labour. But even the product of labour itself has undergone a change in our hands. If we make abstraction from its use-value, we make abstraction at the same time from the material elements and shapes that make the product a use-value; we see in it no longer a table, a house, yarn, or any other useful thing. Its existence as a material thing is put out of sight. Neither can it any longer be regarded as the product of the labour of the joiner, the mason, the spinner, or of any other definite kind of productive labour. Along with the useful qualities of the products themselves, we put out of sight both the useful character of the various kinds of labour embodied in them, and the concrete forms of that labour; there is nothing left but what is common to them all; all are reduced to one and the same sort of labour, human labour in the abstract.

Let us now consider the residue of each of these products; it consists of the same unsubstantial reality in each, a mere congelation of homogeneous human labour, of labour-power expended without regard to the mode of its expenditure. All that these things now tell us is, that human labour-power has been expended in their production, that human labour is embodied in them. When looked at as crystals of this social substance, common to them all, they are – Values.

We have seen that when commodities are exchanged, their exchange-value manifests itself as something totally independent of their use-value. But if we abstract from their use-value, there remains their Value as defined above. Therefore, the common substance that manifests itself in the exchange-value of commodities, whenever they are exchanged, is their value. The progress of our investigation will show that exchange-value is the only form in which the value of commodities can manifest itself or be expressed. For the present, however, we have to consider the nature of value independently of this, its form.

A use-value, or useful article, therefore, has value only because human labour in the abstract has been embodied or materialised in it. How, then, is the magnitude of this value to be measured? Plainly, by the quantity of the value-creating substance, the labour, contained in the article. The quantity of labour, however, is measured by its duration, and labour-time in its turn finds its standard in weeks, days, and hours.

Some people might think that if the value of a commodity is determined by the quantity of labour spent on it, the more idle and unskilful the labourer, the more valuable would his commodity be, because more time would be required in its production. The labour, however, that forms the substance of value, is homogeneous human labour, expenditure of one uniform labour-power. The total labour-power of society, which is embodied in the sum total of the values of all commodities produced by that society, counts here as one homogeneous mass of human labour-power, composed though it be of innumerable individual units. Each of these units is the same as any other, so far as it has the character of the average labour-power of society, and takes effect as such; that is, so far as it requires for producing a commodity, no more time than is needed on an average, no more than is socially necessary. The labour-time socially necessary is that required to produce an article under the normal conditions of production, and with the average degree of skill and intensity prevalent at the time. The introduction of power-looms into England probably reduced by one-half the labour required to weave a given quantity of yarn into cloth. The hand-loom weavers, as a matter of fact, continued to require the same time as before; but for all that, the product of one hour of their labour represented after the change only half an hour's social labour, and consequently fell to one-half its former value.

We see then that that which determines the magnitude of the value of any article is the amount of labour socially necessary, or the labour-time socially necessary for its production. Each individual commodity, in this connexion, is to be considered as an average sample of its class. Commodities, therefore, in which equal quantities of labour are embodied, or which can be produced in the same time, have the same value. The value of one commodity is to the value of any other, as the labour-time necessary for the production of the one is to that necessary for the production of the other. 'As values, all commodities are only definite masses of congealed labour-time.'

The value of a commodity would therefore remain constant, if the labour-time required for its production also remained constant. But the latter changes with every variation in the productiveness of labour. This productiveness is determined by various circumstances, amongst others, by the average amount of skill of the workmen, the state of science, and the degree of its practical application, the social organisation of production, the extent and capabilities of the means of production, and by physical conditions. For example, the same amount of labour in favourable seasons is embodied in 8 bushels of corn, and in unfavourable, only in four. The same labour extracts from rich mines more metal than from poor mines. Diamonds are of very rare occurrence on the earth's surface, and hence their discovery costs, on an average, a great deal of labour-time. Consequently much labour is represented in a small compass. Jacob doubts whether gold has ever been paid for at its full value. This applies still more to diamonds. According to Eschwege, the total produce of the Brazilian diamond mines for the eighty years, ending in 1823, had not realised the price of one-and-a-half years' average produce of the sugar and coffee plantations of the same country, although the diamonds cost much more labour, and therefore represented more value. With richer mines, the same quantity of labour would embody itself in more diamonds, and their value would fall. If we could succeed at a small expenditure of labour, in converting carbon into diamonds, their value might fall below that of bricks. In general, the greater the productiveness of labour, the less is the labour-time required for the production of an article, the less is the amount of labour crystallised in that article, and the less is its value; and *vice versa*, the less the productiveness of labour, the greater is the labour-time required for the production of an article, and the greater is its value. The value of a commodity, therefore, varies directly as the quantity, and inversely as the productiveness, of the labour incorporated in it.

A thing can be a use-value, without having value. This is the case whenever its utility to man is not due to labour. Such are air, virgin soil, natural meadows, etc. A thing can be useful, and the product of human labour, without being a commodity. Whoever directly satisfies his wants with the produce of his own labour, creates, indeed, use-values, but not commodities. In order to produce the latter, he must not only produce use-values, but use-values for others, social use-values. (And not only for others, without more. The mediaeval peasant produced quit-rent-corn for his feudal lord and tithe-corn for his parson. But neither the quit-rent-corn nor the tithe-corn became commodities by reason of the fact that they had been produced for others. To become a commodity a product must be transferred to another, whom it will serve as a use-value, by means of an exchange.) Lastly nothing can have value, without being an object of utility. If the thing is useless, so is the labour contained in it; the labour does not count as labour, and therefore creates no value.

[. . .]

At first sight a commodity presented itself to us as a complex of two things – use-value and exchange-value. Later on, we saw also that labour, too, possesses the same two-fold nature; for, so far as it finds expression in value, it does not possess the same characteristics that belong to it as a creator of use-values. I was the first to point out and to examine critically this two-fold nature of the labour contained in commodities. As this point is the pivot on which a clear comprehension of Political Economy turns, we must go more into detail.

Let us take two commodities such as a coat and 10 yards of linen, and let the former be double the value of the latter, so that, if 10 yards of linen = W, the coat = $2W$.

The coat is a use-value that satisfies a particular want. Its existence is the result of a special sort of productive activity, the nature of which is determined by its aim, mode of operation, subject, means, and result. The labour, whose utility is thus represented by the value in use of its product, or which manifests itself by making its product a use-value, we call useful labour. In this connexion we consider only its useful effect.

As the coat and the linen are two qualitatively different use-values, so also are the two forms of labour that produce them, tailoring and weaving. Were these two objects not qualitatively different, not produced respectively by labour of different quality, they could not stand to each other in the relation of commodities. Coats are not exchanged for coats, one use-value is not exchanged for another of the same kind.

To all the different varieties of values in use there correspond as many different kinds of useful labour, classified according to the order, genus, species, and variety to which they belong in the social division of labour. This division of labour is a necessary condition for the production of commodities, but it does not follow, conversely, that the production of commodities is a necessary condition for the division of labour. In the primitive Indian community there is social division of labour, without production of commodities. Or, to take an example nearer home, in every factory the labour is divided according to a system, but this division is not brought about by the operatives mutually exchanging their individual products. Only such products can become commodities with regard to each other, as result from different kinds of labour, each kind being carried on independently and for the account of private individuals.

To resume, then: In the use-value of each commodity there is contained useful labour, *i.e.*, productive activity of a definite kind and exercised with a definite aim. Use-values cannot confront each other as commodities, unless the useful labour embodied in them is qualitatively different in each of them. In a community, the produce of which in general takes the form of commodities, *i.e.*, in a community of commodity producers, this qualitative difference between the useful forms of labour that are carried on independently by individual producers, each on their own account, develops into a complex system, a social division of labour.

Anyhow, whether the coat be worn by the tailor or by his customer, in either case it operates as a use-value. Nor is the relation between the coat and the labour that produced it altered by the circumstance that tailoring may have become a special trade, an independent branch of the social division of labour. Wherever the want of clothing forced them to it, the human race made clothes for thousands of years, without a single man becoming a tailor. But coats and linen, like every other element of material wealth that is not the spontaneous produce of Nature, must invariably owe their existence to a special productive activity, exercised with a definite aim, an activity that appropriates particular nature-given materials to particular human wants. So far therefore as labour is a creator of use-value, is useful labour, it is a necessary condition, independent of all forms of society, for the existence of the human race; it is an eternal nature-imposed necessity, without which there can be no material exchanges between man and Nature, and therefore no life.

The use-values, coat, linen, etc., *i.e.*, the bodies of commodities, are combinations of two elements – matter and labour. If we take away the useful labour expended upon them, a material substratum is always left, which is furnished by Nature without the help of man. The latter can work only as Nature does, that is by changing the form of matter. Nay more, in this work of changing the form he is constantly helped by natural forces. We see, then, that labour is not the only source of material wealth, of use-values produced by labour. As William Petty puts it, labour is its father and the earth its mother.

Let us now pass from the commodity considered as a use-value to the value of commodities.

By our assumption, the coat is worth twice as much as the linen. But this is a mere quantitative difference, which for the present does not concern us. We bear in mind, however, that if the value of the coat is double that of 10 yds. of linen, 20 yds. of linen must have the same value as one coat. So far as they are values, the coat and the linen are things of a like substance, objective expressions of essentially identical labour. But tailoring and weaving are, qualitatively, different kinds of labour. There are, however, states of society in which one and the same man does tailoring and weaving alternately, in which case these two forms of labour are mere modifications of the labour of the same individual, and no special and fixed functions of different persons; just as the coat which our tailor makes one day, and the trousers which he makes another day, imply only a variation in the labour of one and the same individual. Moreover, we see at a glance that, in our capitalist society, a given portion of human labour is, in accordance with the varying demand, at one time supplied in the form of tailoring, at another in the form of weaving. This change may possibly not take place without friction, but take place it must.

Productive activity, if we leave out of sight its special form, viz., the useful character of the labour, is nothing but the expenditure of human labour-power. Tailoring and weaving, though qualitatively different productive activities, are each a productive expenditure of human brains, nerves, and muscles, and in this sense are human labour. They are but two different modes of expending human labour-power. Of course, this labour-power, which remains the same under all its modifications, must have attained a certain pitch of development before it can be expended in a multiplicity of modes. But the value of a commodity represents human labour in the abstract, the expenditure of human labour in general. And just as in society, a general or a banker plays a great part, but mere man, on the other hand, a very shabby part, so here with mere human labour. It is the expenditure of simple labour-power, *i.e.*, of the labour-power which, on an average, apart from any special development, exists in the organism of every ordinary individual. Simple average labour, it is true, varies in character in different countries and at different times, but in a particular society it is given. Skilled labour counts only as simple labour intensified, or rather, as multiplied simple labour, a given quantity of skilled being considered equal to a greater quantity of simple labour. Experience shows that this reduction is constantly being made. A commodity may be the product of the most skilled labour, but its value, by equating it to the product of simple unskilled labour, represents a definite quantity of the latter labour alone. The different proportions in which different sorts of labour are reduced to unskilled labour as their standard, are established by a social process that goes on behind the backs of the producers, and, consequently, appear to be fixed by custom. For simplicity's sake we shall henceforth account every kind of labour to be unskilled, simple labour; by this we do no more than save ourselves the trouble of making the reduction.

Just as, therefore, in viewing the coat and linen as values, we abstract from their different use-values, so it is with the labour represented by those values: we disregard the difference between its useful forms, weaving and tailoring. As the use-values, coat and linen, are combinations of special productive activities with cloth and yarn, while the values, coat and linen, are, on the other hand, mere homogeneous congelations of undifferentiated labour, so the labour embodied in these latter values does not count by virtue of its productive relation to cloth and yarn, but only as being expenditure of human labour-power. Tailoring and weaving are necessary factors in the creation of the use-values, coat and linen, precisely because these two kinds of labour are of different qualities; but only in so far as abstraction is made from their special qualities, only in so far as both possess the same quality of being human labour, do tailoring and weaving form the substance of the values of the same articles.

Coats and linen, however, are not merely values, but values of definite magnitude, and according to our assumption, the coat is worth twice as much as the ten yards of linen. Whence this difference in their values? It is owing to the fact that the linen contains only half as much labour as the coat, and consequently, that in the production of the latter, labour-power must have been expended during twice the time necessary for the production of the former.

While, therefore, with reference to use-value, the labour contained in a commodity counts only qualitatively, with reference to value it counts only quantitatively, and must first be reduced to human labour pure and simple. In the former case, it is a question of How and What, in the latter of How much? How long a time? Since the magnitude of the value of a commodity represents only the quantity of labour embodied in it, it follows that all commodities, when taken in certain proportions, must be equal in value.

If the productive power of all the different sorts of useful labour required for the production of a coat remains unchanged, the sum of the values of the coats produced increases with their number. If one coat represents x days' labour, two coats represent $2x$ days' labour, and so on. But assume that the duration of the labour necessary for the production of a coat becomes doubled or halved. In the first case, one coat is worth as much as two coats were before; in the second case, two coats are only worth as much as one was before, although in both cases one coat renders the same service as before, and the useful labour embodied in it remains of the same quality. But the quantity of labour spent on its production has altered.

An increase in the quantity of use-values is an increase of material wealth. With two coats two men can be clothed, with one coat only one man. Nevertheless, an increased quantity of material wealth may correspond to a simultaneous fall in the magnitude of its value. This antagonistic movement has its origin in the two-fold character of labour. Productive power has reference, of course, only to labour of some useful concrete form, the efficacy of any special productive activity during a given time being dependent on its productiveness. Useful labour becomes, therefore, a more or less abundant source of products, in proportion to the rise or fall of its productiveness. On the other hand, no change in this productiveness affects the labour represented by value. Since productive power is an attribute of the concrete useful forms of labour, of course it can no longer have any bearing on that labour, so soon as we make abstraction from those concrete useful forms. However then productive power may vary, the same labour, exercised during equal periods of time, always yields equal amounts of value. But it will yield, during equal periods of time, different quantities of values in use; more, if the productive power rise, fewer, if it fall. The same change in productive power, which increases the fruitfulness of labour, and, in consequence, the quantity of use-values produced by that labour, will diminish the total value of this increased quantity of use-values, provided such change shorten the total labour-time necessary for their production; and *vice versa*.

On the one hand all labour is, speaking physiologically, an expenditure of human labour-power, and in its character of identical abstract human labour, it creates and forms the value of commodities. On the other hand, all labour is the expenditure of human labour-power in a special form and with a definite aim, and in this, its character of concrete useful labour, it produces use-values.

The form of value or exchange-value

Commodities come into the world in the shape of use-values, articles, or goods, such as iron, linen, corn, etc. This is their plain, homely, bodily form. They are, however, commodities, only because they are something two-fold, both objects of utility, and, at the same time, depositories of value. They manifest themselves therefore as commodities, or have the form of commodities, only in so far as they have two forms, a physical or natural form, and a value-form.

The reality of the value of commodities differs in this respect from Dame Quickly, that we don't know 'where to have it'. The value of commodities is the very opposite of the coarse materiality of their substance, not an atom of matter enters into its composition. Turn and examine a single commodity, by itself, as we will, yet in so far as it remains an object of value, it seems impossible to grasp it. If, however, we bear in mind that the value of commodities has a purely social reality, and that they acquire this reality only in so far as they are expressions or embodiments of one identical social substance, viz., human labour, it follows as a matter of course, that value can only manifest itself in the social relation of commodity to commodity. In fact we started from exchange-value, or the exchange relation of commodities, in order to get at the value that lies hidden behind it. We must now return to this form under which value first appeared to us.

Every one knows, if he knows nothing else, that commodities have a value-form common to them all, and presenting a marked contrast with the varied bodily forms of their use-values. I mean their money-form. Here, however, a task is set us, the performance of which has never yet even been attempted by *bourgeois* economy, the task of tracing the genesis of this money-form, of developing the expression of value implied in the value-relation of commodities, from its simplest, almost imperceptible outline, to the dazzling money-form. By doing this we shall, at the same time, solve the riddle presented by money.

The simplest value-relation is evidently that of one commodity to some one other commodity of a different kind. Hence the relation between the values of two commodities supplies us with the simplest expression of the value of a single commodity. [. . .] The whole mystery of the form of value lies hidden in this elementary form. Its analysis, therefore, is our real difficulty.

[. . .]

If we say that, as values, commodities are mere congelations of human labour, we reduce them by our analysis, it is true, to the abstraction, value; but we ascribe to this value no form apart from their bodily form. It is otherwise in the value-relation of one commodity to another. Here, the one stands forth in its character of value by reason of its relation to the other.

By making the coat the equivalent of the linen, we equate the labour embodied in the former to that in the latter. Now, it is true that the tailoring, which makes the coat, is concrete labour of a different sort from the weaving which makes the linen. But the act of equating it to the weaving, reduces the tailoring to that which is really equal in the two kinds of labour, to their common character of human labour. In this roundabout way, then, the fact is expressed, that weaving also, in so far as it weaves value, has nothing to distinguish it from tailoring, and, consequently, is abstract human labour. It is the expression of equivalence between different sorts of commodities that alone brings into relief the specific character of value-creating labour, and this it does by actually reducing the different varieties of labour embodied in the different kinds of commodities to their common quality of human labour in the abstract.

There is, however, something else required beyond the expression of the specific character of the labour of which the value of the linen consists. Human labour-power in motion, or human labour, creates value, but is not itself value. It becomes value only in its congealed state, when embodied in the form of some object. In order to express the value of the linen as a congelation of human labour, that value must be expressed as having objective existence, as being a something materially different from the linen itself, and yet a something common to the linen and all other commodities. The problem is already solved.

[. . .]

We see, then, all that our analysis of the value of commodities has already told us, is told us by the linen itself, so soon as it comes into communication with another commodity, the coat. Only it betrays its thoughts in that language with which alone it is familiar, the language of commodities. In order to tell us that its own value is created by labour in its abstract character of human labour, it says that the coat, in so far as it is worth as much as the linen, and therefore is value, consists of the same labour as the linen. In order to inform us that its sublime reality as value is not the same as its buckram body, it says that value has the appearance of a coat, and consequently that so far as the linen is value, it and the coat are as like as two peas.

[. . .]

The fetishism of commodities and the secret thereof

A commodity appears, at first sight, a very trivial thing, and easily understood. Its analysis shows that it is, in reality, a very queer thing, abounding in metaphysical subtleties and theological niceties. [. . .] The mystical character of commodities does not originate . . . in their use-value. Just as little does it proceed from the nature of the determining factors of value. For, in the first place, however varied the useful kinds of labour, or productive activities, may be, it is a physiological fact, that they are functions of the human organism, and that each such function, whatever may be its nature or form, is essentially the expenditure of human brain, nerves, muscles, etc. Secondly, with regard to that which forms the ground-work for the quantitative determination of value, namely, the duration of that expenditure, or the quantity of labour, it is quite clear that there is a palpable difference between its quantity and quality. In all states of society, the labour-time that it costs to produce the means of subsistence, must necessarily be an object of interest to mankind, though not of equal interest in different stages of development. And lastly, from the moment that men in any way work for one another, their labour assumes a social form.

Whence, then, arises the enigmatical character of the product of labour, so soon as it assumes the form of commodities? Clearly from this form itself. The equality of all sorts of human labour is expressed objectively by their products all being equally values; the measure of the expenditure of labour-power by the duration of that expenditure, takes the form of the quantity of value of the products of labour; and finally, the mutual relations of the producers, within which the social character of their labour affirms itself, take the form of a social relation between the products.

A commodity is therefore a mysterious thing, simply because in it the social character of men's labour appears to them as an objective character stamped upon the product of that labour; because the relation of the producers to the sum total of their own labour is presented to them as a social relation, existing not between themselves, but between the products of their labour. This is the reason why the products of labour become commodities, social things whose qualities are at the same time perceptible and imperceptible by the senses. In the same way the light from an object is perceived by us not as the subjective excitation of our optic nerve, but as the objective form of something outside the eye itself. But, in the act of seeing, there is at all events, an actual passage of light from one thing to another, from the external object to the eye. There is a physical relation between physical things. But it is different with commodities. There, the existence of the things *qua* commodities, and the value-relation between the products of labour which stamps them as commodities, have absolutely no connexion with their physical properties and with the material relations arising therefrom. There it is a definite social relation between men, that assumes, in their eyes, the fantastic form of a relation between things. In order, therefore, to find an analogy, we must have recourse to the mist-enveloped regions of the religious world. In that world the productions of the human brain appear as independent beings endowed with life, and entering into relation both with one another and the human race. So it is in the world of commodities with the products of men's hands. This I call the Fetishism which attaches itself to the products of labour, so soon as they are produced as commodities, and which is therefore inseparable from the production of commodities.

This Fetishism of commodities has its origin, as the foregoing analysis has already shown, in the peculiar social character of the labour that produces them.

As a general rule, articles of utility become commodities, only because they are products of the labour of private individuals or groups of individuals who carry on their work independently of each other. The sum total of the labour of all these private individuals forms the aggregate labour of society. Since the producers do not come into social contact with each other until they exchange their products, the specific social character of each producer's labour does not show itself except in the act of exchange. In other words, the labour of the individual asserts itself as a part of the labour of society, only by means of the relations which the act of exchange establishes directly between the products, and indirectly, through them, between the producers. To the latter, therefore, the relations connecting the labour of one individual with that of the rest appear, not as direct social relations between individuals at work, but as what they really are, material relations between persons and social relations between things. It is only by being exchanged that the products of labour acquire, as values, one uniform social status, distinct from their varied forms of existence as objects of utility. This division of a product into a useful thing and a value becomes practically important, only when exchange has acquired such an extension that useful articles are produced for the purpose of being exchanged, and their character as values has therefore to be taken into account, beforehand, during production. From this moment the labour of the individual producer acquires socially a two-fold character. On the one hand, it must, as a definite useful kind of labour, satisfy a definite social want, and thus hold its place as part and parcel of the collective labour of all, as a branch of a social division of labour that has sprung up spontaneously. On the other hand, it can satisfy the manifold wants of the individual producer himself, only in so far as the mutual exchangeability of all kinds of useful private labour is an established social fact, and therefore the private useful labour of each producer ranks on an equality with that of all others. The equalisation of the most different kinds of labour can be the result only of an abstraction from their inequalities, or of reducing them to their common denominator, viz., expenditure of human labour-power or human labour in the abstract. The two-fold social character of the labour of the individual appears to him, when reflected in his brain, only under those forms which are impressed upon that labour in every-day practice by the exchange of products. In this way, the character that his own labour possesses of being socially useful takes the form of the condition, that the product must be not only useful, but useful for others, and the social character that his particular labour has of being the equal of all other particular kinds of labour, takes the form that all the physically different articles that are the products of labour, have one common quality, viz., that of having value.

Hence, when we bring the products of our labour into relation with each other as values, it is not because we see in these articles the material receptacles of homogeneous human labour. Quite the contrary: whenever, by an exchange, we equate as values our different products, by that very act, we also equate, as human labour, the different kinds of labour expended upon them. We are not aware of this, nevertheless we do it. Value, therefore, does not stalk about with a label describing what it is. It is value, rather, that converts every product into a social hieroglyphic. Later on, we try to decipher the hieroglyphic, to get behind the secret of our own social products; for to stamp an object of utility as a value, is just as much a social product as language. The recent scientific discovery, that the products of labour, so far as they are values, are but material expressions of the human labour spent in their production, marks, indeed, an epoch in the history of the development of the human race, but, by no means, dissipates the mist through which the social character of labour appears to us to be an objective character of the products themselves. The fact, that in the particular form of production with which we are dealing, viz., the production of commodities, the specific social character of private labour carried on independently, consists in the equality of every kind of that labour, by virtue of its being human labour, which character, therefore, assumes in the product the form of value – this fact appears to the producers, notwithstanding the discovery above referred to, to be just as real and final, as the fact, that, after the discovery by science of the component gases of air, the atmosphere itself remained unaltered.

[. . .]

Part II

The transformation of money into capital

The general formula for capital

The circulation of commodities is the starting-point of capital. The production of commodities, their circulation, and that more developed form of their circulation called commerce, these form the historical ground-work from which it rises. The modern history of capital dates from the creation in the 16th century of a world-embracing commerce and a world-embracing market.

If we abstract from the material substance of the circulation of commodities, that is, from the exchange of the various use-values, and consider only the economic forms produced by this process of circulation, we find its final result to be money: this final product of the circulation of commodities is the first form in which capital appears.

As a matter of history, capital, as opposed to landed property, invariably takes the form at first of money; it appears as moneyed wealth, as the capital of the merchant and of the usurer. But we have no need to refer to the origin of capital in order to discover that the first form of appearance of capital is money. We can see it daily under our very eyes. All new capital, to commence with, comes on the stage, that is, on the market, whether of commodities, labour, or money, even in our days, in the shape of money that by a definite process has to be transformed into capital.

The first distinction we notice between money that is money only, and money that is capital, is nothing more than a difference in their form of circulation.

The simplest form of the circulation of commodities is C–M–C, the transformation of commodities into money, and the change of the money back again into commodities; or selling in order to buy. But alongside of this form we find another specifically different form: M–C–M, the transformation of money into commodities, and the change of commodities back again into money; or buying in order to sell. Money that circulates in the latter manner is thereby transformed into, becomes capital, and is already potentially capital.

Now let us examine the circuit M–C–M a little closer. It consists, like the other, of two antithetical phases. In the first phase, M–C, or the purchase, the money is changed into a commodity. In the second phase, C–M, or the sale, the commodity is changed back again into money. The combination of these two phases constitutes the single movement whereby money is exchanged for a commodity, and the same commodity is again exchanged for money; whereby a commodity is bought in order to be sold, or, neglecting the distinction in form between buying and selling, whereby a commodity is bought with money, and then money is bought with a commodity. The result, in which the phases of the process vanish, is the exchange of money for money, M–M. If I purchase 2,000 lbs. of cotton for £100, and resell the 2,000 lbs. of cotton for £110, I have, in fact, exchanged £100 for £110, money for money.

Now it is evident that the circuit M–C–M would be absurd and without meaning if the intention were to exchange by this means two equal sums of money, £100 for £100. The miser's plan would be far simpler and surer; he sticks to his £100 instead of exposing it to the dangers of circulation. And yet, whether the merchant who has paid £100 for his cotton sells it for £110, or lets it go for £100, or even £50, his money has, at all events, gone through a characteristic and original movement, quite different in kind from that which it goes through in the hands of the peasant who sells corn, and with the money thus set free buys clothes. We have therefore to examine first the distinguishing characteristics of the forms of the circuits M–C–M and C–M–C, and in doing this the real difference that underlies the mere difference of form will reveal itself.

Let us see, in the first place, what the two forms have in common.

Both circuits are resolvable into the same two antithetical phases, C–M, a sale, and M–C, a purchase. In each of these phases the same material elements – a commodity, and money, and the same economic dramatis personae, a buyer and a seller – confront one another. Each circuit is the unity of the same two antithetical phases, and in each case this unity is brought about by the intervention of three contracting parties, of whom one only sells, another only buys, while the third both buys and sells.

What, however, first and foremost distinguishes the circuit C–M–C from the circuit M–C–M, is the inverted order of succession of the two phases. The simple circulation of commodities begins with a sale and ends with a purchase, while the circulation of money as capital begins with a purchase and ends with a sale. In the one case both the starting-point and the goal are commodities, in the other they are money. In the first form the movement is brought about by the intervention of money, in the second by that of a commodity.

In the circulation C–M–C, the money is in the end converted into a commodity, that serves as a use-value; it is spent once for all. In the inverted form, M–C–M, on the contrary, the buyer lays out money in order that, as a seller, he may recover money. By the purchase of his commodity he throws money into circulation, in order to withdraw it again by the sale of the same commodity. He lets the money go, but only with the sly intention of getting it back again. The money, therefore, is not spent, it is merely advanced.

In the circuit C–M–C, the same piece of money changes its place twice. The seller gets it from the buyer and pays it away to another seller. The complete circulation, which begins with the receipt, concludes with the payment, of money for commodities. It is the very contrary in the circuit M–C–M. Here it is not the piece of money that changes its place twice, but the commodity. The buyer takes it from the hands of the seller and passes it into the hands of another buyer. Just as in the simple circulation of commodities the double change of place of the same piece of money effects its passage from one hand into another, so here the double change of place of the same commodity brings about the reflux of the money to its point of departure.

Such reflux is not dependent on the commodity being sold for more than was paid for it. This circumstance influences only the amount of the money that comes back. The reflux itself takes place, so soon as the purchased commodity is resold, in other words, so soon as the circuit M–C–M is completed. We have here, therefore, a palpable difference between the circulation of money as capital, and its circulation as mere money.

The circuit C–M–C comes completely to an end, so soon as the money brought in by the sale of one commodity is abstracted again by the purchase of another.

If, nevertheless, there follows a reflux of money to its starting-point, this can only happen through a renewal or repetition of the operation. If I sell a quarter of corn for £3, and with this £3 buy clothes, the money, so far as I am concerned, is spent and done with. It belongs to the clothes merchant. If I now sell a second quarter of corn, money indeed flows back to me, not however as a sequel to the first transaction, but in consequence of its repetition. The money again leaves me, so soon as I complete this second transaction by a fresh purchase. Therefore, in the circuit C–M–C, the expenditure of money has nothing to do with its reflux. On the other hand, in M–C–M, the reflux of the money is conditioned by the very mode of its expenditure. Without this reflux, the operation fails, or the process is interrupted and incomplete, owing to the absence of its complementary and final phase, the sale.

The circuit C–M–C starts with one commodity, and finishes with another, which falls out of circulation and into consumption. Consumption, the satisfaction of wants, in one word, use-value, is its end and aim. The circuit M–C–M, on the contrary, commences with money and ends with money. Its leading motive, and the goal that attracts it, is therefore mere exchange-value.

In the simple circulation of commodities, the two extremes of the circuit have the same economic form. They are both commodities, and commodities of equal value. But they are also use-values differing in their qualities, as, for example, corn and clothes. The exchange of products, of the different materials in which the labour of society is embodied, forms here the basis of the movement. It is otherwise in the circulation M–C–M, which at first sight appears purposeless, because tautological. Both extremes have the same economic form. They are both money, and therefore are not qualitatively different use-values; for money is but the converted form of commodities, in which their particular use-values vanish. To exchange £100 for cotton, and then this same cotton again for £100, is merely a roundabout way of exchanging money for money, the same for the same, and appears to be an operation just as purposeless as it is absurd. One sum of money is distinguishable from another only by its amount. The character and tendency of the process M–C–M, is therefore not due to any qualitative difference between its extremes, both being money, but solely to their quantitative difference. More money is withdrawn from circulation at the finish than was thrown into it at the start. The cotton that was bought for £100 is perhaps resold for £100+ £10 or £110. The exact form of this process is therefore M–C–M′, where M′ = M + ∆M = the original sum advanced, plus an increment. This increment or excess over the original value I call 'surplus-value'. The value originally advanced, therefore, not only remains intact while in circulation, but adds to itself a surplus-value or expands itself. It is this movement that converts it into capital.

Of course, it is also possible, that in C–M–C, the two extremes C–C, say corn and clothes may represent different quantities of value. The farmer may sell his corn above its value, or may buy the clothes at less than their value. He may, on the other hand, 'be done' by the clothes merchant. Yet, in the form of circulation now under consideration, such differences in value are purely accidental. The fact that the corn and the clothes are equivalents, does not deprive the process of all meaning, as it does in

M–C–M. The equivalence of their values is rather a necessary condition to its normal course.

The repetition or renewal of the act of selling in order to buy, is kept within bounds by the very object it aims at, namely, consumption or the satisfaction of definite wants, an aim that lies altogether outside the sphere of circulation. But when we buy in order to sell, we, on the contrary, begin and end with the same thing, money, exchange-value; and thereby the movement becomes interminable. No doubt, M becomes M + ΔM, £100 become £110. But when viewed in their qualitative aspect alone, £110 are the same as £100, namely money; and considered quantitatively, £110 is, like £100, a sum of definite and limited value. If now, the £110 be spent as money, they cease to play their part. They are no longer capital. Withdrawn from circulation, they become petrified into a hoard, and though they remained in that state till doomsday, not a single farthing would accrue to them. If, then, the expansion of value is once aimed at, there is just the same inducement to augment the value of the £110 as that of the £100; for both are but limited expressions for exchange-value, and therefore both have the same vocation to approach, by quantitative increase, as near as possible to absolute wealth. Momentarily, indeed, the value originally advanced, the £100 is distinguishable from the surplus-value of £10 that is annexed to it during circulation; but the distinction vanishes immediately. At the end of the process, we do not receive with one hand the original £100, and with the other, the surplus-value of £10. We simply get a value of £110, which is in exactly the same condition and fitness for commencing the expanding process, as the original £100 was. Money ends the movement only to begin it again. Therefore, the final result of every separate circuit, in which a purchase and consequent sale are completed, forms of itself the starting-point of a new circuit. The simple circulation of commodities – selling in order to buy – is a means of carrying out a purpose unconnected with circulation, namely, the appropriation of use-values, the satisfaction of wants. The circulation of money as capital is, on the contrary, an end in itself, for the expansion of value takes place only within this constantly renewed movement. The circulation of capital has therefore no limits.

As the conscious representative of this movement, the possessor of money becomes a capitalist. His person, or rather his pocket, is the point from which the money starts and to which it returns. The expansion of value, which is the objective basis or main-spring of the circulation M–C–M, becomes his subjective aim, and it is only in so far as the appropriation of ever more and more wealth in the abstract becomes the sole motive of his operations, that he functions as a capitalist, that is, as capital personified and endowed with consciousness and a will. Use-values must therefore never be looked upon as the real aim of the capitalist; neither must the profit on any single transaction. The restless never-ending process of profit-making alone is what he aims at. This boundless greed after riches, this passionate chase after exchange-value, is common to the capitalist and the miser; but while the miser is merely a capitalist gone mad, the capitalist is a rational miser. The never-ending augmentation of exchange-value, which the miser strives after, by seeking to save his money from circulation, is attained by the more acute capitalist, by constantly throwing it afresh into circulation.

The independent form, *i.e.*, the money-form, which the value of commodities assumes in the case of simple circulation, serves only one purpose, namely, their exchange, and vanishes in the final result of the movement. On the other hand, in the circulation M–C–M, both the money and the commodity represent only different modes of existence of value itself, the money its general mode, and the commodity its particular, or, so to say, disguised mode. It is constantly changing from one form to the other without thereby becoming lost, and thus assumes an automatically active character. If now we take in turn each of the two different forms which self-expanding value successively assumes in the course of its life, we then arrive at these two propositions: Capital is money: Capital is commodities. In truth, however, value is here the active factor in a process, in which, while constantly assuming the form in turn of money and commodities, it at the same time changes in magnitude, differentiates itself by throwing off surplus-value from itself; the original value, in other words, expands spontaneously. For the movement, in the course of which it adds surplus-value, is its own movement, its expansion, therefore, is automatic expansion. Because it is value, it has acquired the occult quality of being able to add value to itself. It brings forth living offspring, or, at the least, lays golden eggs.

Value, therefore, being the active factor in such a process, and assuming at one time the form of money, at another that of commodities, but through all these changes preserving itself and expanding, it requires some independent form, by means of which its identity may at any time be established. And this form it possesses only in the shape of money. It is under the form of money that value begins and ends, and begins again, every act of its own spontaneous generation. It began by being £100, it is now £110, and so on. But the money itself is only one of the two forms of value. Unless it takes the form of some commodity, it does not become capital. There is here no antagonism, as in the case of hoarding, between the money and commodities. The capitalist knows that all commodities, however scurvy they may look, or however badly they may smell, are in faith and in truth money, inwardly circumcised Jews, and what is more, a wonderful means whereby out of money to make more money.

In simple circulation, C–M–C, the value of commodities attained at the most a form independent of their use-values; *i.e.*, the form of money; but that same value now in the circulation M–C–M, or the circulation of capital, suddenly presents itself as an independent substance, endowed with a motion of its own, passing through a life-process of its own, in which money and commodities are mere forms which it assumes and casts off in turn. Nay, more: instead of simply representing the relations of commodities, it enters now, so to say, into private relations with itself. It differentiates itself as original value from itself as surplus-value; as the father differentiates himself from himself qua the son, yet both are one and of one age: for only by the surplus-value of £10 does the £100 originally advanced become capital, and so soon as this takes place, so soon as the son, and by the son, the father, is begotten, so soon does their difference vanish, and they again become one, £110.

Value therefore now becomes value in process, money in process, and, as such, capital. It comes out of circulation, enters into it again, preserves and multiplies itself within its circuit, comes back out of it with expanded bulk, and begins the same round ever afresh. M–M', money which begets money, such is the description of Capital from the mouths of its first interpreters, the Mercantilists.

Buying in order to sell, or, more accurately, buying in order to sell dearer, M–C–M', appears certainly to be a form peculiar to one kind of capital alone, namely, merchants' capital. But industrial capital too is money, that is changed into commodities, and by the sale of these commodities, is re-converted into more money. The events that take place outside the sphere of circulation, in the interval between the buying and selling, do not affect the form of this movement. Lastly, in the case of interest-bearing capital, the circulation M–C–M' appears abridged. We have its result without the intermediate stage, in the form M–M', 'en style lapidaire' so to say, money that is worth more money, value that is greater than itself.

M–C–M' is therefore in reality the general formula of capital as it appears prima facie within the sphere of circulation.

[. . .]

The buying and selling of labour-power

The change of value that occurs in the case of money intended to be converted into capital, cannot take place in the money itself, since in its function of means of purchase and of payment, it does no more than realise the price of the commodity it buys or pays for; and, as hard cash, it is value petrified, never varying. Just as little can it originate in the second act of circulation, the re-sale of the commodity, which does no more than transform the article from its bodily form back again into its money-form. The change must, therefore, take place in the commodity bought by the first act, M–C, but not in its value, for equivalents are exchanged, and the commodity is paid for at its full value. We are, therefore, forced to the conclusion that the change originates in the use-value, as such, of the commodity, *i.e.*, in its consumption. In order to be able to extract value from the consumption of a commodity, our friend, Moneybags, must be so lucky as to find, within the sphere of circulation, in the market, a commodity, whose use-value possesses the peculiar property of being a source of value, whose actual consumption, therefore, is itself an embodiment of labour, and, consequently, a creation of value. The possessor of money does find on the market such a special commodity in capacity for labour or labour-power.

By labour-power or capacity for labour is to be understood the aggregate of those mental and physical capabilities existing in a human being, which he exercises whenever he produces a use-value of any description.

But in order that our owner of money may be able to find labour-power offered for sale as a commodity, various conditions must first be fulfilled. The exchange of commodities of itself implies no other relations of dependence than those which result from its own nature. On this assumption, labour-power can appear upon the market as a commodity, only if, and so far as, its possessor, the individual whose labour-power it is, offers it for sale, or sells it, as a commodity. In order that he may be able to do this, he must have it at his disposal, must be the untrammelled owner of his capacity for labour, *i.e.*, of his person. He and the owner of money meet in the market, and deal with each other as on the basis of equal rights, with this difference alone, that one is buyer, the other seller; both, therefore, equal in the eyes of the law. The continuance of this relation demands that the owner of the labour-power should sell it only for a definite period, for if he were to sell it rump and stump, once for all, he would be selling himself, converting himself from a free man into a slave, from an owner of a commodity into a commodity. He must constantly look upon his labour-power as his own property, his own commodity, and this he can only do by placing it at the disposal of the buyer temporarily, for a definite period of time. By this means alone can he avoid renouncing his rights of ownership over it.

The second essential condition to the owner of money finding labour-power in the market as a commodity is this – that the labourer instead of being in the position to sell commodities in which his labour is incorporated, must be obliged to offer for sale as a commodity that very labour-power, which exists only in his living self.

In order that a man may be able to sell commodities other than labour-power, he must of course have the means of production, as raw material, implements, etc. No boots can be made without leather. He requires also the means of subsistence. Nobody – not even 'a musician of the future' –

can live upon future products, or upon use-values in an unfinished state; and ever since the first moment of his appearance on the world's stage, man always has been, and must still be a consumer, both before and while he is producing. In a society where all products assume the form of commodities, these commodities must be sold after they have been produced, it is only after their sale that they can serve in satisfying the requirements of their producer. The time necessary for their sale is superadded to that necessary for their production.

For the conversion of his money into capital, therefore, the owner of money must meet in the market with the free labourer, free in the double sense, that as a free man he can dispose of his labour-power as his own commodity, and that on the other hand he has no other commodity for sale, is short of everything necessary for the realisation of his labour-power.

The question why this free labourer confronts him in the market, has no interest for the owner of money, who regards the labour-market as a branch of the general market for commodities. And for the present it interests us just as little. We cling to the fact theoretically, as he does practically. One thing, however, is clear – Nature does not produce on the one side owners of money or commodities, and on the other men possessing nothing but their own labour-power. This relation has no natural basis, neither is its social basis one that is common to all historical periods. It is clearly the result of a past historical development, the product of many economic revolutions, of the extinction of a whole series of older forms of social production.

So, too, the economic categories, already discussed by us, bear the stamp of history. Definite historical conditions are necessary that a product may become a commodity. It must not be produced as the immediate means of subsistence of the producer himself. Had we gone further, and inquired under what circumstances all, or even the majority of products take the form of commodities, we should have found that this can only happen with production of a very specific kind, capitalist production. Such an inquiry, however, would have been foreign to the analysis of commodities. Production and circulation of commodities can take place, although the great mass of the objects produced are intended for the immediate requirements of their producers, are not turned into commodities, and consequently social production is not yet by a long way dominated in its length and breadth by exchange-value. The appearance of products as commodities pre-supposes such a development of the social division of labour, that the separation of use-value from exchange-value, a separation which first begins with barter, must already have been completed. But such a degree of development is common to many forms of society, which in other respects present the most varying historical features. On the other hand, if we consider money, its existence implies a definite stage in the exchange of commodities. The particular functions of money which it performs, either as the mere equivalent of commodities, or as means of circulation, or means of payment, as hoard or as universal money, point, according to the extent and relative preponderance of the one function or the other, to very different stages in the process of social production. Yet we know by experience that a circulation of commodities relatively primitive, suffices for the production of all these forms. Otherwise with capital. The historical conditions of its existence are by no means given with the mere circulation of money and commodities. It can spring into life, only when the owner of the means of production and subsistence meets in the market with the free labourer selling his labour-power. And this one historical condition comprises a world's history. Capital, therefore, announces from its first appearance a new epoch in the process of social production.

We must now examine more closely this peculiar commodity, labour-power. Like all others it has a value. How is that value determined?

The value of labour-power is determined, as in the case of every other commodity, by the labour-time necessary for the production, and consequently also the reproduction, of this special article. So far as it has value, it represents no more than a definite quantity of the average labour of society incorporated in it. Labour-power exists only as a capacity, or power of the living individual. Its production consequently pre-supposes his existence. Given the individual, the production of labour-power consists in his reproduction of himself or his maintenance. For his maintenance he requires a given quantity of the means of subsistence. Therefore the labour-time requisite for the production of labour-power reduces itself to that necessary for the production of those means of subsistence; in other words, the value of labour-power is the value of the means of subsistence necessary for the maintenance of the labourer. Labour-power, however, becomes a reality only by its exercise; it sets itself in action only by working. But thereby a definite quantity of human muscle, nerve, brain, etc., is wasted, and these require to be restored. This increased expenditure demands a larger income. If the owner of labour-power works to-day, to-morrow he must again be able to repeat the same process in the same conditions as regards health and strength. His means of subsistence must therefore be sufficient to maintain him in his normal state as a labouring individual. His natural wants, such as food, clothing, fuel, and housing, vary according to the climatic and other physical conditions of his country. On the other hand, the number and extent of his so-called necessary wants, as also the modes of satisfying them, are themselves the product of historical development, and depend therefore to a great extent on the degree of civilisation of a country, more particularly on the conditions under which, and consequently on the habits and degree of comfort in which, the class of free labourers has been formed. In contradistinction therefore to the case of other commodities, there enters into the determination of the value of labour-power a historical and moral element. Nevertheless, in a given country, at a given period, the average quantity of the means of subsistence necessary for the labourer is practically known.

The owner of labour-power is mortal. If then his appearance in the market is to be continuous, and the continuous conversion of money into capital assumes this, the seller of labour-power must perpetuate himself, 'in the way that every living individual perpetuates himself, by procreation.' The labour-power withdrawn from the market by wear and tear and death, must be continually replaced by, at the very least, an equal amount of fresh labour-power. Hence the sum of the means of subsistence necessary for the production of labour-power must include the means necessary for the labourer's substitutes, i.e., his children, in order that this race of peculiar commodity-owners may perpetuate its appearance in the market.

In order to modify the human organism, so that it may acquire skill and handiness in a given branch of industry, and become labour-power of a special kind, a special education or training is requisite, and this, on its part, costs an equivalent in commodities of a greater or less amount. This amount varies according to the more or less complicated character of the labour-power. The expenses of this education (excessively small in the case of ordinary labour-power), enter pro tanto into the total value spent in its production.

The value of labour-power resolves itself into the value of a definite quantity of the means of subsistence. It therefore varies with the value of these means or with the quantity of labour requisite for their production.

[. . .]

Part III

The production of absolute surplus-value

The labour-process

The capitalist buys labour-power in order to use it; and labour-power in use is labour itself. The purchaser of labour-power consumes it by setting the seller of it to work. By working, the latter becomes actually, what before he only was potentially, labour-power in action, a labourer. In order that his labour may re-appear in a commodity, he must, before all things, expend it on something useful, on something capable of satisfying a want of some sort. Hence, what the capitalist sets the labourer to produce, is a particular use-value, a specified article. The fact that the production of use-values, or goods, is carried on under the control of a capitalist and on his behalf, does not alter the general character of that production.

[. . .]

Our would-be capitalist . . . [has] purchased, in the open market, all the necessary factors of the labour-process; its objective factors, the means of production, as well as its subjective factor, labour-power. With the keen eye of an expert, he has selected the means of production and the kind of labour-power best adapted to his particular trade, be it spinning, bootmaking, or any other kind. He then proceeds to consume the commodity, the labour-power that he has just bought, by causing the labourer, the impersonation of that labour-power, to consume the means of production by his labour. The general character of the labour-process is evidently not changed by the fact, that the labourer works for the capitalist instead of for himself; moreover, the particular methods and operations employed in bootmaking or spinning are not immediately changed by the intervention of the capitalist. He must begin by taking the labour-power as he finds it in the market, and consequently be satisfied with labour of such a kind as would be found in the period immediately preceding the rise of capitalists. Changes in the methods of production by the subordination of labour to capital, can take place only at a later period, and therefore will have to be treated of in a later chapter.

The labour-process, turned into the process by which the capitalist consumes labour-power, exhibits two characteristic phenomena. First, the labourer works under the control of the capitalist to whom his labour belongs; the capitalist taking good care that the work is done in a proper manner, and that the means of production are used with intelligence, so that there is no unnecessary waste of raw material, and no wear and tear of the implements beyond what is necessarily caused by the work.

Secondly, the product is the property of the capitalist and not that of the labourer, its immediate producer. Suppose that a capitalist pays for a day's labour-power at its value; then the right to use that power for a day belongs to him, just as much as the right to use any other commodity, such as a horse that he has hired for the day. To the purchaser of a commodity belongs its use, and the seller of labour-power, by giving his labour, does no more, in reality, than part with the use-value that he has sold. From the instant he steps into the workshop, the use-value of his labour-power, and therefore also its use, which is labour, belongs to the capitalist. By the purchase of labour-power, the capitalist incorporates labour, as a living ferment, with the lifeless constituents of the product. From his point of view, the labour-process is nothing more than the consumption of the commodity purchased, *i.e.*, of labour-power; but this consumption cannot be effected except by supplying the labour-power with the means of production. The labour-process is a process between things that the capitalist has purchased, things that have become his property. The product of this process belongs, therefore, to him, just as much as does the wine which is the product of a process of fermentation completed in his cellar.

The production of surplus-value

The product appropriated by the capitalist is a use-value, as yarn, for example, or boots. But, although boots are, in one sense, the basis of all social progress, and our capitalist is a decided 'progressist,' yet he does not manufacture boots for their own sake. Use-value is, by no means, the thing 'qu'on aime pour lui-même' in the production of commodities. Use-values are only produced by capitalists, because, and in so far as, they are the material substratum, the depositories of exchange-value. Our capitalist has two objects in view: in the first place, he wants to produce a use-value that has a value in exchange, that is to say, an article destined to be sold, a commodity; and secondly, he desires to produce a commodity whose value shall be greater than the sum of the values of the commodities used in its production, that is, of the means of production and the labour-power, that he purchased with his good money in the open market. His aim is to produce not only a use-value, but a commodity also, not only use-value, but value; not only value, but at the same time surplus-value.

It must be borne in mind, that we are now dealing with the production of commodities, and that, up to this point, we have only considered one aspect of the process. Just as commodities are, at the same time, use-values and values, so the process of producing them must be a labour-process, and at the same time, a process of creating value.

Let us now examine production as a creation of value.

We know that the value of each commodity is determined by the quantity of labour expended on and materialised in it, by the working-time necessary, under given social conditions, for its production. This rule also holds good in the case of the product that accrued to our capitalist, as the result of the labour-process carried on for him. [. . .] But the past labour that is embodied in the labour-power, and the living labour that it can call into action; the daily cost of maintaining it, and its daily expenditure in work, are two totally different things. The former determines the exchange-value of the labour-power, the latter is its use-value. The fact that half a day's labour is necessary to keep the labourer alive during 24 hours, does not in any way prevent him from working a whole day. Therefore, the value of labour-power, and the value which that labour-power creates in the labour-process, are two entirely different magnitudes; and this difference of the two values was what the capitalist had in view, when he was purchasing the labour-power. The useful qualities that labour-power possesses, and by virtue of which it makes yarn or boots, were to him nothing more than a conditio sine qua non; for in order to create value, labour must be expended in a useful manner. What really influenced him was the specific use-value which this commodity possesses of being *a source not only of value, but of more value than it has itself.* This is the special service that the capitalist expects from labour-power, and in this transaction he acts in accordance with the 'eternal laws' of the exchange of commodities. The seller of labour-power, like the seller of any other commodity, realises its exchange-value, and parts with its use-value. He cannot take the one without giving the other. The use-value of labour-power, or in other words, labour, belongs just as little to its seller, as the use-value of oil after it has been sold belongs to the dealer who has sold it. The owner of the money has paid the value of a day's labour-power; his, therefore, is the use of it for a day; a day's labour belongs to him. The circumstance, that on the one hand the daily sustenance of labour-power costs only half a day's labour, while on the other hand the very same labour-power can work during a whole day, that consequently the value which its use during one day creates, is double what he pays for that use, this circumstance is, without doubt, a piece of good luck for the buyer, but by no means an injury to the seller.

[. . .]

We now see, that the difference between labour, considered on the one hand as producing utilities, and on the other hand, as creating value, a difference which we discovered by our analysis of a commodity, resolves itself into a distinction between two aspects of the process of production.

The process of production, considered on the one hand as the unity of the labour-process and the process of creating value, is production of commodities; considered on the other hand as the unity of the labour-process and the process of producing surplus-value, it is the capitalist process of production, or capitalist production of commodities.

[. . .]

By our explanation of the different parts played by the various factors of the labour-process in the formation of the product's value, we have, in fact, disclosed the characters of the different functions allotted to the different elements of capital in the process of expanding its own value. The surplus of the total value of the product, over the sum of the values of its constituent factors, is the surplus of the expanded capital over the capital originally advanced. The means of production on the one hand, labour-power on the other, are merely the different modes of existence which the value of the original capital assumed when from being money it was transformed into the various factors of the labour-process. That part of capital then, which is represented by the means of production, by the raw material, auxiliary material and the instruments of labour, does not, in the process of production, undergo any quantitative alteration of value. I therefore call it the constant part of capital, or, more shortly, *constant capital*.

On the other hand, that part of capital, represented by labour-power, does, in the process of production, undergo an alteration of value. It both reproduces the equivalent of its own value, and also produces an excess, a surplus-value, which may itself vary, may be more or less according to circumstances. This part of capital is continually being transformed from a constant into a variable magnitude. I therefore call it the variable part of capital, or, shortly, *variable capital*. The same elements of capital which, from the point of view of the labour-process, present themselves respectively as the objective and subjective factors, as means of production and labour-power, present themselves, from the point of view of the process of creating surplus-value, as constant and variable capital.

[. . .]

A change in the proportion of constant to variable capital does not affect the respective functions of these two kinds of capital. The technical conditions of the labour-process may be revolutionised to such an extent, that where formerly ten men using ten implements of small value worked up a relatively small quantity of raw material, one man may now, with the aid of one expensive machine, work up one hundred times as much raw material. In the latter case we have an enormous increase in the constant capital, that is represented by the total value of the means of production used, and at the same time a great reduction in the variable capital, invested in labour-power. Such a revolution, however, alters only the quantitative relation between the constant and the variable capital, or the proportions in which the total capital is split up into its constant and variable constituents; it has not in the least degree affected the essential difference between the two.

We have seen that the labourer, during one portion of the labour-process, produces only the value of his labour-power, that is, the value of his means of subsistence. Now since his work forms part of a system, based on the social division of labour, he does not directly produce the actual necessaries which he himself consumes; he produces instead a particular commodity, yarn for example, whose value is equal to the value of those necessaries or of the money with which they can be bought. The portion of his day's labour devoted to this purpose, will be greater or less, in proportion to the value of the necessaries that he daily requires on an average, or, what amounts to the same thing, in proportion to the labour-time required on an average to produce them. If the value of those necessaries represent on an average the expenditure of six hours' labour, the workman must on an average work for six hours to produce that value. If instead of working for the capitalist, he worked independently on his own account, he would, other things being equal, still be obliged to labour for the same number of hours, in order to produce the value of his labour-power, and thereby to gain the means of subsistence necessary for his conservation or continued reproduction. But as we have seen, during that portion of his day's labour in which he produces the value of his labour-power, say three shillings, he produces only an equivalent for the value of his labour-power already advanced by the capitalist; the new value created only replaces the variable capital advanced. It is owing to this fact, that the production of the new value of three shillings takes the semblance of a mere reproduction. That portion of the working-day, then, during which this reproduction takes place, I call 'necessary' labour-time, and the labour expended during that time I call 'necessary' labour. Necessary, as regards the labourer, because independent of the particular social form of his labour; necessary, as regards capital, and the world of capitalists, because on the continued existence of the labourer depends their existence also.

During the second period of the labour-process, that in which his labour is no longer necessary labour, the workman, it is true, labours, expends labour-power; but his labour, being no longer necessary labour, he creates no value for himself. He creates surplus-value which, for the capitalist, has all the charms of a creation out of nothing. This portion of the working-day, I name surplus labour-time, and to the labour expended during that time, I give the name of surplus-labour. It is every bit as important, for a correct understanding of surplus-value, to conceive it as a mere congelation of surplus labour-time, as nothing but materialised surplus-labour, as it is, for a proper comprehension of value, to conceive it as a mere congelation of so many hours of labour, as nothing but materialised labour. The essential difference between the various economic forms of society, between, for instance, a society based on slave-labour, and one based on wage-labour, lies only in the mode in which this surplus-labour is in each case extracted from the actual producer, the labourer.

Since, on the one hand, the values of the variable capital and of the labour-power purchased by that capital are equal, and the value of this labour-power determines the necessary portion of the working-day; and since, on the other hand, the surplus-value is determined by the surplus portion of the working-day, it follows that surplus-value bears the same ratio to variable capital, that surplus-labour does to necessary labour, or in other words, the rate of surplus-value $\frac{s}{v} = \frac{\text{surplus-labour}}{\text{necessary labour}}$. Both ratios, $\frac{s}{v}$ and $\frac{\text{surplus-labour}}{\text{necessary labour}}$, express the same thing in different ways; in the one case by reference to materialised, incorporated labour, in the other by reference to living, fluent labour.

The rate of surplus-value is therefore an exact expression for the degree of exploitation of labour-power by capital, or of the labourer by the capitalist.

[. . .]

The working day

What experience shows to the capitalist generally is a constant excess of population, *i.e.*, an excess in relation to the momentary requirements of surplus-labour-absorbing capital, although this excess is made up of generations of human beings stunted, short-lived, swiftly replacing each other, plucked, so to say, before maturity. And, indeed, experience shows to the intelligent observer with what swiftness and grip the capitalist mode of production, dating, historically speaking, only from yesterday, has seized the vital power of the people by the very root – shows how the degeneration of the industrial population is only retarded by the constant absorption of primitive and physically uncorrupted elements from the country – shows how even the country labourers, in spite of fresh air and the principle of natural selection, that works so powerfully amongst them, and only permits the survival of the strongest, are already beginning to die off. Capital that has such good reasons for denying the sufferings of the legions of workers that surround it, is in practice moved as much and as little by the sight of the coming degradation and final depopulation of the human race, as by the probable fall of the earth into the sun. In every stock-jobbing swindle every one knows that some time or other the crash must come, but every one hopes that it may fall on the head of his neighbour, after he himself has caught the shower of gold and placed it in safety. *Après moi le déluge!* is the watchword of every capitalist and of every capitalist nation. Hence Capital is reckless of the health or length of life of the labourer, unless under compulsion from society. To the out-cry as to the physical and mental degradation, the premature death, the torture of over-work, it answers: Ought these to trouble us since they increase our profits? But looking at things as a whole, all this does not, indeed, depend on the good or ill will of the individual capitalist. Free competition brings out the inherent laws of capitalist production, in the shape of external coercive laws having power over every individual capitalist.

[. . .]

It must be acknowledged that our labourer comes out of the process of production other than he entered. In the market he stood as owner of the commodity 'labour-power' face to face with other owners of commodities, dealer against dealer. The contract by which he sold to the capitalist his labour-power proved, so to say, in black and white that he disposed of himself freely. The bargain concluded, it is discovered that he was no 'free agent', that the time for which he is free to sell his labour-power is the time for which he is forced to sell it, that in fact the vampire will not lose its hold on him 'so long as there is a muscle, a nerve, a drop of blood to be exploited'. For 'protection' against 'the serpent of their agonies', the labourers must put their heads together, and, as a class, compel the passing of a law, an all-powerful social barrier that shall prevent the very workers from selling, by voluntary contract with capital, themselves and their families into slavery and death. In place of the pompous catalogue of the 'inalienable rights of man' comes the modest Magna Charta of a legally limited working-day, which shall make clear 'when the time which the worker sells is ended, and when his own begins'. What a transformation!

[. . .]

The so-called primitive accumulation

The secret of primitive accumulation

We have seen how money is changed into capital; how through capital surplus-value is made, and from surplus-value more capital. But the accumulation of capital pre-supposes surplus-value; surplus-value pre-supposes capitalistic production; capitalistic production pre-supposes the pre-existence of considerable masses of capital and of labour-power in the hands of producers of commodities. The whole movement, therefore, seems to turn in a vicious circle, out of which we can only get by supposing a primitive accumulation (previous accumulation of Adam Smith) preceding capitalistic accumulation; an accumulation not the result of the capitalist mode of production, but its starting-point.

This primitive accumulation plays in Political Economy about the same part as original sin in theology. Adam bit the apple, and thereupon sin fell on the human race. Its origin is supposed to be explained when it is told as an anecdote of the past. In times long gone by there were two sorts of people; one, the diligent, intelligent, and, above all, frugal élite; the other, lazy rascals, spending their substance, and more, in riotous living. The legend of theological original sin tells us certainly how man came to be condemned to eat his bread in the sweat of his brow; but the history of economic original sin reveals to us that there are people to whom this is by no means essential. Never mind! Thus it came to pass that the former sort accumulated wealth, and the latter sort had at last nothing to sell except their own skins. And from this original sin dates the poverty of the great majority that, despite all its labour, has up to now nothing to sell but itself, and the wealth of the few that increases constantly although they have long ceased to work. Such insipid childishness is every day preached to us in the defence of property. M. Thiers, *e.g.*, had the assurance to repeat it with all the solemnity of a statesman, to the French people, once so *spirituel*. But as soon as the question of property crops up, it becomes a sacred duty to proclaim the intellectual food of the infant as the one thing fit for all ages and for all stages of development. In actual history it is notorious that conquest, enslavement, robbery, murder, briefly force, play the great part. In the tender annals of Political Economy, the idyllic reigns from time immemorial. Right and 'labour' were from all time the sole means of enrichment, the present year of course always excepted. As a matter of fact, the methods of primitive accumulation are anything but idyllic.

In themselves money and commodities are no more capital than are the means of production and of subsistence. They want transforming into capital. But this transformation itself can only take place under certain circumstances that centre in this, viz., that two very different kinds of commodity-possessors must come face to face and into contact; on the one hand, the owners of money, means of production, means of subsistence, who are eager to increase the sum of values they possess, by buying other people's labour-power; on the other hand, free labourers, the sellers of their own labour-power, and therefore the sellers of labour. Free labourers, in the double sense that neither they themselves form part and parcel of the means of production, as in the case of slaves, bondsmen, etc, nor do the means of production belong to them, as in the case of peasant-proprietors; they are, therefore, free from, unencumbered by, any means of production of their own. With this polarisation of the market for commodities, the fundamental conditions of capitalist production are given. The capitalist system pre-supposes the complete separation of the labourers from all property in the means by which they can realise their labour. As soon as capitalist production is once on its own legs, it not only maintains this separation, but reproduces it on a continually extending scale. The process, therefore, that clears the way for the capitalist system, can be none other than the process which takes away from the labourer the possession of his means of production; a process that transforms, on the one hand, the social means of subsistence and of production into capital, on the other, the immediate producers into wage-labourers. The so-called primitive accumulation, therefore, is nothing else than the historical process of divorcing the producer from the means of production. It appears as primitive, because it forms the pre-historic stage of capital and of the mode of production corresponding with it.

The economic structure of capitalistic society has grown out of the economic structure of feudal society. The dissolution of the latter set free the elements of the former.

The immediate producer, the labourer, could only dispose of his own person after he had ceased to be attached to the soil and ceased to be the slave, serf, or bondman of another. To become a free seller of labour-power, who carries his commodity wherever he finds a market, he must further have escaped from the regime of the guilds, their rules for apprentices and journeymen, and the impediments of their labour regulations. Hence, the historical movement which changes the producers into wage-workers, appears, on the one hand, as their emancipation from serfdom and from the fetters of the guilds, and this side alone exists for our bourgeois historians. But, on the other hand, these new freedmen became sellers of themselves only after they had been robbed of all their own means of production, and of all the guarantees of existence afforded by the old feudal arrangements. And the history of this, their expropriation, is written in the annals of mankind in letters of blood and fire.

The industrial capitalists, these new potentates, had on their part not only to displace the guild masters of handicrafts, but also the feudal lords, the possessors of the sources of wealth. In this respect their conquest of social power appears as the fruit of a victorious struggle both against feudal lordship and its revolting prerogatives, and against the guilds and the fetters they laid on the free development of production and the free exploitation of man by man. The chevaliers d'industrie, however, only succeeded in supplanting the chevaliers of the sword by making use of events of which they themselves were wholly innocent. They have risen by means as vile as those by which the Roman freedman once on a time made himself the master of his *patronus*.

The starting-point of the development that gave rise to the wage-labourer as well as to the capitalist, was the servitude of the labourer. The advance consisted in a change of form of this servitude, in the transformation of feudal exploitation into capitalist exploitation. To understand its march, we need not go back very far. Although we come across the first beginnings of capitalist production as early as the 14th or 15th century, sporadically, in certain towns of the Mediterranean, the capitalistic era dates from the 16th century. Wherever it appears, the abolition of serfdom has been long effected, and the highest development of the middle ages, the existence of sovereign towns, has been long on the wane.

In the history of primitive accumulation, all revolutions are epoch-making that act as levers for the capitalist class in course of formation; but, above all, those moments when great masses of men are suddenly and forcibly torn from their means of subsistence, and hurled as free and 'unattached' proletarians on the labour-market. The expropriation of the agricultural producer, of the peasant, from the soil, is the basis of the whole process. The history of this expropriation, in different countries, assumes different aspects, and runs through its various phases in different orders of succession, and at different periods. In England alone, which we take as our example, has it the classic form.

[. . .]

Historical tendency of capitalist accumulation

What does the primitive accumulation of capital, i.e., its historical genesis, resolve itself into? In so far as it is not immediate transformation of slaves and serfs into wage-labourers, and therefore a mere change of form, it only means the expropriation of the immediate producers, i.e., the dissolution of private property based on the labour of its owner. Private property, as the antithesis to social, collective property, exists only where the means of labour and the external conditions of labour belong to private individuals. But according as these private individuals are labourers or not labourers, private property has a different character. The numberless shades, that it at first sight presents, correspond to the intermediate stages lying between these two extremes. The private property of the labourer in his means of production is the foundation of petty industry, whether agricultural, manufacturing, or both; petty industry, again, is an essential condition for the development of social production and of the free individuality of the labourer himself. Of course, this petty mode of production exists also under slavery, serfdom, and other states of dependence. But it flourishes, it lets loose its whole energy, it attains its adequate classical form, only where the labourer is the private owner of his own means of labour set in action by himself: the peasant of the land which he cultivates, the artisan of the tool which he handles as a virtuoso. This mode of production pre-supposes parcelling of the soil, and scattering of the other means of production. As it excludes the concentration of these means of production, so also it excludes co-operation, division of labour within each separate process of production, the control over, and the productive application of the forces of Nature by society, and the free development of the social productive powers. It is compatible only with a system of production, and a society, moving within narrow and more or less primitive bounds. To perpetuate it would be, as Pecqueur rightly says, 'to decree universal mediocrity'. At a certain stage of development it brings forth the material agencies for its own dissolution. From that moment new forces and new passions spring up in the bosom of society; but the old social organisation fetters them and keeps them down. It must be annihilated; it is annihilated. Its annihilation, the transformation of the individualised and scattered means of production into socially concentrated ones, of the pigmy property of the many into the huge property of the few, the expropriation of the great mass of the people from the soil, from the means of subsistence, and from the means of labour, this fearful and painful expropriation of the mass of the people forms the prelude to the history of capital. It comprises a series of forcible methods, of which we have passed in review only those that have been epoch-making as methods of the primitive accumulation of capital. The expropriation of the immediate producers was accomplished with merciless Vandalism, and under the stimulus of passions the most infamous, the most sordid, the pettiest, the most meanly odious. Self-earned private property, that is based, so to say, on the fusing together of the isolated, independent labouring-individual with the conditions of his labour, is supplanted by capitalistic private property, which rests on exploitation of the nominally free labour of others, i.e., on wage-labour.

As soon as this process of transformation has sufficiently decomposed the old society from top to bottom, as soon as the labourers are turned into proletarians, their means of labour into capital, as soon as the capitalist mode of production stands on its own feet, then the further socialisation of labour and further transformation of the land and other means of production into socially exploited and, therefore, common means of production, as well as the further expropriation of private proprietors, takes a new form. That which is now to be expropriated is no longer the labourer working for himself, but the capitalist exploiting many labourers. This expropriation is accomplished by the action of the immanent laws of capitalistic production itself, by the centralisation of capital. One capitalist always kills many. Hand in hand with this centralisation, or this expropriation of many capitalists by few, develop, on an ever-extending scale, the co-operative form of the labour-process, the conscious technical application of science, the methodical cultivation of the soil, the transformation of the instruments of labour into instruments of labour only usable in common, the economising of all means of production by their use as the means of production of combined, socialised labour, the entanglement of all peoples in the net of the world-market, and with this, the international character of the capitalistic régime. Along with the constantly diminishing number of the magnates of capital, who usurp and monopolise all advantages of this process of transformation, grows the mass of misery, oppression, slavery, degradation, exploitation; but with this too grows the revolt of the working-class, a class always increasing in numbers, and disciplined, united, organised by the very mechanism of the process of capitalist production itself. The monopoly of capital becomes a fetter upon the mode of production, which has sprung up and flourished along with, and under it. Centralisation of the means of production and socialisation of labour at last reach a point where they become incompatible with their capitalist integument. This integument is burst asunder. The knell of capitalist private property sounds. The expropriators are expropriated.

The capitalist mode of appropriation, the result of the capitalist mode of production, produces capitalist private property. This is the first negation of individual private property, as founded on the labour of the proprietor. But capitalist production begets, with the inexorability of a law of Nature, its own negation. It is the negation of negation. This does not re-establish private property for the producer, but gives him individual property based on the acquisitions of the capitalist era: *i.e.*, on co-operation and the possession in common of the land and of the means of production.

The transformation of scattered private property, arising from individual labour, into capitalist private property is, naturally, a process, incomparably more protracted, violent, and difficult, than the transformation of capitalistic private property, already practically resting on socialised production, into socialised property. In the former case, we had the expropriation of the mass of the people by a few usurpers; in the latter, we have the expropriation of a few usurpers by the mass of the people.

[. . .]

Capital Vol 3.

The law of the tendency of the rate of profit to fall

Assuming a given wage and working-day, a variable capital, for instance of 100, represents a certain number of employed labourers. It is the index of this number. Suppose £ 100 are the wages of 100 labourers for, say, one week. If these labourers perform equal amounts of necessary and surplus-labour, if they work daily as many hours for themselves, i.e., for the reproduction of their wage, as they do for the capitalist, i.e., for the production of surplus-value, then the value of their total product = £200, and the surplus-value they produce would amount, to £100. The rate of surplus-value, $\frac{s}{v}$, would = 100%. But . . . this rate of surplus-value would nonetheless express itself in very different rates of profit, depending on the different volumes of constant capital c and consequently of the total capital C, because the rate of profit = $\frac{s}{C}$. The rate of surplus-value is 100%:

$$\text{If } c = 50, \quad \text{and } v = 100, \text{ then } p' = \frac{100}{150} = 66\frac{2}{3}\%;$$

$$\text{,, } c = 100, \text{ and } v = 100, \text{ then } p' = \frac{100}{200} = 50\%;$$

$$\text{,, } c = 200, \text{ and } v = 100, \text{ then } p' = \frac{100}{300} = 33\frac{1}{3}\%;$$

$$\text{,, } c = 300, \text{ and } v = 100, \text{ then } p' = \frac{100}{400} = 25\%;$$

$$\text{,, } c = 400, \text{ and } v = 100, \text{ then } p' = \frac{100}{500} = 20\%.$$

This is how the same rate of surplus-value would express itself under the same degree of labour exploitation in a falling rate of profit, because the material growth of the constant capital implies also a growth – albeit not in the same proportion – in its value, and consequently in that of the total capital.

If it is further assumed that this gradual change in the composition of capital is not confined only to individual spheres of production, but that it occurs more or less in all, or at least in the key spheres of production, so that it involves changes in the average organic composition of the total capital of a certain society, then the gradual growth of constant capital in relation to variable capital must necessarily lead to *a gradual fall of the general rate of profit*, so long as the rate of surplus-value, or the intensity of exploitation of labour by capital, remain the same. Now we have seen that it is a law of capitalist production that its development is attended by a relative decrease of variable in relation to constant capital, and consequently to the total capital set in motion. This is just another way of saying that owing to the distinctive methods of production developing in the capitalist system the same number of labourers, i.e., the same quantity of labour-power set in motion by a variable capital of a given value, operate, work up and productively consume in the same time span an ever-increasing quantity of means of labour, machinery and fixed capital of all sorts, raw and auxiliary materials – and consequently a constant capital of an ever-increasing value. This continual relative decrease of the variable capital vis-à-vis the constant, and consequently the total capital, is identical with the progressively higher organic composition of the social capital in its average. It is likewise just another expression for the progressive development of the social productivity of labour, which is demonstrated precisely by the fact that the same number of labourers, in the same time, i.e., with less labour, convert an ever-increasing quantity of raw and auxiliary materials into products, thanks to the growing application of machinery and fixed capital in general. To this growing quantity of value of the constant capital – although indicating the growth of the real mass of use-values of which the constant capital materially consists only approximately – corresponds a progressive cheapening of products. Every individual product, considered by itself, contains a smaller quantity of labour than it did on a lower level of production, where the capital invested in wages occupies a far greater place compared to the capital invested in means of production. The hypothetical series drawn up at the beginning of this chapter expresses, therefore, the actual tendency of capitalist production. This mode of production produces a progressive relative decrease of the variable capital as compared to the constant capital, and consequently a continuously rising organic composition of the total capital. The immediate result of this is that the rate of surplus-value, at the same, or even a rising, degree of labour exploitation, is represented by a continually falling general rate of profit. (. . . This fall does not manifest itself in an absolute form, but rather as a tendency toward a progressive fall.) The progressive tendency of the general rate of profit to fall is, therefore, just *an expression peculiar to the capitalist mode of production* of the progressive development of the social productivity of labour. This does not mean to say that the rate of profit may not fall temporarily for other reasons. But proceeding from the nature of the capitalist mode of production, it is thereby proved a logical necessity that in its development the general average rate of surplus-value must express itself in a falling general rate of profit. Since the mass of the employed living labour is continually on the decline as compared to the mass of materialised labour set in motion by it, i.e., to the productively consumed means of production, it follows that the portion of living labour, unpaid and congealed in surplus-value, must also be continually on the decrease compared to the amount of value represented by the invested total capital. Since the ratio of the mass of surplus-value to the value of the invested total capital forms the rate of profit, this rate must constantly fall.

[. . .]

Counteracting influences

If we consider the enormous development of the productive forces of social labour in the last 30 years alone as compared with all preceding periods; if we consider, in particular, the enormous mass of fixed capital, aside from the actual machinery, which goes into the process of social production as a whole, then the difficulty which has hitherto troubled the economist, namely to explain the falling rate of profit, gives place to its opposite, namely to explain why this fall is not greater and more rapid. There must be some counteracting influences at work, which cross and annul the effect of the general law, and which give it merely the characteristic of a tendency, for which reason we have referred to the fall of the general rate of profit as a tendency to fall.

The following are the most general counterbalancing forces:

1 Increasing intensity of exploitation . . .
2 Depression of wages below the value of labour-power . . .
3 Cheapening of elements of constant capital . . .
4 Relative over-population . . .
5 Foreign trade . . .
6 The increase of stock capital.

[. . .]

On the formation of stock companies

1 An enormous expansion of the scale of production and of enterprises, that was impossible for individual capitals. At the same time, enterprises that were formerly government enterprises, become public.

2 The capital, which in itself rests on a social mode of production and presupposes a social concentration of means of production and labour-power, is here directly endowed with the form of social capital (capital of directly associated individuals) as distinct from private capital, and its undertakings assume the form of social undertakings as distinct from private undertakings. It is the abolition of capital as private property within the frame-work of capitalist production itself.

3 Transformation of the actually functioning capitalist into a mere manager, administrator of other people's capital, and of the owner of capital into a mere owner, a mere money-capitalist. Even if the dividends which they receive include the interest and the profit of enterprise, i.e., the total profit (for the salary of the manager is, or should be, simply the wage of a specific type of skilled labour, whose price is regulated in the labour-market like that of any other labour), this total profit is henceforth received only in the form of interest, i.e., as mere compensation for owning capital that now is entirely divorced from the function in the actual process of reproduction, just as this function in the person of the manager is divorced from ownership of capital. Profit thus appears (no longer only that portion of it, the interest, which derives its justification from the profit of the

borrower) as a mere appropriation of the surplus-labour of others, arising from the conversion of means of production into capital, i.e., from their alienation vis-à-vis the actual producer, from their antithesis as another's property to every individual actually at work in production, from manager down to the last day-labourer. In stock companies the function is divorced from capital ownership, hence also labour is entirely divorced from ownership of means of production and surplus-labour. This result of the ultimate development of capitalist production is a necessary transitional phase towards the reconversion of capital into the property of producers, although no longer as the private property of the individual producers, but rather as the property of associated producers, as outright social property. On the other hand, the stock company is a transition toward the conversion of all functions in the reproduction process which still remain linked with capitalist property, into mere functions of associated producers, into social functions.

Before we go any further, there is still the following economically important fact to be noted: Since profit here assumes the pure form of interest, undertakings of this sort are still possible if they yield bare interest, and this is one of the causes, stemming the fall of the general rate of profit, since such undertakings, in which the ratio of constant capital to the variable is so enormous, do not necessarily enter into the equalisation of the general rate of profit.

[. . .]

This is the abolition of the capitalist mode of production within the capitalist mode of production itself, and hence a self-dissolving contradiction, which *prima facie* represents a mere phase of transition to a new form of production. It manifests itself as such a contradiction in its effects. It establishes a monopoly in certain spheres and thereby requires state interference. It reproduces a new financial aristocracy, a new variety of parasites in the shape of promoters, speculators and simply nominal directors; a whole system of swindling and cheating by means of corporation promotion, stock issuance, and stock speculation. It is private production without the control of private property.

Aside from the stock-company business, which represents the abolition of capitalist private industry on the basis of the capitalist system itself and destroys private industry as it expands and invades new spheres of production, credit offers to the individual capitalist, or to one who is regarded a capitalist, absolute control within certain limits over the capital and property of others, and thereby over the labour of others. The control over social capital, not the individual capital of his own, gives him control of social labour. The capital itself, which a man really owns or is supposed to own in the opinion of the public, becomes purely a basis for the superstructure of credit. This is particularly true of wholesale commerce, through which the greatest portion of the social product passes. All standards of measurement, all excuses more or less still justified under capitalist production, disappear here. What the speculating wholesale merchant risks is social property, not *his own*. Equally sordid becomes the phrase relating the origin of capital to savings, for what he demands is that *others* should save for him. The other phrase concerning abstention is squarely refuted by his luxury, which is now itself a means of credit. Conceptions which have some meaning on a less developed stage of capitalist production, become quite meaningless here. Success and failure both lead here to a centralisation of capital, and thus to expropriation on the most enormous scale. Expropriation extends here from the direct producers to the smaller and the medium-sized capitalists themselves. It is the point of departure for the capitalist mode of production; its accomplishment is the goal of this production. In the last instance, it aims at the expropriation of the means of production from all individuals. With the development of social production the means of production cease to be means of private production and products of private production, and can thereafter be only means of production in the hands of associated producers, i.e., the latter's social property, much as they are their social products. However, this expropriation appears within the capitalist system in a contradictory form, as appropriation of social property by a few; and credit lends the latter more and more the aspect of pure adventurers. Since property here exists in the form of stock, its movement and transfer become purely a result of gambling on the stock exchange, where the little fish are swallowed by the sharks and the lambs by the stock-exchange wolves. There is antagonism against the old form in the stock companies, in which social means of production appear as private property; but the conversion to the form of stock still remains ensnared in the trammels of capitalism; hence, instead of overcoming the antithesis between the character of wealth as social and as private wealth, the stock companies merely develop it in a new form.

The co-operative factories of the labourers themselves represent within the old form the first sprouts of the new, although they naturally reproduce, and must reproduce, everywhere in their actual organisation all the shortcomings of the prevailing system. But the antithesis between capital and labour is overcome within them, if at first only by way of making the associated labourers into their own capitalist, i.e., by enabling them to use the means of production for the employment of their own labour. They show how a new mode of production naturally grows out of an old one, when the development of the material forces of production and of the corresponding forms of social production have reached a particular stage.

Without the factory system arising out of the capitalist mode of production there could have been no co-operative factories. Nor could these have developed without the credit system arising out of the same mode of production. The credit system is not only the principal basis for the gradual transformation of capitalist private enterprises into capitalist stock companies, but equally offers the means for the gradual extension of co-operative enterprises on a more or less national scale. The capitalist stock companies, as much as the co-operative factories, should be considered as transitional forms from the capitalist mode of production to the associated one, with the only distinction that the antagonism is resolved negatively in the one and positively in the other.

[. . .]

Classes

The owners merely of labour-power, owners of capital, and land-owners, whose respective sources of income are wages, profit and ground-rent, in other words, wage-labourers, capitalists and land-owners, constitute then three big classes of modern society based upon the capitalist mode of production.

In England, modern society is indisputably most highly and classically developed in economic structure. Nevertheless, even here the stratification of classes does not appear in its pure form. Middle and intermediate strata even here obliterate lines of demarcation everywhere (although incomparably less in rural districts than in the cities). However, this is immaterial for our analysis. We have seen that the continual tendency and law of development of the capitalist mode of production is more and more to divorce the means of production from labour, and more and more to concentrate the scattered means of production into large groups, thereby transforming labour into wage-labour and the means of production into capital. And to this tendency, on the other hand, corresponds the independent separation of landed property from capital and labour, or the transformation of all landed property into the form of landed property corresponding to the capitalist mode of production.

The first question to be answered is this: What constitutes a class? – and the reply to this follows naturally from the reply to another question, namely: What makes wage-labourers, capitalists and landlords constitute the three great social classes?

At first glance – the identity of revenues and sources of revenue. There are three great social groups whose members, the individuals forming them, live on wages, profit and ground-rent respectively, on the realisation of their labour-power, their capital, and their landed property.

However, from this standpoint, physicians and officials, e.g., would also constitute two classes, for they belong to two distinct social groups, the members of each of these groups receiving their revenue from one and the same source. The same would also be true of the infinite fragmentation of interest and rank into which the division of social labour splits labourers as well as capitalists and landlords – the latter, e.g., into owners of vineyards, farm owners, owners of forests, mine owners and owners of fisheries.

[Here the manuscript breaks off.]

From: *Capital,* Vol. 1, pp. 18–21, 43–55, 57–8, 76–9, 145–53, 164–9, 173, 179–81, 188, 201–3, 208–9, 256–7, 285–6, 667–70, 713–5; Vol. 3, pp. 211–3, 232, 235–40, 436–40, 885–6

17

The Civil War in France

It is frequently observed that Marx had a very great deal to say about capitalism, but surprising little to offer on the character of a future socialist society. The brief interlude of the Commune in Paris (in 1871) furnished Marx with a model for a transitional workers' regime. Here, Marx outlines this form of government, insisting that in it we can find 'the political form at last discovered under which to work out the economical emancipation of Labour'.

[. . .]

On the dawn of the 18th of March, Paris arose to the thunderburst of 'Vive la Commune!' What is the Commune, that sphinx so tantalizing to the bourgeois mind?

> The proletarians of Paris, said the Central Committee in its manifesto of the 18th March, amidst the failures and treasons of the ruling classes, have understood that the hour has struck for them to save the situation by taking into their own hands the direction of public affairs. . . . They have understood that it is their imperious duty and their absolute right to render themselves masters of their own destinies, by seizing upon the governmental power.

But the working class cannot simply lay hold of the ready-made State machinery, and wield it for its own purposes.

The centralized State power, with its ubiquitous organs of standing army, police, bureaucracy, clergy, and judicature – organs wrought after the plan of a systematic and hierarchic division of labour – originates from the days of absolute monarchy, serving nascent middle-class society as a mighty weapon in its struggles against feudalism. Still, its development remained clogged by all manner of mediaeval rubbish, seignorial rights, local privileges, municipal and guild monopolies and provincial constitutions. The gigantic broom of the French Revolution of the eighteenth century swept away all these relics of bygone times, thus clearing simultaneously the social soil of its last hindrances to the superstructure of the modern State edifice raised under the First Empire, itself the offspring of the coalition wars of old semi-feudal Europe against modern France. During the subsequent *régimes* the Government, placed under parliamentary control – that is, under the direct control of the propertied classes – became not only a hotbed of huge national debts and crushing taxes; with its irresistible allurements of place, pelf, and patronage, it became not only the bone of contention between the rival factions and adventurers of the ruling classes; but its political character changed simultaneously with the economic changes of society. At the same pace at which the progress of modern industry developed, widened, intensified the class antagonism between capital and labour, the State power assumed more and more the character of the national power of capital over labour, of a public force organized for social enslavement, of an engine of class despotism. After every revolution marking a progressive phase in the class struggle, the purely repressive character of the State power stands out in bolder and bolder relief. The Revolution of 1830, resulting in the transfer of Government from the landlords to the capitalists, transferred it from the more remote to the more direct antagonists of the working men. The bourgeois Republicans, who, in the name of the Revolution of February, took the State power, used it for the June massacres, in order to convince the working class that 'social' republic meant the republic ensuring their social subjection, and in order to convince the royalist bulk of the bourgeois and landlord class that they might safely leave the cares and emoluments of government to the bourgeois 'Republicans'. However, after their one heroic exploit of June, the bourgeois Republicans had, from the front, to fall back to the rear of the 'Party of Order' – a combination formed by all the rival fractions and factions of the appropriating class in their now openly declared antagonism to the producing classes. The proper form of their joint-stock Government was the *Parliamentary Republic*, with Louis Bonaparte for its President. Theirs was a *régime* of avowed class terrorism and deliberate insult towards the 'vile multitude'. If the Parliamentary Republic, as M. Thiers said, 'divided them (the different fractions of the ruling class) least,' it opened an abyss between that class and the whole body of society outside their spare ranks. The restraints by which their own divisions had under former *régimes* still checked the State power, were removed by their union; and in view of the threatening upheaval of the proletariat, they now used that State power mercilessly and ostentatiously as the national war-engine of capital against labour. In their uninterrupted crusade against the producing masses they were, however, bound not only to invest the executive with continually increased powers of repression, but at the same time to divest their own parliamentary stronghold – the National Assembly – one by one, of all its own means of defence against the Executive. The Executive, in the person of Louis Bonaparte, turned them out. The natural offspring of the 'Party-of-Order' Republic was the Second Empire.

The Empire, with the *coup d'état* for its certificate of birth, universal suffrage for its sanction, and the sword for its sceptre, professed to rest upon the peasantry, the large mass of producers not directly involved in the struggle of capital and labour. It professed to save the working class by breaking down Parliamentarism, and, with it, the undisguised subserviency of Government to the propertied classes. It professed to save the propertied classes by upholding their economic supremacy over the working class; and, finally, it professed to unite all classes by reviving for all the chimera of national glory. In reality, it was the only form of government possible at a time when the bourgeoisie had already lost, and the working class had not yet acquired, the faculty of ruling the nation. It was acclaimed throughout the world as the saviour of society. Under its sway, bourgeois society, freed from political cares, attained a development unexpected even by itself. Its industry and commerce expanded to colossal dimensions; financial swindling celebrated cosmopolitan orgies; the misery of the masses was set off by a shameless display of gorgeous, meretricious, and debased luxury. The State power, apparently soaring high above society, was at the same time itself the greatest scandal of that society and the very hotbed of all its corruptions. Its own rottenness, and the rottenness of the society it had saved, were laid bare by the bayonet of Prussia, herself eagerly bent upon transferring the supreme seat of that *régime* from Paris to Berlin. Imperialism is, at the same time, the most prostitute and the ultimate form of the State power which nascent middle-class society had commenced to elaborate as a means of its own emancipation from feudalism, and which full-grown bourgeois society had finally transformed into a means for the enslavement of labour by capital.

The direct antithesis to the Empire was the Commune. The cry of 'Social Republic', with which the revolution of February was ushered in by the Paris proletariat, did but express a vague aspiration after a Republic that was not only to supersede the monarchical form of class-rule, but class-rule itself. The Commune was the positive form of that Republic.

Paris, the central seat of the old governmental power, and, at the same time, the social stronghold of the French working class, had risen in arms against the attempt of Thiers and the Rurals to restore and perpetuate that old governmental power bequeathed to them by the Empire. Paris could resist only because, in consequence of the siege, it had got rid of the army, and replaced it by a National Guard, the bulk of which consisted of working men. This fact was now to be transformed into an institution. The first decree of the Commune, therefore, was the suppression of the standing army, and the substitution for it of the armed people.

The Commune was formed of the municipal councillors, chosen by universal suffrage in the various wards of the town, responsible and revocable at short terms. The majority of its members were naturally working men, of acknowledged representatives of the working class. The Commune was to be a working, not a parliamentary, body, executive and legislative at the same time. Instead of continuing to be the agent of the Central Government, the police was at once stripped of its political attributes, and turned into the responsible and at all times revocable agent of the Commune. So were the officials of all other branches of the Administration. From the members of the Commune downwards, the public service had to be done at *workmen's wages*. The vested interests and the representation allowances of the high dignitaries of State disappeared along with the high dignitaries themselves. Public functions ceased to be the private property of the tools of the Central Government. Not only municipal administration, but the whole initiative hitherto exercised by the State was laid into the hands of the Commune.

Having once got rid of the standing army and the police, the physical force elements of the old Government, the Commune was anxious to break the spiritual force of repression, the 'parson-power', by the disestablishment and disendowment of all churches as proprietary bodies. The priests were sent back to the recesses of private life, there to feed upon the alms of the faithful in imitation of their predecessors, the Apostles. The whole of the educational institutions were opened to the people gratuitously, and at the same time cleared of all interference of Church and State. Thus, not only was education made accessible to all, but science itself freed from the fetters which class prejudice and governmental force had imposed upon it.

The judicial functionaries were to be divested of that sham independence which had but served to mask their abject subserviency to all succeeding governments to which, in turn, they had taken, and broken, the oaths of allegiance. Like the rest of public servants, magistrates and judges were to be elective, responsible, and revocable.

The Paris Commune was, of course, to serve as a model to all the great industrial centres of France. The communal *régime* once established in Paris and the secondary centres, the old centralized Government would in the provinces, too, have to give way to the self-government of the producers. In a rough sketch of national organization which the Commune had no time to develop, it states clearly that the Commune was to be the political form of even the smallest country hamlet, and that in the rural districts the standing army was to be replaced by a national militia, with an extremely short term of service. The rural communes of every district were to administer their common affairs by an assembly of delegates in the central town, and these district assemblies were again to send deputies to the National Delegation in Paris, each delegate to be at any time revocable and bound by the *mandat impératif* (formal instructions) of his constituents. The few but important functions which still would remain for a central government were not to be suppressed, as has been intentionally misstated, but were to be discharged by Communal, and therefore strictly responsible agents. The unity of the nation was not to be broken, but, on the contrary, to be organized by the Communal constitution, and to become a reality by the destruction of the State power which claimed to be the embodiment of that unity independent of, and superior to, the nation itself, from which it was but a parasitic excrescence. While the merely repressive organs of the old governmental power were to be amputated, its legitimate functions were to be wrested from an authority usurping preeminence over society itself, and restored to the responsible agents of society. Instead of deciding once in three or six years which member of the ruling class was to misrepresent the people in Parliament, universal suffrage was to serve the people, constituted in Communes, as individual suffrage serves every other employer in the search for the workmen and managers in his business. And it is well known that companies, like individuals, in matters of real business generally know how to put the right man in the right place, and, if they for once make a mistake, to redress it promptly. On the other hand, nothing could be more foreign to the spirit of the Commune than to supersede universal suffrage by hierarchic investiture.

It is generally the fate of completely new historical creations to be mistaken for the counterpart of older and even defunct forms of social life, to which they may bear a certain likeness. Thus, this new Commune, which breaks the modern State power, has been mistaken for a reproduction of the mediaeval Communes, which first preceded, and afterwards became the substratum of, that very State power. – The communal constitution has been mistaken for an attempt to break up into a federation of small States, as dreamt of by Montesquieu and the Girondins, that unity of great nations which, if originally brought about by political force, has now become a powerful coefficient of social production. – The antagonism of the Commune against the State power has been mistaken for an exaggerated form of the ancient struggle against over-centralization. Peculiar historical circumstances may have prevented the classical development, as in France, of the bourgeois form of government, and may have allowed, as in England, to complete the great central State organs by corrupt vestries, jobbing councillors, and ferocious poor-law guardians in the towns, and virtually hereditary magistrates in the counties. The Communal Constitution would have restored to the social body all the forces hitherto absorbed by the State parasite feeding upon, and clogging the free movement of,

society. By this one act it would have initiated the regeneration of France.
– The provincial French middle-class saw in the Commune an attempt to
restore the sway their order had held over the country under Louis
Philippe, and which, under Louis Napoleon, was supplanted by the
pretended rule of the country over the towns. In reality, the Communal
Constitution brought the rural producers under the intellectual lead of the
central towns of their districts, and there secured to them, in the working
men, the natural trustees of their interests. – The very existence of the
Commune involved, as a matter of course, local municipal liberty, but no
longer as a check upon the, now superseded, State power. It could only
enter into the head of a Bismarck, who, when not engaged on his intrigues
of blood and iron, always likes to resume his old trade, so befitting his
mental calibre, of contributor to *Kladderadatsch* (the Berlin *Punch*), it
could only enter into such a head, to ascribe to the Paris Commune
aspirations after that caricature of the old French municipal organization
of 1791, the Prussian municipal constitution which degrades the town
governments to mere secondary wheels in the police-machinery of the
Prussian State. The Commune made that catch-word of bourgeois
revolutions, cheap government, a reality, by destroying the two greatest
sources of expenditure – the standing army and State functionarism. Its
very existence presupposed the non-existence of monarchy, which, in
Europe at least, is the normal incumbrance and indispensable cloak of
class-rule. It supplied the Republic with the basis of really democratic
institutions. But neither cheap government nor the 'true Republic' was its
ultimate aim; they were its mere concomitants.

The multiplicity of interpretations to which the Commune has been
subjected, and the multiplicity of interests which construed it in their
favour, show that it was a thoroughly expansive political form, while all
previous forms of government had been emphatically repressive. Its true
secret was this. It was essentially a working-class government, the produce
of the struggle of the producing against the appropriating class, the
political form at last discovered under which to work out the economical
emancipation of Labour.

Except on this last condition, the Communal Constitution would have
been an impossibility and a delusion. The political rule of the producer
cannot coexist with the perpetuation of his social slavery. The Commune
was therefore to serve as a lever for uprooting the economical foundations
upon which rests the existence of classes, and therefore of class rule. With
labour emancipated, every man becomes a working man, and productive
labour ceases to be a class attribute.

It is a strange fact. In spite of all the tall talk and all the immense
literature, for the last sixty years, about Emancipation of Labour, no
sooner do the working men anywhere take the subject into their own hands

with a will, than uprises at once all the apologetic phraseology of the mouthpieces of present society with its two poles of Capital and Wage-slavery (the landlord now is but the sleeping partner of the capitalist), as if capitalist society was still in its purest state of virgin innocence, with its antagonisms still undeveloped, with its delusions still unexploded, with its prostitute realities not yet laid bare. The Commune, they exclaim, intends to abolish property, the basis of all civilization! Yes, gentlemen, the Commune intended to abolish that class-property which makes the labour of the many the wealth of the few. It aimed at the expropriation of the expropriators. It wanted to make individual property a truth by transforming the means of production, land and capital, now chiefly the means of enslaving and exploiting labour, into mere instruments of free and associated labour. – But this is Communism, 'impossible' Communism! Why, those members of the ruling classes who are intelligent enough to perceive the impossibility of continuing the present system – and they are many – have become the obtrusive and full-mouthed apostles of co-operative production. If co-operative production is not to remain a sham and a snare; if it is to supersede the Capitalist system; if united co-operative societies are to regulate national production upon a common plan, thus taking it under their own control, and putting an end to the constant anarchy and periodical convulsions which are the fatality of Capitalist production – what else, gentlemen, would it be but Communism, 'possible' Communism?

The working class did not expect miracles from the Commune. They have no ready-made utopias to introduce by the people's decree. They know that in order to work out their own emancipation, and along with it that higher form to which present society is irresistibly tending by its own economical agencies, they will have to pass through long struggles, through a series of historic processes, transforming circumstances and men. They have no ideals to realize, but to set free elements of the new society with which old collapsing bourgeois society itself is pregnant. In the full consciousness of their historic mission, and with the heroic resolve to act up to it, the working class can afford to smile at the coarse invective of the gentlemen's gentlemen with the pen and inkhorn, and at the didactic patronage of well-wishing bourgeois-doctrinaires, pouring forth their ignorant platitudes and sectarian crotchets in the oracular tone of scientific infallibility.

When the Paris Commune took the management of the revolution in its own hands; when plain working men for the first time dared to infringe upon the Governmental privilege of their 'natural superiors', and, under circumstances of unexampled difficulty, performed their work modestly, conscientiously, and efficiently – performed it at salaries the highest of which barely amounted to one-fifth of what, according to high scientific authority, is the minimum required for a secretary to a certain metropolitan school-board – the old world writhed in convulsions of rage at the sight of the Red Flag, the symbol of the Republic of Labour, floating over the Hôtel de Ville.

And yet, this was the first revolution in which the working class was openly acknowledged as the only class capable of social initiative, even by the great bulk of the Paris middle class – shopkeepers, tradesmen, merchants – the wealthy capitalists alone excepted. The Commune had saved them by a sagacious settlement of that ever-recurring cause of dispute among the middle classes themselves – the debtor and creditor accounts. The same portion of the middle class, after they had assisted in putting down the working men's insurrection of June, 1848, had been at once unceremoniously sacrificed to their creditors by the then Constituent Assembly. But this was not their motive for now rallying round the working class. They felt that there was but one alternative – the Commune, or the Empire – under whatever name it might reappear. The Empire had ruined them economically by the havoc it made of public wealth, by the wholesale financial swindling it fostered, by the props it lent to the artificially accelerated centralization of capital, and the concomi-tant expropriation of their own ranks. It had suppressed them politically, it had shocked them morally by its orgies, it had insulted their Voltairianism by handing over the education of their children to the *frères Ignorantins*, it had revolted their national feeling as Frenchmen by precipitating them headlong into a war which left only one equivalent for the ruins it made – the disappearance of the Empire. In fact, after the exodus from Paris of the high Bonapartist and capitalist *Bohême*, the true middle-class Party of Order came out in the shape of the 'Union Républicaine', enrolling themselves under the colours of the Commune and defending it against the willful misconstruction of Thiers. Whether the gratitude of this great body of the middle class will stand the present severe trial, time must show.

The Commune was perfectly right in telling the peasants that 'its victory was their only hope'. Of all the lies hatched at Versailles and re-echoed by the glorious European penny-a-liner, one of the most tremendous was that the Rurals represented the French peasantry. Think only of the love of the French peasant for the men to whom, after 1815, he had to pay the milliard of indemnity! In the eyes of the French peasant, the very existence of a great landed proprietor is in itself an encroachment on his conquests of 1789. The bourgeois, in 1848, had burthened his plot of land with the additional tax of forty-five cents in the franc; but then he did so in the name of the revolution; while now he had fomented a civil war against the revolution, to shift on to the peasant's shoulders the chief load of the five milliards of indemnity to be paid to the Prussians. The Commune, on the other hand, in one of its first proclamations, declared that the true originators of the war would be made to pay its cost. The Commune would have delivered the peasant of the blood tax, – would have given him a cheap government, – transformed his present blood-suckers, the notary, advocate, executor, and other judicial vampires, into salaried communal agents, elected by, and responsible to, himself. It would have freed him of the tyranny of the village police, the gendarme, and the prefect, would have put enlightenment by the schoolmaster in the place of stuntification by the priest. And the French peasant is, above all, a man of reckoning. He would find it extremely reasonable that the pay of the priest, instead of being extorted by the tax-gatherer, should only depend upon the spontaneous action of the parishioners' religious instincts. Such were the great immediate boons which the rule of the Commune – and that rule alone – held out to the French peasantry. It is, therefore, quite superfluous here to expatiate upon the more complicated but vital problems which the Commune alone was able, and at the same time compelled, to solve in favour of the peasant, viz., the hypothecary debt, lying like an incubus upon his parcel of soil, the *prolétariat foncier* (the rural proletariat), daily growing upon it, and his expropriation from it enforced, at a more and more rapid rate, by the very development of modern agriculture and the competition of capitalist farming.

The French peasant had elected Louis Bonaparte president of the Republic; but the Party of Order created the Empire. What the French peasant really wants he commenced to show in 1849 and 1850, by opposing his maire to the Government's prefect, his schoolmaster to the Government's priest, and himself to the Government's gendarme. All the laws made by the Party of Order in January and February, 1850, were avowed measures of repression against the peasant. The peasant was a Bonapartist, because the great Revolution, with all its benefits to him, was, in his eyes, personified in Napoleon. This delusion, rapidly breaking down under the Second Empire (and in its very nature hostile to the Rurals), this prejudice of the past, how could it have withstood the appeal of the Commune to the living interests and urgent wants of the peasantry?

The Rurals – this was, in fact, their chief apprehension – knew that three months' free communication of Communal Paris with the provinces would bring about a general rising of the peasants, and hence their anxiety to establish a police blockade around Paris, so as to stop the spread of the rinderpest.

If the Commune was thus the true representative of all the healthy elements of French society, and therefore the truly national Government, it was, at the same time, as a working men's Government, as the bold champion of the emancipation of labour, emphatically international. Within sight of the Prussian army, that had annexed to Germany two

French provinces, the Commune annexed to France the working people all over the world.

The Second Empire had been the jubilee of cosmopolitan blackleggism, the rakes of all countries rushing in at its call for a share in its orgies and in the plunder of the French people. Even at this moment the right hand of Thiers is Ganesco, the foul Wallachian, and his left hand is Markowski, the Russian spy. The Commune admitted all foreigners to the honour of dying for an immortal cause. Between the foreign war lost by their treason, and the civil war fomented by their conspiracy with the foreign invader, the bourgeoisie had found the time to display their patriotism by organizing police-hunts upon the Germans in France. The Commune made a German working-man its Minister of Labour. Thiers, the bourgeoisie, the Second Empire, had continually deluded Poland by loud professions of sympathy, while in reality betraying her to, and doing the dirty work of, Russia. The Commune honoured the heroic sons of Poland by placing them at the head of the defenders of Paris. And, to broadly mark the new era of history it was conscious of initiating, under the eyes of the conquering Prussians on the one side, and of the Bonapartist army, led by Bonapartist generals, on the other, the Commune pulled down that colossal symbol of martial glory, the Vendôme column.

The great social measure of the Commune was its own working existence. Its special measures could but betoken the tendency of a government of the people by the people. Such were the abolition of the nightwork of journeymen bakers; the prohibition, under penalty, of the employers' practice to reduce wages by levying upon their workpeople fines under manifold pretexts, – a process in which the employer combines in his own person the parts of legislator, judge, and executor, and filches the money to boot. Another measure of this class was the surrender, to associations of workmen, under reserve of compensation, of all closed workshops and factories, no matter whether the respective capitalists had absconded or preferred to strike work.

The financial measures of the Commune, remarkable for their sagacity and moderation, could only be such as were compatible with the state of a besieged town. Considering the colossal robberies committed upon the city of Paris by the great financial companies and contractors, under the protection of Haussmann, the Commune would have had an incomparably better title to confiscate their property than Louis Napoleon had against the Orléans family. The Hohenzollern and the English oligarchs who both have derived a good deal of their estates from Church plunder, were, of course, greatly shocked at the Commune clearing but 8,000f. out of secularisation.

While the Versailles Government, as soon as it had recovered some spirit and strength, used the most violent means against the Commune; while it put down the free expression of opinion all over France, even to the forbidding of meetings of delegates from the large towns; while it subjected Versailles and the rest of France to an espionage far surpassing that of the Second Empire; while it burned by its gendarme inquisitors all papers printed at Paris, and sifted all correspondence from and to Paris; while in the National Assembly the most timid attempts to put in a word for Paris were howled down in a manner unknown even to the *Chambre introuvable* of 1816; with the savage warfare of Versailles outside, and its attempts at corruption and conspiracy inside Paris – would the Commune not have shamefully betrayed its trust by affecting to keep up all the decencies and appearances of liberalism as in a time of profound peace? Had the Government of the Commune been akin to that of M. Thiers, there would have been no more occasion to suppress Party-of-Order papers at Paris than there was to suppress Communal papers at Versailles.

It was irritating indeed to the Rurals that at the very same time they declared the return to the Church to be the only means of salvation for France, the infidel Commune unearthed the peculiar mysteries of the Picpus nunnery, and of the Church of Saint Laurent. It was a satire upon M. Thiers that, while he showered grand crosses upon the Bonapartist generals in acknowledgment of their mastery in losing battles, signing capitulations, and turning cigarettes at Wilhelmshöhe, the Commune dismissed and arrested its generals whenever they were suspected of neglecting their duties. The expulsion from, and arrest by, the Commune of one of its members who had slipped in under a false name, and had undergone at Lyons six days' imprisonment for simple bankruptcy, was it not a deliberate insult hurled at the forger, Jules Favre, then still the foreign minister of France, still selling France to Bismarck, and still dictating his orders to that paragon Government of Belgium? But indeed the Commune did not pretend to infallibility, the invariable attribute of all governments of the old stamp. It published its doings and sayings, it initiated the public into all its shortcomings.

In every revolution there intrude, at the side of its true agents, men of a different stamp; some of them survivors of and devotees to past revolutions, without insight into the present movement, but preserving popular influence by their known honesty and courage, or by the sheer force of tradition; others mere bawlers, who, by dint of repeating year after year the same set of stereotyped declamations against the Government of the day, have sneaked into the reputation of revolutionists of the first water. After the 18th of March, some such men did also turn up, and in some cases contrived to play pre-eminent parts. As far as their power went, they hampered the real action of the working class, exactly as men of that sort have hampered the full development of every previous revolution.

They are an unavoidable evil; with time they are shaken off; but time was not allowed to the Commune.

Wonderful, indeed, was the change the Commune had wrought in Paris! No longer any trace of the meretricious Paris of the Second Empire. No longer was Paris the rendezvous of British landlords, Irish absentees, American ex-slaveholders and shoddy men, Russian ex-serfowners, and Wallachian boyards. No more corpses at the Morgue, no nocturnal burglaries, scarcely any robberies; in fact, for the first time since the days of February, 1848, the streets of Paris were safe, and that without any police of any kind.

> We (said a member of the Commune) hear no longer of assassination, theft, and personal assault; it seems indeed as if the police had dragged along with it to Versailles all its Conservative friends.

The *cocottes* had refound the scent of their protectors – the absconding men of family, religion, and, above all, of property. In their stead, the real women of Paris showed again at the surface – heroic, noble, and devoted, like the women of antiquity. Working, thinking, fighting, bleeding Paris – almost forgetful, in its incubation of a new society, of the cannibals at its gates – radiant in the enthusiasm of its historic initiative!

Opposed to this new world at Paris, behold the old world at Versailles – that assembly of the ghouls of all defunct *régimes*, Legitimists and Orleanists, eager to feed upon the carcass of the nation, – with a tail of antediluvian Republicans, sanctioning, by their presence in the Assembly, the slaveholders' rebellion, relying for the maintenance of their Parliamentary Republic upon the vanity of the senile mountebank at its head, and caricaturing 1789 by holding their ghastly meetings in the *Jeu de Paume*.[1] There it was, this Assembly, the representative of everything dead in France, propped up to the semblance of life by nothing but the swords of the generals of Louis Bonaparte. Paris all truth, Versailles all lie; and that lie vented through the mouth of Thiers.

Thiers tells a deputation of the mayors of the Seine-et-Oise, –

> You may rely upon my word, which I have *never* broken!

He tells the Assembly itself that 'it was the most freely elected and most Liberal Assembly France ever possessed'; he tells his motley soldiery that it was 'the admiration of the world, and the finest army France ever possessed'; he tells the provinces that the bombardment of Paris by him was a myth:

> If some cannon-shots have been fired, it is not the deed of the army of

Versailles, but of some insurgents trying to make believe that they are fighting, while they dare not show their faces.

He again tells the provinces that

the artillery of Versailles does not bombard Paris, but only cannonades it.

He tells the Archbishop of Paris that the pretended executions and reprisals (!) attributed to the Versailles troops were all moonshine. He tells Paris that he was only anxious 'to free it from the hideous tyrants who oppress it', and that, in fact, the Paris of the Commune was 'but a handful of criminals'.

The Paris of M. Thiers was not the real Paris of the 'vile multitude', but a phantom Paris, the Paris of the *francs-fileurs*, the Paris of the Boulevards, male and female – the rich, the capitalist, the gilded, the idle Paris, now thronging with its lackeys, its blacklegs, its literary *bohême*, and its *cocottes* at Versailles, Saint-Denis, Rueil, and Saint-Germain; considering the civil war but an agreeable diversion, eyeing the battle going on through telescopes, counting the rounds of cannon, and swearing by their own honour and that of their prostitutes, that the performance was far better got up than it used to be at the Porte St. Martin. The men who fell were really dead; the cries of the wounded were cries in good earnest; and, besides, the whole thing was so intensely historical.

This is the Paris of M. Thiers as the Emigration of Coblenz was the France of M. de Calonne.

[. . .]

From: *Collected Works*, Vol. 22, pp. 328–43

Notes

1 'The tennis court where the National Assembly of 1789 adopted its famous decisions'. (*Engels' Note to the 1871 German edition*)

18

Critique of the Gotha Programme

Marx was sharply critical of the political programme adopted at Gotha in 1875 by the newly merged German Socialist Workers Party. In these passages, Marx shows that he does not expect an immediate transition from capitalism to a classless and stateless communist condition. The postcapitalist order will be one 'still stamped with the birthmarks of the old society' and in which the laws of commodity exchange are not wholly overcome. To the consternation of some of his readers, Marx describes this transitional period as constituting 'the revolutionary dictatorship of the proletariat'.

[. . .]

I

1. Labour is the source of all wealth and all culture, and since useful labour is possible only in society and through society, the proceeds of labour belong undiminished with equal right to all members of society.

First Part of the Paragraph: 'Labour is the source of all wealth and all culture'.

Labour is *not the source* of all wealth. *Nature* is just as much the source of use values (and it is surely of such that material wealth consists!) as labour, which itself is only the manifestation of a force of nature, human labour power. The above phrase is to be found in all children's primers and is correct in so far as it is *implied* that labour is performed with the appurtenant subjects and instruments. But a socialist programme cannot allow such bourgeois phrases to pass over in silence the *conditions* that alone give them meaning. And in so far as man from the beginning behaves towards nature, the primary source of all instruments and subjects of labour, as an owner, treats her as belonging to him, his labour becomes the source of use values, therefore also of wealth. The bourgeois have very good grounds for falsely ascribing *supernatural creative power* to labour; since precisely from the fact that labour depends on nature it follows that the man who possesses no other property than his labour power must, in all conditions of society and culture, be the slave of other men who have made themselves the owners of the material conditions of labour. He can work only with their permission, hence live only with their permission.

Let us now leave the sentence as it stands, or rather limps. What would one have expected in conclusion? Obviously this: 'Since labour is the source of all wealth, no one in society can appropriate wealth except as the product of labour. Therefore, if he himself does not work, he lives by the labour of others and also acquires his culture at the expense of the labour of others.'

Instead of this, by means of the verbal rivet *'and since'* a second proposition is added in order to draw a conclusion from this and not from the first one.

Second Part of the Paragraph: 'Useful labour is possible only in society and through society'.

According to the first proposition, labour was the source of all wealth and all culture; therefore no society is possible without labour. Now we learn, conversely, that no 'useful' labour is possible without society.

One could just as well have said that only in society can useless and even socially harmful labour become a branch of gainful occupation, that only in society can one live by being idle, etc., etc. – in short, one could just as well have copied the whole of Rousseau.

And what is 'useful' labour? Surely only labour which produces the intended useful result. A savage – and man was a savage after he had ceased to be an ape – who has killed an animal with a stone, who collects fruits, etc., performs 'useful' labour.

Thirdly. The conclusion: 'And since useful labour is possible only in society and through society, the proceeds of labour belong undiminished with equal right to all members of society'.

A fine conclusion! If useful labour is possible only in society and through society, the proceeds of labour belong to society – and only so much therefrom accrues to the individual worker as is not required to maintain the 'condition' of labour, society.

In fact, this proposition has at all times been made use of by the champions of the *state of society prevailing* at any given time. First come the claims of the government and everything that sticks to it, since it is the social organ for the maintenance of the social order; then come the claims of the various kinds of private property, for the various kinds of private property are the foundations of society, etc. One sees that such hollow phrases can be twisted and turned as desired.

The first and second parts of the paragraph have some intelligible connection only in the following wording: 'Labour becomes the source of wealth and culture only as social labour', or, what is the same thing, 'in and through society'.

This proposition is incontestably correct, for although isolated labour (its material conditions presupposed) can also create use values, it can create neither wealth nor culture.

But equally incontestable is this other proposition: 'In proportion as labour develops socially, and becomes thereby a source of wealth and culture, poverty and destitution develop among the workers, and wealth and culture among the non-workers'.

This is the law of all history hitherto. What, therefore, had to be done here, instead of setting down general phrases about 'labour' and 'society', was to prove concretely how in present capitalist society the material, etc., conditions have at last been created which enable and compel the workers to lift this social curse.

In fact, however, the whole paragraph, bungled in style and content, is only there in order to inscribe the Lassallean catchword of the 'undiminished proceeds of labour' as a slogan at the top of the party banner. I shall return later to the 'proceeds of labour', 'equal right', etc., since the same thing recurs in a somewhat different form, further on.

> 2. In present-day society, the instruments of labour are the monopoly of the capitalist class; the resulting dependence of the working class is the cause of misery and servitude in all its forms.

This sentence, borrowed from the Rules of the International, is incorrect in this 'improved' edition.

In present-day society the instruments of labour are the monopoly of the landowners (the monopoly of property in land is even the basis of the monopoly of capital) *and* the capitalists. In the passage in question, the Rules of the International do not mention either the one or the other class of monopolists. They speak of the '*monopolizer of the means of labour*, that is, *the sources of life*'. The addition, '*sources of life*', makes it sufficiently clear that land is included in the instruments of labour.

The correction was introduced because Lassalle, for reasons now generally known, attacked *only* the capitalist class and not the landowners. In England, the capitalist is usually not even the owner of the land on which his factory stands.

3. The emancipation of labour demands the promotion of the instruments of labour to the common property of society and the cooperative regulation of the total labour with a fair distribution of the proceeds of labour.

'Promotion of the instruments of labour to the common property' ought obviously to read their 'conversion into the common property'; but this only in passing.

What are 'proceeds of labour'? The product of labour or its value? And in the latter case, is it the total value of the product or only that part of the value which labour has newly added to the value of the means of production consumed?

'Proceeds of labour' is a loose notion which Lassalle has put in the place of definite economic conceptions.

What is 'a fair distribution'?

Do not the bourgeois assert that the present-day distribution is 'fair'? And is it not, in fact, the only 'fair' distribution on the basis of the present-day mode of production? Are economic relations regulated by legal conceptions or do not, on the contrary, legal relations arise from economic ones? Have not also the socialist sectarians the most varied notions about 'fair' distribution?

To understand what is implied in this connection by the phrase 'fair distribution', we must take the first paragraph and this one together. The latter presupposes a society wherein 'the instruments of labour are common property and the total labour is cooperatively regulated', and from the first paragraph we learn that 'the proceeds of labour belong undiminished with equal right to all members of society'.

'To all members of society'? To those who do not work as well? What remains then of the 'undiminished proceeds of labour'? Only to those members of society who work? What remains then of the 'equal right' of all members of society?

But 'all members of society' and 'equal right' are obviously mere phrases. The kernel consists in this, that in this communist society every worker must receive the 'undiminished' Lassallean 'proceeds of labour'.

Let us take first of all the words 'proceeds of labour' in the sense of the product of labour; then the cooperative proceeds of labour are the *total social product*.

From this must now be deducted:

First, cover for replacement of the means of production used up.

Secondly, additional portion for expansion of production.

Thirdly, reserve or insurance funds to provide against accidents, dislocations caused by natural calamities, etc.

These deductions from the 'undiminished proceeds of labour' are an economic necessity and their magnitude is to be determined according to available means and forces, and partly by computation of probabilities, but they are in no way calculable by equity.

There remains the other part of the total product, intended to serve as means of consumption.

Before this is divided among the individuals, there has to be deducted again, from it:

First, the general costs of administration not belonging to production.

This part will, from the outset, be very considerably restricted in comparison with present-day society and it diminishes in proportion as the new society develops.

Secondly, that which is intended for the common satisfaction of needs such as schools, health services, etc.

From the outset this part grows considerably in comparison with present-day society and it grows in proportion as the new society develops.

Thirdly, funds for those unable to work, etc., in short, for what is included under so-called official poor relief today.

Only now do we come to the 'distribution' which the programme, under Lassallean influence, alone has in view in its narrow fashion, namely, to that part of the means of consumption which is divided among the individual producers of the cooperative society.

The 'undiminished proceeds of labour' have already unnoticeably become converted into the 'diminished' proceeds, although what the producer is deprived of in his capacity as a private individual benefits him directly or indirectly in his capacity as a member of society.

Just as the phrase of the 'undiminished proceeds of labour' has disappeared, so now does the phrase of the 'proceeds of labour' disappear altogether.

Within the cooperative society based on common ownership of the means of production, the producers do not exchange their products; just as little does the labour employed on the products appear here *as the value* of these products, as a material quality possessed by them, since now, in contrast to capitalist society, individual labour no longer exists in an indirect fashion but directly as a component part of the total labour. The phrase 'proceeds of labour', objectionable also today on account of its ambiguity, thus loses all meaning.

What we have to deal with here is a communist society, not as it has *developed* on its own foundations, but, on the contrary, just as it *emerges* from capitalist society; which is thus in every respect, economically, morally and intellectually, still stamped with the birthmarks of the old society from whose womb it emerges. Accordingly, the individual producer receives back from society – after the deductions have been made – exactly what he gives to it. What he has given to it is his individual quantum of labour. For example, the social working day consists of the sum of the individual hours of work; the individual labour time of the individual producer is the part of the social working day contributed by him, his share in it. He receives a certificate from society that he has furnished such and such an amount of labour (after deducting his labour for the common funds), and with this certificate he draws from the social stock of means of consumption as much as costs the same amount of labour. The same amount of labour which he has given to society in one form he receives back in another.

Here obviously the same principle prevails as that which regulates the exchange of commodities, as far as this is exchange of equal values. Content and form are changed, because under the altered circumstances no one can give anything except his labour, and because, on the other hand, nothing can pass to the ownership of individuals except individual means of consumption. But, as far as the distribution of the latter among the individual producers is concerned, the same principle prevails as in the exchange of commodity-equivalents: a given amount of labour in one form is exchanged for an equal amount of labour in another form.

Hence, *equal right* here is still in principle – *bourgeois right*, although principle and practice are no longer at loggerheads, while the exchange of equivalents in commodity exchange only exists *on the average* and not in the individual case.

In spite of this advance, this *equal right* is still constantly stigmatized by a bourgeois limitation. The right of the producers is *proportional* to the labour they supply; the equality consists in the fact that measurement is made with an *equal standard*, labour.

But one man is superior to another physically or mentally and so supplies more labour in the same time, or can labour for a longer time; and labour, to serve as a measure, must be defined by its duration or intensity, otherwise it ceases to be a standard of measurement. This *equal* right is an unequal right for unequal labour. It recognizes no class differences, because everyone is only a worker like everyone else; but it tacitly recognizes unequal individual endowment and thus productive capacity as natural privileges. *It is, therefore, a right of inequality, in its content, like every right.* Right by its very nature can consist only in the application of an equal standard; but unequal individuals (and they would not be different individuals if they were not unequal) are measurable only by an equal standard in so far as they are brought under an equal point of view, are taken from one *definite* side only, for instance, in the present case, are regarded *only as workers*, and nothing more is seen in them, everything else being ignored. Further, one worker is married, another not; one has more children than another, and so on and so forth. Thus, with an equal performance of labour, and hence an equal share in the social consumption fund, one will in fact receive more than another, one will be richer than another, and so on. To avoid all these defects, right instead of being equal would have to be unequal.

But these defects are inevitable in the first phase of communist society as it is when it has just emerged after prolonged birth pangs from capitalist society. Right can never be higher than the economic structure of society and its cultural development conditioned thereby.

In a higher phase of communist society, after the enslaving subordination of the individual to the division of labour, and there-with also the antithesis between mental and physical labour, has vanished; after labour has become not only a means of life but life's prime want; after the productive forces have also increased with the all-round development of the individual, and all the springs of cooperative wealth flow more abundantly – only then can the narrow horizon of bourgeois right be crossed in its entirety and society inscribe on its banners: From each according to his ability, to each according to his needs!

I have dealt more at length with the 'undiminished proceeds of labour', on the one hand, and with 'equal right' and 'fair distribution', on the other, in order to show what a crime it is to attempt, on the one hand, to force on our Party again, as dogmas, ideas which in a certain period had some meaning but have now become obsolete verbal rubbish, while again perverting, on the other, the realistic outlook, which it cost so much effort to instil into the Party but which has now taken root in it, by means of ideological nonsense about right and other trash so common among the democrats and French Socialists.

Quite apart from the analysis so far given, it was in general a mistake to make a fuss about so-called *distribution* and put the principal stress on it.

Any distribution whatever of the means of consumption is only a consequence of the distribution of the conditions of production themselves. The latter distribution, however, is a feature of the mode of production itself. The capitalist mode of production, for example, rests on the fact that the material conditions of production are in the hands of non-workers in the form of property in capital and land, while the masses are only owners of the personal condition of production, of labour power. If the elements of production are so distributed, then the present-day distribution of the means of consumption results automatically. If the material conditions of production are the cooperative property of the workers themselves, then there likewise results a distribution of the means of consumption different from the present one. Vulgar Socialism (and from it in turn a section of the democracy) has taken over from the bourgeois economists the consideration and treatment of distribution as independent of the mode of production and hence the presentation of Socialism as turning principally on distribution. After the real relation has long been made clear, why retrogress again?

4. The emancipation of labour must be the work of the working class, relatively to which all other classes are only one reactionary mass.

The first strophe is taken from the introductory words of the Rules of the International, but 'improved'. There it is said: 'The emancipation of the working class must be the act of the workers themselves'; here, on the contrary, the 'working class' has to emancipate – what? 'Labour'. Let him understand who can.

In compensation, the antistrophe, on the other hand, is a Lassallean quotation of the first water: 'relatively to which (the working class) all other classes are *only one reactionary mass*'.

In the *Communist Manifesto* it is said: 'Of all the classes that stand face to face with the bourgeoisie today, the proletariat alone is a *really revolutionary class*. The other classes decay and finally disappear in the face of modern industry; the proletariat is its special and essential product'.

The bourgeoisie is here conceived as a revolutionary class – as the bearer of large-scale industry – relatively to the feudal lords and the lower middle class, who desire to maintain all social positions that are the creation of obsolete modes of production. Thus they do not form *together* with the *bourgeoisie* only one reactionary mass.

On the other hand, the proletariat is revolutionary relatively to the bourgeoisie because, having itself grown up on the basis of large-scale industry, it strives to strip off from production the capitalist character that the bourgeoisie seeks to perpetuate. But the *Manifesto* adds that the 'lower middle class' . . . is becoming revolutionary 'in view of [its] impending transfer into the proletariat'.

From this point of view, therefore, it is again nonsense to say that it, together with the bourgeoisie, and with the feudal lords into the bargain, 'form only one reactionary mass' relatively to the working class.

Has one proclaimed to the artisans, small manufacturers, etc., and *peasants* during the last elections: Relatively to us you, together with the bourgeoisie and feudal lords, form only one reactionary mass?

Lassalle knew the *Communist Manifesto* by heart, as his faithful followers know the gospels written by him. If, therefore, he has falsified it so grossly, this has occurred only to put a good colour on his alliance with absolutist and feudal opponents against the bourgeoisie.

In the above paragraph, moreover, his oracular saying is dragged in by main force without any connection with the botched quotation from the Rules of the International. Thus it is here simply an impertinence, and indeed not at all displeasing to Herr Bismarck, one of those cheap pieces of insolence in which the Marat of Berlin deals.

5. The working class strives for its emancipation first of all *within the*

framework of the present-day national state, conscious that the necessary result of its efforts, which are common to the workers of all civilized countries, will be the international brotherhood of peoples.

Lassalle, in opposition to the *Communist Manifesto* and to all earlier Socialism, conceived the workers' movement from the narrowest national standpoint. He is being followed in this – and that after the work of the International!

It is altogether self-evident that, to be able to fight at all, the working class must organize itself at home *as a class* and that its own country is the immediate arena of its struggle. In so far its class struggle is national, not in substance, but, as the *Communist Manifesto* says, 'in form'. But the 'framework of the present-day national state', for instance, the German Empire, is itself in its turn economically 'within the framework' of the world market, politically 'within the framework' of the system of states. Every businessman knows that German trade is at the same time foreign trade, and the greatness of Herr Bismarck consists, to be sure, precisely in his pursuing a kind of *international* policy.

And to what does the German workers' party reduce its internationalism? To the consciousness that the result of its efforts will be 'the international brotherhood of peoples' – a phrase borrowed from the bourgeois League of Peace and Freedom, which is intended to pass as equivalent to the international brotherhood of the working classes in the joint struggle against the ruling classes and their governments. Not a word, therefore, *about the international functions* of the German working class! And it is thus that it is to challenge its own bourgeoisie – which is already linked up in brotherhood against it with the bourgeois of all other countries – and Herr Bismarck's international policy of conspiracy!

In fact, the internationalism of the programme stands *even infinitely below* that of the Free Trade Party. The latter also asserts that the result of its efforts will be 'the international brotherhood of peoples'. But it also *does* something to make trade international and by no means contents itself with the consciousness – that all peoples are carrying on trade at home.

The international activity of the working classes does not in any way depend on the existence of the *International Working Men's Association*. This was only the first attempt to create a central organ for that activity; an attempt which was a lasting success on account of the impulse which it gave but which was no longer realizable in its *first historical form* after the fall of the Paris Commune.

Bismarck's *Norddeutsche* was absolutely right when it announced, to the satisfaction of its master, that the German workers' party had sworn off internationalism in the new programme.

II

> Starting from these basic principles, the German workers' party strives by
> all legal means for the *free state – and –* socialist society: the abolition of the
> wage system *together with the iron law of wages –* and – exploitation in every
> form; the elimination of all social and political inequality.

I shall return to the 'free' state later.

So, in future, the German workers' party has got to believe in Lassalle's
'iron law of wages'! That this may not be lost, the nonsense is perpetrated
of speaking of the 'abolition of the wage system' (it should read: system
of wage labour) '*together with* the iron law of wages'. If I abolish wage
labour, then naturally I abolish its laws also, whether they are of 'iron' or
sponge. But Lassalle's attack on wage labour turns almost solely on this
so-called law. In order, therefore, to prove that Lassalle's sect has
conquered, the 'wage system' must be abolished '*together with* the iron law
of wages' and not without it.

It is well known that nothing of the 'iron law of wages' is Lassalle's
except the word 'iron' borrowed from Goethe's 'great, eternal iron laws'.
The word *iron* is a label by which the true believers recognize one another.
But if I take the law with Lassalle's stamp on it and, consequently, in his
sense, then I must also take it with his substantiation for it. And what is
that? As Lange already showed, shortly after Lassalle's death, it is the
Malthusian theory of population (preached by Lange himself). But if this
theory is correct, then again I can *not* abolish the law even if I abolish wage
labour a hundred times over, because the law then governs not only the
system of wage labour but *every* social system. Basing themselves directly
on this, the economists have been proving for fifty years and more that
Socialism cannot abolish poverty, *which has its basis in nature*, but can only
make it *general*, distribute it simultaneously over the whole surface of
society!

But all this is not the main thing. *Quite apart* from the *false* Lassallean
formulation of the law, the truly outrageous retrogression consists in the
following:

Since Lassalle's death there has asserted itself in *our* Party the scientific
understanding that wages are not what they *appear* to be, namely, the *value*,
or *price, of labour*, but only a masked form for the *value*, or *price, of labour*
power. Thereby the whole bourgeois conception of wages hitherto, as well
as all the criticism hitherto directed against this conception, was thrown
overboard once for all and it was made clear that the wage worker has
permission to work for his own subsistence, that is, *to live*, only in so far
as he works for a certain time gratis for the capitalist (and hence also for
the latter's co-consumers of surplus value); that the whole capitalist system

of production turns on the increase of this gratis labour by extending the working day or by developing the productivity, that is, increasing the intensity of labour power, etc.; that, consequently, the system of wage labour is a system of slavery, and indeed of a slavery which becomes more severe in proportion as the social productive forces of labour develop, whether the worker receives better or worse payment. And after this understanding has gained more and more ground in our Party, one returns to Lassalle's dogmas, although one must have known that Lassalle *did not know* what wages were, but following in the wake of the bourgeois economists took the appearance for the essence of the matter.

It is as if, among slaves who have at last got behind the secret of slavery and broken out in rebellion, a slave still in thrall to obsolete notions were to inscribe on the programme of the rebellion: Slavery must be abolished because the feeding of slaves in the system of slavery cannot exceed a certain low maximum!

Does not the mere fact that the representatives of our Party were capable of perpetrating such a monstrous attack on the understanding that has spread among the mass of our Party prove by itself with what criminal levity and with what lack of conscience they set to work in drawing up this compromise programme.

Instead of the indefinite concluding phrase of the paragraph, 'the elimination of all social and political inequality', it . . . ought to have been said that with the abolition of class distinctions all social and political inequality arising from them would disappear of itself.

III

'The German workers' party, in order to pave the way to the solution of the social question, demands the establishment of producers' cooperative societies with state aid under the democratic control of the toiling people. The producers' cooperative societies are to be called into being for industry and agriculture on such a scale that the socialist organization of the total labour will arise from them.

After the Lassallean 'iron law of wages', the physic of the prophet. The way to it is 'paved' in worthy fashion. In place of the existing class struggle appears a newspaper scribbler's phrase: 'the social *question*', to the '*solution*' of which one 'paves the way'. Instead of arising from the revolutionary process of transformation of society, the 'socialist organization of the total labour' 'arises' from the 'state aid' that the state gives to the producers' cooperative societies and which the *state*, not the worker, '*calls into being*'. It is worthy of Lassalle's imagination that with state loans one can build a new society just as well as a new railway!

From the remnants of a sense of shame, 'state aid' has been put – under the democratic control of the 'toiling people'.

In the first place, the majority of the 'toiling people' in Germany consists of peasants, and not of proletarians.

Secondly 'democratic' means in German *'volksherrschaftlich'* ['by the rule of the people']. But what does 'control by the rule of the people of the toiling people' mean? And particularly in the case of a toiling people which, through these demands that it puts to the state, expresses its full consciousness that it neither rules nor is ripe for ruling!

It would be superfluous to deal here with the criticism of the recipe prescribed by Buchez in the reign of Louis Philippe in *opposition* to the French Socialists and accepted by the reactionary workers of the *Atelier*. The chief offence does not lie in having inscribed this specific nostrum in the programme, but in taking, in general, a retrograde step from the standpoint of a class movement to that of a sectarian movement.

That the workers desire to establish the conditions for cooperative production on a social scale, and first of all on a national scale, in their own country, only means that they are working to revolutionize the present conditions of production, and it has nothing in common with the foundation of cooperative societies with state aid. But as far as the present cooperative societies are concerned, they are of value *only* in so far as they are the independent creations of the workers and not protégés either of the governments or of the bourgeois.

IV

I come now to the democratic section.

A. *The free basis of the state.*

First of all, according to II, the German workers' party strives for 'the free state'.

Free state – what is this?

It is by no means the aim of the workers, who have got rid of the narrow mentality of humble subjects, to set the state free. In the German Empire the 'state' is almost as 'free' as in Russia. Freedom consists in converting the state from an organ superimposed upon society into one completely subordinate to it, and today, too, the forms of state are more free or less free to the extent that they restrict the 'freedom of the state'.

The German workers' party – at least if it adopts the programme – shows that its socialist ideas are not even skin-deep; in that, instead of treating existing society (and this holds good for any future one) as the *basis* of the existing state (or of the future state in the case of future society), it treats the state rather as an independent entity that possesses its own *intellectual, ethical and libertarian bases.*

And what of the riotous misuse which the programme makes of the words '*present-day state*', '*present-day society*', and of the still more riotous misconception it creates in regard to the state to which it addresses its demands?

'Present-day society' is capitalist society, which exists in all civilized countries, more or less free from medieval admixture, more or less modified by the special historical development of each country, more or less developed. On the other hand, the 'present-day state' changes with a country's frontier. It is different in the Prusso-German Empire from what it is in Switzerland, it is different in England from what it is in the United States. '*The* present-day state' is, therefore, a fiction.

Nevertheless, the different states of the different civilized countries, in spite of their manifold diversity of form, all have this in common, that they are based on modern bourgeois society, only one more or less capitalistically developed. They have, therefore, also certain essential features in common. In this sense it is possible to speak of the 'present-day state', in contrast with the future, in which its present root, bourgeois society, will have died off.

The question then arises: what transformation will the state undergo in communist society? In other words, what social functions will remain in existence there that are analogous to present functions of the state? This question can only be answered scientifically, and one does not get a flea-hop nearer to the problem by a thousandfold combination of the word people with the word state.

Between capitalist and communist society lies the period of the revolutionary transformation of the one into the other. There corresponds to this also a political transition period in which the state can be nothing but *the revolutionary dictatorship of the proletariat.*

Now the programme does not deal with this nor with the future state of communist society.

Its political demands contain nothing beyond the old democratic litany familiar to all: universal suffrage, direct legislation, popular rights, a people's militia, etc. They are a mere echo of the bourgeois People's Party, of the League of Peace and Freedom. They are all demands which, in so far as they are not exaggerated in fantastic presentation, have already been *realized*. Only the state to which they belong does not lie within the borders of the German Empire, but in Switzerland, the United States, etc. This sort of 'state of the future' is a present-day state, although existing outside the 'framework' of the German Empire.

But one thing has been forgotten. Since the German workers' party expressly declares that it acts within 'the present-day national state', hence within *its own* state, the Prusso-German Empire – its demands would indeed otherwise be largely meaningless, since one only demands what one has not got – it should not have forgotten the chief thing, namely, that all those pretty little gewgaws rest on the recognition of the so-called sovereignty of the people and hence are appropriate only in a *democratic republic*.

Since one has not the courage – and wisely so, for the circumstances demand caution – to demand the democratic republic, as the French workers' programmes under Louis Philippe and under Louis Napoleon did, one should not have resorted, either, to the subterfuge, neither 'honest' nor decent, of demanding things which have meaning only in a democratic republic from a state which is nothing but a police-guarded military despotism, embellished with parliamentary forms, alloyed with a feudal admixture, already influenced by the bourgeoisie and bureaucratically carpentered, and then to assure this state into the bargain that one imagines one will be able to force such things upon it 'by legal means'.

Even vulgar democracy, which sees the millennium in the democratic republic and has no suspicion that it is precisely in this last form of state of bourgeois society that the class struggle has to be fought out to a conclusion – even it towers mountains above this kind of democratism which keeps within the limits of what is permitted by the police and not permitted by logic.

That, in fact, by the word 'state' is meant the government machine, or the state in so far as it forms a special organism separated from society through division of labour, is shown by the words 'the German workers' party demands *as the economic basis of the state*: a single progressive income tax', etc. Taxes are the economic basis of the government machinery and of nothing else. In the state of the future, existing in Switzerland, this demand has been pretty well fulfilled. Income tax presupposes various sources of income of the various social classes, and hence capitalist society. It is, therefore, nothing remarkable that the Liverpool financial reformers, bourgeois headed by Gladstone's brother, are putting forward the same demand as the programme.

B. 'The German workers' party demands as the intellectual and ethical basis of the state:
1. Universal and *equal elementary education* by the state. Universal compulsory school attendance. Free instruction.

Equal elementary education? What idea lies behind these words? Is it believed that in present-day society (and it is only with this one has to deal) education can be *equal* for all classes? Or is it demanded that the upper classes also shall be compulsorily reduced to the modicum of education – the elementary school – that alone is compatible with the economic conditions not only of the wage workers but of the peasants as well?

'Universal compulsory school attendance. Free instruction'. The former exists even in Germany, the second in Switzerland and in the United States in the case of elementary schools. If in some states of the latter country higher educational institutions are also 'free' that only means in fact defraying the cost of the education of the upper classes from the general tax receipts. Incidentally, the same holds good for 'free administration of justice'. The administration of criminal justice is to be had free everywhere; that of civil justice is concerned almost exclusively with conflicts over property and hence affects almost exclusively the possessing classes. Are they to carry on their litigation at the expense of the national coffers?

The paragraph on the schools should at least have demanded technical schools (theoretical and practical) in combination with the elementary school.

'*Elementary education by the state*' is altogether objectionable. Defining by a general law the expenditures on the elementary schools, the qualifications of the teaching staff, the branches of instruction, etc., and, as is done in the United States, supervising the fulfilment of these legal specifications by state inspectors, is a very different thing from appointing the state as the educator of the people! Government and church should rather be equally excluded from any influence on the school. Particularly, indeed, in the Prusso-German Empire (and one should not take refuge in the rotten subterfuge that one is speaking of a 'state of the future'; we have seen how matters stand in this respect) the state has need, on the contrary, of a very stern education by the people.

But the whole programme, for all its democratic clang, is tainted through and through by the Lassallean sect's servile belief in the state, or, what is no better, by a democratic belief in miracles, or rather it is a compromise between these two kinds of belief in miracles, both equally remote from Socialism.

'*Freedom of science*' says a paragraph of the Prussian constitution. Why, then, here?

'*Freedom of conscience!*' If one desired at this time of the *Kulturkamp* to remind liberalism of its old catchwords, it surely could have been done only in the following form: Everyone should be able to attend to his religious as well as his bodily needs without the police sticking their noses in. But the workers' party ought at any rate in this connection to have expressed its awareness of the fact that bourgeois 'freedom of conscience' is nothing but the toleration of all possible kinds of *religious freedom of conscience*, and that for its part it endeavours rather to liberate the conscience from the witchery of religion. But one chooses not to transgress the 'bourgeois' level.

I have now come to the end, for the appendix that now follows in the programme does not constitute a characteristic component part of it. Hence I can be very brief here.

2. *Normal working day.*

In no other country has the workers' party limited itself to such an indefinite demand, but has always fixed the length of the working day that it considers normal under the given circumstances.

3. Restriction of female labour and prohibition of child labour.

The standardization of the working day must include the restriction of female labour, in so far as it relates to the duration, intermissions, etc., of the working day; otherwise it could only mean the exclusion of female labour from branches of industry that are especially unhealthy for the female body or are objectionable morally for the female sex. If that is what was meant, it should have been said so.

'*Prohibition of child labour!*' Here it was absolutely essential to state the age limit.

A *general prohibition* of child labour is incompatible with the existence of large-scale industry and hence an empty, pious wish. Its realization – if it were possible – would be reactionary, since, with a strict regulation of the working time according to the different age groups and other safety measures for the protection of children, an early combination of productive labour with education is one of the most potent means for the transformation of present-day society.

4. State supervision of factory, workshop and domestic industry.

In consideration of the Prusso-German state it should definitely have been demanded that the inspectors are to be removable only by a court of law; that any worker can have them prosecuted for neglect of duty; that they must belong to the medical profession.

5. Regulation of prison labour.

A petty demand in a general workers' programme. In any case, it should have been clearly stated that there is no intention from fear of competition to allow ordinary criminals to be treated like beasts, and especially that there is no desire to deprive them of their sole means of betterment, productive labour. This was surely the least one might have expected from Socialists.

6. An effective liability law.

It should have been stated what is meant by an 'effective' liability law.

Be it noted, incidentally, that in speaking of the normal working day the part of factory legislation that deals with health regulations and safety measures, etc., has been overlooked. The liability law only comes into operation when these regulations are infringed.

In short, this appendix also is distinguished by slovenly editing.

Dixi et salvavi animam meam

(I have spoken and saved my soul.)

From: Marx and Engels *Selected works in Two Volumes*. Vol. 2, pp. 17–34

19

Two Letters on Russia

In these two short extracts, drawn from letters written in 1877 and 1881 respectively, Marx comments on the possibility of a transition to socialism in Russia which 'by-passes' the capitalist period. These brief fragments gained some prominence retrospectively in the light of Russian experience after 1917. In themselves, they tell us more about Marx's insistence that Capital *should not be read mechanistically than about his considered views of the likely future prospects of socialism in Russia.*

Letter to the Editorial Board of the Otechestvenniye Zapiski

[London,] November 1877

[. . .]

The chapter on primitive accumulation [in *Capital*] does not pretend to do more than trace the path by which, in Western Europe, the capitalist order of economy emerged from the womb of the feudal order of economy. It therefore describes the historical movement which by divorcing the producers from their means of production converts them into wage workers (proletarians in the modern sense of the word) while it converts those who possess the means of production into capitalists. In that history 'all revolutions are epoch-making that act as levers for the advancement of the capitalist class in course of formation; above all those which, by stripping great masses of men of their traditional means of production and subsistence, suddenly hurl them on the labour market. But the basis of this whole development is the expropriation of the agricultural producer. This has been accomplished in radical fashion only in England . . . but all the countries of Western Europe are going through the same movement,' etc. At the end of the chapter the historical tendency of production is summed up thus: That it 'itself begets its own negation with the inexorability which governs the metamorphoses of nature'; that it has itself created the elements of a new economic order, by giving the greatest impulse at once to the productive forces of social labour and to the integral development of every individual producer; that capitalist property, resting already, as it actually does, on a collective mode of production, cannot but transform itself into social property. At this point I have not furnished any proof, for the good reason that this statement is itself nothing else but a general summary of long expositions previously given in the chapters on capitalist production.

Now what application to Russia could my critic make of this historical sketch? Only this: If Russia is tending to become a capitalist nation after the example of the West-European countries – and during the last few years she has been taking a lot of trouble in this direction – she will not succeed without having first transformed a good part of her peasants into proletarians; and after that, once taken to the bosom of the capitalist regime, she will experience its pitiless laws like other profane peoples. That is all. But that is too little for my critic. He feels he absolutely must metamorphose my historical sketch of the genesis of capitalism in Western Europe into an historico-philosophic theory of the general path every people is fated to tread, whatever the historical circumstances in which it finds itself, in order that it may ultimately arrive at the form of economy which ensures, together with the greatest expansion of the productive powers of social labour, the most complete development of man. But I beg his pardon. (He is both honouring and shaming me too much.) Let us take an example.

In several parts of *Capital* I allude to the fate which overtook the plebeians of ancient Rome. They were originally free peasants, each cultivating his own piece of land on his own account. In the course of Roman history they were expropriated. The same movement which divorced them from their means of production and subsistence involved the formation not only of big landed property but also of big money capital. And so one fine morning there were to be found on the one hand free men, stripped of everything except their labour power, and on the other, in order to exploit this labour, those who held all the acquired wealth in their possession. What happened? The Roman proletarians became not wage labourers but a *mob* of do-nothings more abject than the former 'poor whites' in the South of the United States, and alongside of them there developed a mode of production which was not capitalist but based on slavery. Thus events strikingly analogous but taking place in different historical surroundings led to totally different results. By studying each of these forms of evolution separately and then comparing them one can easily find the clue to this phenomenon, but one will never arrive there by using as one's master key a general historico-philosophical theory, the supreme virtue of which consists in being super-historical.

[. . .]

Letter to Vera Zasulich

London, 1881

[. . .]

I hope . . . that a few lines will suffice to dispel any doubts you may harbour as to the misunderstanding in regard to my so-called theory.

In analysing the genesis of capitalist production I say:

'At the core of the capitalist system, therefore, lies the complete separation of the producer from the means of production . . . the basis of this whole development is the *expropriation of the agricultural producer*. To date this has not been accomplished in a radical fashion anywhere except in England . . . But *all the other countries of Western Europe* are undergoing the same process'.

Hence the 'historical inevitability' of this process is *expressly* limited to the *countries of Western Europe*. The cause of that limitation is indicated in the following passage from Chapter XXXII of *Capital*:

'*Private property*, based on personal labour . . . will be supplanted by *capitalist private property*, based on the exploitation of the labour of others, on wage labour'.

In this Western movement, therefore, what is taking place is the *transformation of one form of private property into another form of private property*. In the case of the Russian peasants, *their communal property* would, on the contrary, have to be *transformed into private property*.

Hence the analysis provided in *Capital* does not adduce reasons either for or against the viability of the rural commune, but the special study I have made of it, and the material for which I drew from original sources, has convinced me that this commune is the fulcrum of social regeneration in Russia, but in order that it may function as such, it would first be necessary to eliminate the deleterious influences which are assailing it from all sides, and then ensure for it the normal conditions of spontaneous development.

From: *Selected Correspondence*, pp. 378–9; *Collected Works*, Vol. 46, pp. 71–2

Index

Lightning Source UK Ltd.
Milton Keynes UK
UKOW05f0303100217
294074UK00002B/148/P